THE I

Totalitarian Movements and Political Religions
Series Editors: Michael Burleigh, Robert Mallett and Emilio Gentile
ISSN: 1477-058X

This innovative new book series will scrutinise all attempts to totally refashion mankind and society, whether these hailed from the Left or the Right, which, unusually, will receive equal consideration. Although its primary focus will be on the authoritarian and totalitarian politics of the twentieth century, the series will also provide a forum for the wider discussion of the politics of faith and salvation in general, together with an examination of their inexorably catastrophic consequences. There are no chronological or geographical limitations to the books that may be included, and the series will include reprints of classic works and translations, as well as monographs and collections of essays.

International Fascism, 1919–1945
Gert Sørenson and Robert Mallett (eds)

Totalitarian Democracy and After: International Colloquium in Memory of Jacob L. Talmon
Yehoshua Arieli and Nathan Rotenstreich (eds)

The French and Italian Communist Parties: Comrades and Culture
Cyrille Guiat

The Lesser Evil: Moral Approaches to Genocide Practices
Helmut Dubiel and Gabriel Motzkin (eds)

Redefining Stalinism
Harold Shukman (ed.)

Religion, Politics and Ideology in the Third Reich: Selected Essays
Uriel Tal

The Italian Road to Totalitarianism
Emilio Gentile, translated by Robert Mallett

The Seizure of Power: Fascism in Italy, 1919–1929
Adrian Lyttelton

THE LESSER EVIL

Moral Approaches to Genocide Practices

Editors:

HELMUT DUBIEL

Justus-Liebig University, Giessen

and

GABRIEL MOTZKIN

Hebrew University of Jerusalem

Routledge
Taylor & Francis Group

LONDON AND NEW YORK

First published in 2004 in Great Britain
by Routledge
2 Park Square, Milton Park,
Abingdon, Oxon, OX14 4RN

Simultaneously published in the USA and Canada
by Routledge
711 Tird Ave, New York NY 10017

Routledge is an imprint of the Taylor & Francis Group

Transferred to Digital Printing 2005

British Library Cataloguing in Publication Data

The lesser evil: moral approaches to genocide practices. –
(Cass series. Totalitarian movements and political religions)
1. National socialism – Historiography 2. Communism – Historiography
3. Genocide – Historiography 4. History, Modern – 20th century
I. Dubiel, Helmut, 1946– II. Motzkin, Gabriel
320.5'3'0904

ISBN 0-7146-5493-0 (cloth)
ISBN 0-7146-8395-7 (paper)
ISSN 1477-058X

Library of Congress Cataloging-in-Publication Data

The lesser evil: moral approaches to genocide practices / editors Helmut Dubiel
and Gabriel Motzkin.
        p.   cm. – (Cass series – totalitarian movements and political religions,
    ISSN 1477-058X)
Includes bibliographical references and index.
    ISBN 0-7146-5493-0 (cloth) – ISBN 0-7146-8395-7 (paper)
    1. Genocide–Moral and ethical aspects–Congresses. 2. Communism–Moral
and ethical aspects–Congresses. 3. National socialism–Moral and ethical
aspects–Congresses. 4. Totalitarianism–Moral and ethical aspects–Congresses.
I. Dubiel, Helmut, 1946– II. Motzkin, Gabriel Gideon Hillel. III. Series.

HV6322.7.L47 2003
940.53'18–dc21   2003055203

Typeset in 10.25/12pt Sabon by Cambridge Photosetting Services

Contents

Series Editor's Preface

As the generic introduction to this series explains, these books 'will scrutinise all attempts to totally refashion mankind and society, whether these hailed from the Left or the Right, which, unusually, will receive equal consideration'. Unusually, because, although the history of the twentieth century should not be reduced to a competition between the merely gruesome, it is transparently the case that the crimes of Communism, admirable chronicled in the recent   Black Book of Communism and most recently by the journalist Anne Applebaum in her stunning book   GULAG, have been neglected in favour of what almost amounts to a pathological and unsavoury addiction to the atrocities of Nazism.

This addiction, represented in my own limited acquaintance by the computer programmer who devours every new book on Hitler, the local butcher who watches every Second World War TV documentary, and Oxford political-science colleagues who spend each interview with prospective students discussing Hitler (as opposed to Hobbes, Locke or Burke), the only subject adolescents can talk about with any fluency, is fuelled by the media and Hollywood as well as by scholarship of quasi-industrial proportions.

The imbalance is obvious to both plain and sophisticated people, many of whom, at least in Europe, are growing weary of having the crimes of Nazism perpetually put before their eyes, especially since this is being done in a crudely instrumental and minatory fashion by people who wish to reduce Europe to little more than a graveyard patrolled by allegedly ever larger numbers of antisemites. The USA, by contrast, remains miraculously immune to this contagion. Paradoxically, as Maurice Cowling has remarked, such heavy insinuations may be contributing to the disturbing recrudescence of the very sentiments they ostensibly aim to check.

The reasons for this systematic imbalance include a residual subscription to 'anti-fascist' mythology on the part of some of the liberal-Left as well as former Stalinists; an inability to identify with the sort of people imprisoned or murdered by Marxists, such as Kazakh herdsmen or Ukrainian farmers; the bizarre notion that criticising Communist tyranny somehow detracts from a wider 'progressive' agenda and hence aids and abets conservatives, or, horror of horrors, neo- or post-Fascists; as well as, finally, an understandable preoccupation among citizens of post-Communist societies, notably in Russia, with daily survival after a 70-year man-made disaster, and a less excusable nostalgia for the times when the USSR was at least 'big' as well as 'bad', with 'badness' being re-construed as a bit of excessive social 'discipline'.

There are various recent attempts to compare and contrast Nazism and Stalinism – one of which found no room for comparing them as sinister police states with ramified concentration camp industrial complexes. The present book, whose contributors include several of the major historical thinkers of our time, such as Martin Malia and Tzvetan Todorov, is important because it reflects both on the terms of any comparison and on what those who write in good faith hope to achieve by it, without seeking to shape a spurious consensus. It is an important book that deserves a wide readership.

Michael Burleigh
Series Co-Editor

Introduction

Helmut Dubiel and Gabriel Motzkin

Any reader looking for a consensus on the topic of the comparison between Nazism and Communism will not find it here. The editors had the idea that this volume should include essays by scholars who disagree about the purpose, the methods, and the assumptions behind such a comparison. The disagreement extends even to the analyses and interpretations of the different ways in which these movements continue to have an impact on our culture even after they have ceased to threaten us.

The necessity for analyzing these comparisons first struck one of the editors, Gabriel Motzkin, when he read a review of   Le livre noir du Communisme (The Black Book of Communism) in the Times Literary Supplement from 27 March 1998, entitled 'The Lesser Evil?' The review was written by Martin Malia, an eminent historian and contributor to this volume who has written works on Russia's cultural and intellectual relations with the West. Reading that review, the editors felt that it would be problematic if two isolated discourses were to develop side-by-side: one about the reception of Nazism and the other about the reception of Communism. A competition for significance would develop between the experts on Nazism and the experts on Communism. Such an approach could easily distort the historical and ethical evaluation of these movements. Indeed, when experts who study Nazism or Communism make comparisons between different aspects of the two, they often do so without a sufficient acquaintance with the history of the other movement.

Serendipitously, at the same time that Malia's review appeared, Avishai Margalit, with whom Motzkin had collaborated on several articles, read an essay by Alain de Benoist, 'Nazism and Communism: Evil Twins?', published in the summer 1998 issue of   Telos. The essay outraged him, and he suggested to Motzkin to do an article together on the meaning of this very comparison. While that project never came to fruition, its spirit, which took the form

1

of long and intense discussions with Margalit, is adopted in the collection that we now offer to the interested public.

Being at the time the Director of the Franz-Rosenzweig Center for German–Jewish Literature and Cultural History at the Hebrew University in Jerusalem, Motzkin conceived of doing a conference on the subject and shared his idea with Dietmar Müller-Elmau of Schloss Elmau in Bavaria. The conference took place in August 2000.

One of the participants in the Elmau conference was Helmut Dubiel, whom Motzkin had met the previous spring at a conference organized by a group of scholars working on a collective research project on 'Cultures of Memory' and sponsored by the German Research Authority and the University of Gießen. Dubiel's most recent book,   No One is Free from History, examined the debates in the German Bundestag about dealing with the Nazi past. At the Elmau conference, Dubiel was so taken by the subject that he suggested doing a second conference. As Dubiel then became the Max Weber Professor for European Studies at New York University, it was decided that New York University and the Rosenzweig Center would co-host this second conference in New York City. The conference took place in April 2001. We are indebted to Professor Richard Foley, the Dean of New York University's Faculty of Arts and Sciences, for his unwavering support. Most of the immediate organization of the conference fell on the staff of the Center for European Studies at New York University. We express our gratitude to its members and particularly to Ms Alamanda Griffin.

Dietmar Müller-Elmau suggested that this second conference required a preliminary discussion, for which he generously offered financial support. That pre-conference was held in December 2000 at the Van Leer Institute in Jerusalem and was aided by the contribution of Shimshon Zelniker, the Director of the institute.

This volume, therefore, is the outcome of three scholarly discussions: Elmau, August 2000, Jerusalem, December 2000, and New York City, April 2001. Each conference had its own focus. Nonetheless, the meetings shared several themes. The themes deserve to be mentioned at the outset, for they are the bones of contention in the arguments between the different essays in this collection.

The first issue concerns the different academic reception of Nazism and Communism. Martin Malia argues that we know much more about Nazi atrocities than about Communist atrocities and this difference in knowledge has colored our historical interpretation. Lukes implies the opposite: he holds that the atrocities of Communism have been well known for a long time, and that actually there were periods in which greater attention has been paid to Communist atrocities than to Nazi atrocities.

INTRODUCTION

The second issue can be defined as the issue of rationality. It has three aspects: the rationality of the victims; the rationality of the actual actions undertaken by the perpetrators; and the alleged rationality of the perpetrators' worldview. Dan Diner has held elsewhere, in opposition to Hannah Arendt's thesis, that the Judenräte behaved in a 'rational' way. At the conference in Jerusalem, Margalit argued for the rationality of the way the Communists conceived of what they were doing. The issue of the supposed rationality and instrumentality of Nazi actions during the Holocaust is well known. Then there is the question of the allegedly greater rationality of the Communist worldview in comparison with the Nazi worldview. It is commonly held that the Communists were less fantastic in their world plans. Malia's, Meuschel's and Margolin's interpretations might well lead to the questioning of this assumption.

Third, there is another problem intertwined with the multi-dimensional issue of rationality. Malia captured it perhaps best in his original review in the Times Literary Supplement, when he intimated that in some quarters degrading the ideals of the Enlightenment would be regarded as worse than denying them. In other words, the Communists' allegedly greater rationality could easily lead them to create an even more imaginary system, one in which lies would be institutionalized so that the apparent rationality of the system would remain unquestioned. In that case, the Nazis' allegedly greater irrationality would actually make it possible for them to be more open about their terrible aims. In relation to the implications of rationality and irrationality for systemic honesty and dishonesty, one question that emerged was whether there was a distinction between lying to others and lying to oneself. Several of the participants in the conference understood the Communists as having lied to themselves, while the Nazis felt no obligation of integrity to others.

Fourth, a larger issue that hovered above all discussions was the relation between memory and history. In this context, 'memory' is shorthand for the way we choose to remember and commemorate the atrocities perpetrated in the name of these two movements. History here refers not so much to what actually happened, but rather to the place of intellectuals and scholars in reconstructing what happened, a role that has academic, ethical and cultural aspects. The essays by Diner, Malia, Motzkin, Aschheim, Lang, Ackermann, Ben-Ghiat and Todorov all address this issue.

Finally, there is the question of the role of the intellectual in preserving and analyzing the past. This problem is well reflected in the intellectuals' biographies and identities. Several essays – Wohlfahrt's and Lukes' most poignantly – raise this question. It should be pointed out that many of the participants in the conferences, among them Dubiel, Diner, Ackermann, Lukes and Margolin, were in their student days sympathizers with the left, and some still are. A consideration of the issue of Communist atrocities therefore functions for them in ways that are partially comparable with the Germans' acknowledgements of Nazi atrocities, namely a painful questioning of one's own values and identities. Behind this particular question of one's own allegiances is a larger issue, the question of whether the comparison, as it is addressed in this collection, can be misused by political movements for their own goals. The argument could all too easily be made that such a comparison is really intended to rehabilitate the one or the other movement, and that therefore it is politically implicated with the movement that it excuses. Here is the place to state emphatically that nothing could be further from the intentions of the editors or of any of the contributors. We are all aware of the danger, but we also think that it would be a dereliction of responsibility if we neglected the comparison, for several reasons. First, because it has played such an important role in twentieth-century history: Nazism and Communism have been compared since the inception of both movements. Second, because the comparison will be made by irresponsible people, if not by responsible people. A sense of responsibility implies being sensitive to the fuzzy border between self-critique and apologetic, between critique of one's own actions and letting oneself off the hook. And, third, because the different ways in which comparisons can be and have been used and abused by both right and left have not always been so distinct.

It is our responsibility to understand our culture. In relation to the traumas of the twentieth century, which invite comparison if only because of their traumatic effects, that responsibility has two aspects: our obligation to understand what happened and our obligation to understand how we have dealt with it ever since.

Part I

Approaches

1

Nazism–Communism: Delineating the Comparison

Martin Malia

When we ask whether it is Communism or Nazism that must be judged the greater evil, what exactly should we compare in order to frame an answer? The usual procedure is to contrast inventories of horror: numbers of victims, means and circumstances of their deaths, types of concentration camps. Yet how do we make the transition from the raw facts of atrocity to a judgment of their moral meaning? Just why, for example, is the industrialized extermination mounted by Hitler more 'evil' than the 'pharaonic technology' employed by Stalin and Mao Zedong?[1] It would be an error to suppose there can exist a simple or direct answer to such a question. Rather, this greatest of vexed issues handed down from the twentieth century must be approached on three inter-related levels: moral, political and historical.

On the first level, we are concerned with the philosophical matter of ascertaining degrees of evil; and it is this exercise that arouses the greatest passion and has produced the most extensive literature. On the second level, we are enquiring whether the two systems may be legitimately equated as totalitarian polities; and since totalitarianism is clearly a bad thing, this subject also has moral ramifications that make it almost as contentious as the first. Yet, to give convincing answers to either of these questions, the indispensable preliminary is to confront some basic historical problems: Nazism and Communism's two-decade relationship, their organizational structures, their ideological purposes, and their actual res gestae.

It is to delineating a perspective on this third level that the present chapter is basically devoted. The first level will be touched on only by implication: we will be lucky if the volume as a whole can establish standards of evidence compelling enough to yield a consensual moral evaluation. The second level, which is more easily grounded in history, is given greater direct attention and evaluation; and something like a concept of generic totalitarianism will emerge by the end. As for the central subject of this chapter, the third level, the emphasis here is not on substantive, still less systematic, historical comparison, but on the parameters of such an investigation. Yet even within this narrowed-down task we encounter a complex mixture of overlapping and asymmetry.

There is, first, an obvious temporal overlapping: Hitler and Stalin were contemporaries; Nazism developed in part in opposition to Communism while Communism's primary defining adversary was always 'Fascism'; and in this interlocking relationship the two went to Armageddon together in the most traumatic moment of the century. Conversely, there is a major temporal asymmetry: Nazism lasted only 12 years and in a single country, spreading outward only by conquest, whereas Soviet Communism lasted 74 years, and eventually cloned itself over a third of the planet. Indeed, Communism is still with us, though in anemic form, in East Asia and just offshore from Miami.

Then, too, there are asymmetries of a conceptual sort. Is Nazism a unique case or part of a generic 'Fascism', beginning with Mussolini's March on Rome in 1922 and embracing the Nationalists in the Spanish Civil War, the Romanian Iron Guard, and Tojo's generals in Japan? After all, Hitler and Mussolini intervened together to aid Franco, they formed a Rome–Berlin Axis and eventually, with Japan, an Anti-Comintern Pact. Until well after the war, the term 'Axis' was colloquial shorthand for everyone on the 'Fascist' side (only Finland escaped obloquy for its involvement).

With the passage of time, however, this picture was significantly blurred. Throughout the century the Communists alone adhered consistently to the category of generic Fascism (which they had indeed invented in the 1920s). Thus, from the mid-1930s onward the slogan 'anti-Fascism' beckoned liberals to their side in one or another 'popular front', and even today it remains a mobilizing watchword. Non-Communist historians, for their part, wavered on this issue, though most would distinguish 'national authoritarian' regimes, such as Franco's Spain or Salazar's Portugal, with their commitment to social conservatism, a purely defensive foreign policy and traditional religion, from the 'neo-pagan' and imperialistic 'mobilization regimes' of Germany and Italy.[2] Finally, the exceptional nature of the Nazi death camps and the growing postwar awareness of the Holocaust, in conjunction with the thesis of its world-historical uniqueness, have increasingly argued for Nazism's singularity among European 'Fascisms'.

By contrast, the existence of a generic Communism can scarcely be questioned. It exists everywhere a Leninist party with the mission of 'building socialism' is in power, said socialism requiring the suppression of private property and the market in favor of institutional dictatorship and a command economy. Even so, this formula has in practice yielded significantly different results from one case and period to another. Thus, within the Soviet matrix there were marked fluctuations in coercive power from Lenin's War Communism of 1918–21, to the semi-market New Economic Policy (NEP) of 1921–29, to Stalin's 'revolution from above' of the early 1930s and his Great Terror of the decade's end and so on to the perilous wartime and imperial postwar periods (Nazism, on the other hand, subdivides chiefly into prewar and wartime periods, and public attention has focused overwhelmingly on the latter). Finally, in the Soviet case, the Khrushchev and Brezhnev eras are distinguished from Stalinism by diminished revolutionary vigor and a much-reduced level of terror.

Outside the Russian matrix, variations in the Leninist formula are even more notable. The Soviets' postwar 'outer empire' in eastern Europe was significantly different from the 'inner empire' of the Union itself. There were no real revolutions in eastern Europe (outside of Yugoslavia, which soon left the Soviet orbit), but instead a diversified process of conquest and absorption. Postwar Poland, for example, where the peasantry was never collectivized, is hardly comparable with Russia under Stalin, or even with Romania under Nicolae Ceauşescu (which was no longer really in the 'outer empire'). And although the political police were active everywhere, there was simply not space enough for real Gulags.

When we move from the Soviet zone in Europe to the Communisms of East Asia, we find greater differences still. Not only were all these regimes institutionally independent of Moscow, but each was different from the other. Kim Il Sung's socialism meant a hermetically closed family dictatorship as surreal as that of Ceauşescu; yet the 'Great Leader' also retained the Soviet alliance as a shield against China. Mao Zedong, on the other hand, was Moscow's greatest enemy on the left; so to prove his superiority over Khrushchev and his 'capitalist roaders', he outdid even Stalin's terror in seeking socialism through the Great Leap Forward of 1959–61 and the Cultural Revolution of 1966–76. Ho Chi Minh, by contrast, though as authentically Leninist as his predecessors to the north, at least channeled his party's energy into a war his population supported. Pol Pot, finally, produced the demented reductio ad absurdum of the whole Communist enterprise, as he attempted to out-radical not just Moscow, but Beijing and Hanoi as well. All these Communisms, moreover, varied in the intensity of their fury from one period to another, most notably as Maoism gave way to Deng Xiaoping's 'market Leninism'.

Still another variation on the generic Communist formula is introduced by the overlap of Leninism with nationalism, not only in the Soviet zone and East Asia but also in Cuba. It has often been noted that 'proletarian internationalism' has been a very weak competitor to modern nationalism; and, indeed, ever since European socialist parties in 1914 voted for war credits in their respective parliaments, in almost any crisis workers have put patriotism first. Consequently, it has been claimed that Stalinism was

9

basically a new species of messianic Russian nationalism, that Maoism was an exacerbated Chinese reply to Soviet 'hegemonic' pretensions, that Ho Chi Minh was a kind of Vietnamese George Washington, and that the sui-genocidal rampage of Pol Pot was a product of traditional Cambodian hatred of Vietnam. Obviously, also, Castro's revolution was a reaction to Yankee imperialism. Nationalism has, of course, played a role in all these cases. The real question, however, is whether that role is sufficient to demote generic Communism to secondary rank.

The answer depends on what we consider to be Communism's 'social base'. If we take the rhetoric of the 'international workers' movement' literally, then worker addiction to nationalism argues against generic Communism's importance.[3] In fact, however, that 'movement' has always been a movement of parties, not of proletariats. These parties, moreover, were founded by intellectuals and largely run by them, at least in their heroic phase, not by their alleged worker base; only later were these parties run by such ex-worker-apparatchiki as Khrushchev or Brezhnev. By then, of course, the full administrative autonomy of the East Asian parties (and the relative autonomy of the East European ones) had fragmented Stalin's genuinely international movement into sovereign entities. Even so, each entity preserved its Leninist structure and goals.

Resolution of the question of nationalism prevailing over Communism also depends on historical period: in the case of Lenin's, and indeed Stalin's, Russia, the answer is definitely no; in the case of Jiang Zemin's China it may still turn out to be yes. Yet we will not know for sure until we see how the last Leninist regimes disappear. An even deeper answer to this question, however, is that Leninist parties, whether united or at odds, have been able to master their populations' nationalism only so long as millenarian zeal lasted; but when zeal waned, nationalism returned to the fore. Indeed, the withering away of zeal is what explains the fate of both the former Soviet Union and the Yugoslav Federation. For in each case it was the prior death of the party that produced the collapse of the unitary state, with former apparatchiki, such as Slobodan Milosevic or Nursultan Nazarbayev, taking up the nationalist cause to retain power.

Given this range of asymmetries between Nazism (and/or 'Fascism') and Communism, as well as the differences among the Leninist cases, what then should we compare in assessing their political kinship or the depth of their criminality? Psychologically satisfying though it may be for some to find sharp distinctions between the two systems and for others to find close kinship, it should be obvious that the vagaries of history will force us to settle for a mixture of similarities and differences.[4]

The basic similarity is that both movements, whatever they claimed to be themselves, had the same enemy: liberal democracy. Both emerged in the

wake of World War I as explicit negations of Europe's long-term movement toward constitutional government founded on universal suffrage;
and so both replaced rule-of-law parliamentarianism with a one-party
regime under a supreme leader, exercising dictatorial power and employing
police terror. Both regimes, furthermore, instituted command economies,
whether through outright nationalization as in Russia or by administrative
pressure as in Germany. Finally, both were driven by millenarian ideologies:
in the case of the Nazis, the quest for the world hegemony of an
Aryan Volksgemeinschaft ('community of people'); in the case of the
Communists, the triumph of world socialist revolution.

These political and ideological characteristics, of course, amount to
what is known as the 'totalitarian model', as this was defined in the wake
of World War II (which was also the beginning of the Cold War) by such
figures as Hannah Arendt and the political scientists Carl J. Friedrich
and Zbigniew Brzezinski.[5] In fact, however, this perception of similarity
antedates the war. In the 1930s it was commonplace to refer to Mussolini,
Hitler and Stalin collectively as 'the dictatorships'. Indeed, this perception
had been given scholarly conceptualization as early as in 1937 by Elie
Halévy in his The Era of Tyrannies, which explained the emergence of
the dictatorships by a conjunction of the socialist ideal with the mass
mobilization of modern war.[6]

When modern war actually came a second time it confirmed the 1930s'
prior judgment, first of all in the collusion between the two chief dictators
in the Ribbentrop–Molotov Pact of 1939. Even more important, however,
was the revelation of the Nazi death camps, which made it starkly clear
that modern 'dictatorship' was an unprecedented phenomenon in world
politics. At the same time, Communism's victory did nothing to mitigate its
own, equally unprecedented terrorist power. In the face of these realities
the classical terms 'tyranny' and 'despotism' were totally inadequate, as
was the limp modern label 'authoritarianism'; so 'totalitarianism' carried
the definitional day. This choice was confirmed as militant Communism
spread during the next five years over a third of the planet to reach its
historical apogee. Thus, as World War II gave way almost immediately to
the Cold War, Stalin came to fill the whole totalitarian space, becoming
in the eyes of the liberal world Hitler's moral heir.[7]

This unitary perception of totalitarianism, however, progressively lost
ground after Stalin's death in 1953. As Khrushchev attempted limited
reform and as open dissidence appeared under Brezhnev, the Soviet party-
state, though it clearly remained tyrannical, appeared distinctly less total
and monolithic. Concurrently, as scholarship accumulated about the Third
Reich, the Nazi dictatorship came to seem less Behemoth-like and more
'polycratic' than had earlier been supposed. Finally, as public awareness of
the Holocaust grew after the 1960s, the Nazi case came to be increasingly

distinguished from the Soviet one until it was widely regarded as a historically unique manifestation of 'absolute evil'. In this perspective, Mussolini, with a weak party-state, no camp system, and only belated anti-Semitism, came to be treated as distinctly less evil than Hitler, and the concept of generic Fascism retreated into the background.

Concurrently, throughout the postwar period the evil of Nazism was increasingly dramatized to the world: the Nuremberg Trials of 1945–46, the Eichmann trial of 1961–62, Claude Lanzman's film Shoah of 1986, and so on to Steven Spielberg's Schindler's List of 1993. But, beyond the writings of Soviet dissidents such as Evgeniia Ginzburg, and especially Aleksandr Solzhenitsyn, there have been no comparable popular drama-tizations of the Gulag to world opinion. Nor has any major Communist figure ever stood trial. East Germany's Erich Honecker was permitted to leave for Chile, and sensitive souls, later so zealous in pursuing General Pinochet, were not at all disturbed. The second-rank figures now being considered for trial in Cambodia (who even knows their names?) will surely not be brought to justice in any foreseeable future.

Thus, by European Communism's collapse in 1989–91, most specialists of both Nazism and Sovietism had renounced not only generic Fascism but the totalitarian model as well, emphasizing instead the absolute singularity of Hitler's Reich. And this may well be the historically justified evaluation. Yet for present purposes the relevant point is that the disproportion between the attention accorded Nazi and Communist crimes has been so great as to constitute, a priori, a double standard in judging them; indeed, the disproportion has made comparison per se a sign of political bad taste.

This double standard, however, was challenged by the Communist collapse. And it has not been sufficiently emphasized that this collapse was not just Soviet, but eminently generic. It began with Deng Xiaoping's conversion to the market in 1979 and the 16-month 'self-limiting revolution' of Solidarity in Poland the following year; it became irreversible in 1989 with the simultaneous destruction of the Maoist mystique on Tiananmen Square and the fall of the Soviet 'outer empire' in Europe; and it culminated in 1991 with the disintegration of the Soviet matrix itself. Not only were the geopolitical results of World War II undone, but the 'short twentieth century', as inaugurated by World War I and Lenin's October, was brought to a close.

The impact of this revolution on our understanding of the old century was not that it revealed the full extent of Communist crime: this had long been no mystery to researchers who really wanted to know. The impact came, rather, from the liberating effect that the system's universal failure had on Western minds: it at last became possible to discuss Communism's record realistically and yet remain in good taste. Hence, the 1930s question of comparing it with Communism's Fascist adversary inevitably returned.

The publication of The Black Book of Communism in 1997 was only the boldest and most systematic expression of this change. A work of solid scholarship, its greatest originality was to treat the subject of Communist crime, not just in terms of the Soviet case but worldwide. And in this perspective, of course, Communism turned out to be far bloodier than Nazism, totaling roughly 85–100 million as opposed to 20–30 million victims, depending on who is counting and what manner of death is being considered.[8]

Moreover, this unavoidable – and to most people startling – fact raises the question of whether such a quantitative difference translates into a qualitative difference in the degrees of evil embodied by the two systems. At the same time, the geographical extension of the problem affected existing arguments for distinguishing, or conflating, the two systems, in particular as regards the viability of the concept 'generic Communism'. Is urban, European Communism comparable with rural, Asian Communism?[9] Must generic Communism therefore be broken down, once again, into more basic national and cultural units? Or does the already-noted fact that Communist leaders everywhere were neither workers nor peasants but intellectuals outweigh this sociological consideration? For there indeed exists a human bridge between the Red East and its Western godfather: Chou En-lai embraced Communism in France in 1921, and Ho Chi Minh and Pol Pot were actual members of the French Party in Stalin's time.

As of the twentieth century's calendar end, however, the verdict of 1989–91 had not really been absorbed into our historical consciousness. The Black Book, in particular, has provoked a mixed reaction. Although almost a million copies have been sold worldwide, including in both Russian and Chinese (Hong Kong) translations, thus indicating widespread interest, intelligentsia reception has been distinctly chilly, beginning in France itself but especially in the United States.[10] For reasons to be addressed below, this split reaction is indeed part of the problem of comparison itself.

In this confused situation, then, the first step toward clarification must be to compare, not actual historical cases, but historiographies. Benedetto Croce once famously declared that all history is contemporary history; and though it is going too far to embrace the post-modern inflation of this point, which would make the past a mere mental construct or 'text', it is certainly true that we invariably read that past through the prism of the present and all its political, cultural and ethical passions. This circumstance has bequeathed us radically asymmetrical historiographies for Nazism (and/or 'Fascism') and the different varieties of Communism.

The basic factor in explaining this asymmetry is that the Nazis lost World War II while the Soviets won it. Beginning in 1945, therefore,

Nazism's disastrous balance sheet was clear to everyone and historians had all its archives to boot. By contrast, the future of the Soviet 'experiment' appeared open-ended until 1991; its records remained secret; and for another half century the liberal world was confronted with the global challenge of its power. Moreover, Nazism's historiography was developed primarily by Germans who had to live with the consequences of the disaster, and hence could not avoid treating it for what it was. The historiography of the various Communisms, on the other hand, offers the bizarre case of a scholarly corpus developed almost entirely by foreigners (we may ignore the official, heroic histories of the various Communist regimes). These outsiders, moreover, were deeply divided over the Red revolution's meaning as it moved from Stalin to Mao to Castro.

Some of them, who for simplicity's sake we may call Cold Warriors, sought to mobilize Western opinion against Communism's progression, while others, ranging from cautious doves to outright fellow travelers, sought to justify either détente with the adversary or active sympathy for its 'achievements', even 'convergence' with its institutions. Our historiography of Communism, therefore, has always been as much a debate between the domestic left and right about Western hopes and fears as it was an enquiry into Soviet and Maoist realities.[11] So, for almost a century intelligentsia 'political pilgrims'[12] trudged from Lenin and Trotsky to Mao and Ho and on to Castro and Che. Nazism, on the other hand, after 1945 has found foreign admirers only among fringe figures seeking to diminish or deny outright the magnitude of the Holocaust.

The result of these contrasting circumstances is that we have radically different 'databases' for our two cases: the historiography of Nazism is voluminous, rich and varied, whereas the historiography of Communism, though copious (at least for the Soviet case) is fragmentary, thin and defective. In fact, much of it is out-and-out misleading.

This historiography's weakest link is East Asia. Although the Maoist mystique in the West never rivaled that of Lenin and Stalin, the premier American school of Sinology, that of John K. Fairbank, was, to say the least, lacking in lucidity about the Chinese regime while the Great Helmsman was still in charge. It is thus no exaggeration to claim that the Western-language historiography of twentieth-century East Asia (except for defeated Japan) has developed seriously only in the past two decades; and even then the archives of all the East Asian Communist regimes remained closed. Nor was the historical investigation of modern East Asia driven by the quest to measure evil that the Holocaust has provided to the Nazism–Stalinism comparison: Hitler and Auschwitz, or even Stalin and the Gulag, have never been a focus of moral debate in East Asia. These issues are not a universal preoccupation but a European or Western one.

So we are returned to our point of departure in the Nazi–Communist confrontation in Europe during the period 1930–45 and its treatment in German and Western Soviet historiography. In both bodies of literature, the first mode of explanation was Marxist, or at least marxisant. In the Russian case, this was for the obvious reason that the Revolution was supposedly 'proletarian', and Westerners wanted to find out if this were really true. So émigré Mensheviks, until 1939 in Berlin and Paris and after the war in New York, were prominent in spreading this perspective, powerfully aided by the Revolution's great loser (who nonetheless remained its prophet), Trotsky, and such of his disciples as Isaac Deutscher. In the German case, émigré Social Democrats or other leftists, such as Franz Neumann or Arthur Rosenberg, played a similar role in molding Western perceptions, with the result that Nazism, when it was not explained in the Communist manner as the product of 'finance capital', was given a social base in 'lower middle classes threatened by proletarianization'.[13]

After the war, however, the two historiographies diverged, with that of Nazism emerging as by far the more complex and variegated.[14] If this scholarly corpus has a leitmotif, it may be called Vergangenheitsbewältigung, that is, mastering or overcoming the past. In broad outline, this enterprise developed as follows.

After an initial postwar phase of conservative resistance to facing up squarely to that past, in the 1970s a new generation produced a 'Hitler Welle' ('Hitler Wave') and an increasingly probing body of literature, as researchers moved from classical prewar Marxism to the para-Marxist Frankfurt School, to Max Weber, to the French Annales School or American structural-functionalism. The first fruit of this methodological mix was a sophisticated elaboration of the totalitarian thesis's emphasis on politics and ideology. This effort in turn, and in conjunction with extensive explorations in social history, fueled a debate over Nazism as the product of a long-term German Sonderweg, or special path of development. In due course, the first of these interpretations was challenged for exaggerating the Nazi regime's internal coherence and the second for oversimplifying German historical development.

All these debates, moreover, were stimulated by the Holocaust's growing centrality in the national consciousness, a problem clearly resistant to ordinary political or social interpretations. This issue, therefore, engendered still another debate, this time between intentionalists, who emphasized Hitler's racist ideology, and functionalists, who emphasized the regime's institutional dynamics and the unfolding of the war – that is, politics. As was only to be expected, in the late 1980s these developments produced a conservative reaction explaining Nazism as a response to Bolshevism, though in the ensuing Historikerstreit, or historians' quarrel, these dissenters clearly lost out. Down to the present, therefore, political, ideological and indeed millenarian explanations have been further refined, and the thesis of Nazi singularity has essentially prevailed. The conclusions of this historiography, moreover, are known in general outline to social scientists in other fields. Who has not heard of the German Sonderweg, the intentionalist-functionalist debate or the Historikerstreit? If anyone needs a refresher course on these matters, there exist whole books that sum them up.[15]

By contrast, Soviet Communism has never been integrated into the common historical culture of Western academia. For example, a prominent historian of Nazism, in commenting on a recent book venturing some comparisons of Hitler and Stalin, objected that the author 'tends to rely more on older scholarship more closely associated with the politicized arguments of the Cold War than on the heavily documented studies by younger scholars of the Soviet Union who have worked extensively in recently opened former Soviet archives'.[16] In other words, this Germanist believes that scholarship on Soviet Russia in recent decades has been non-political, 'value-free' and archivally based to the same degree as the scholarship on Nazism.[17] This is decidedly not the case. When comparing Nazism with Communism, Westerners are in fact hobbled by a great disparity in our knowledge of the two regimes.

Thus, although Soviet specialists are literate in what academia's common historical culture tells us about Nazism, specialists of Nazism have no comparable literacy about the development of Soviet studies. Who knows that calling October a 'coup d'état' was long a fighting matter within the profession? Who understands what was at stake in the debate over the 'Bukharin alternative' versus the 'Cultural Revolution' of 1928–31? Or how many non-specialists are aware that Sovietology's still-dominant explanations of Stalinism were laid down in the 1970s, two decades before Moscow's archives were opened? In consequence, the comparison of Nazism and Communism has been largely the affair of people who know a great deal about the former but precious little about the latter – if they are not downright misinformed regarding it.

The development of Soviet historiography, consequently, requires a much fuller primer here than for Nazism; nor does there exist any handy short course of Sovietology to which an outsider might turn.[18] A still more crucial difference is conceptual: if the Sovietological corpus has a leitmotif, it is not overcoming a painful past; it is mining it to divine a future in which the 'experiment' would at last turn out all right (an enterprise, to be sure, requiring some measure of Stalinismusbewältigung, or dealing with Stalinism).

Accordingly, postwar Soviet historiography overall developed in the reverse direction from that of Nazism: that is, it moved from the primacy of politics and ideology, acting 'from above', to the primacy of socio-economic processes, particularly popular radicalism, acting 'from below'. Or, in the field's shorthand, it moved from the 'totalitarian model' to social-history 'revisionism'. This shift occurred in part for the professional reason that, beginning in the 1960s, social history predominated in all branches of the discipline. And who can deny the necessity of knowing the social facts in any historical configuration? In the Soviet case, though, this trend was pushed to an extreme by politics. For the Soviet Union was then mellowing while the Western cause was turning sour in Vietnam; so the totalitarian model was denounced as mere Cold War ideology and a gross caricature of Soviet complexities. In its place, social process was enthroned as the basic explanatory principle of Communism. To be sure, 'Cold Warriors' such as Robert Conquest continued to write about Communist terror, but such concerns were now viewed by the mainstream as archaic and superficial.

So, revisionism proceeded to discover a Soviet Union that was at the same time social and sociable. As the new narrative ran, the Leninist record, though flawed by Stalin's excesses, was nonetheless an overall achievement and a durable feature of modernity. The Communist system thus must be understood as an alternative form of 'modernization', one promising moreover a social-democratic fulfillment internally and enduring détente internationally.

The ideological subtext of this picture should be readily apparent. The new narrative, after all, began with the thesis that October 1917 was not a Bolshevik coup d'état, as the 'totalitarians' claimed, but a social revolution of workers and peasants; and in 1917 the masses indeed revolted against the possessing classes.[19] Yet it is equally obvious that they themselves did not come to power; a party of Marxist ideologues did. After such a beginning, it ought not be surprising that revisionism followed October's heirs in real history by developing in two divergent directions.

Thus, the movement divided into what might be called 'soft' and 'hard' versions – the cause of the divorce being those troublesome Stalinist excesses. To the soft revisionists, true Leninism was the semi-market NEP of the 1920s, an allegedly humane path to socialism defended after the Founder's death by Nikolai Bukharin; and in view of this 'Bukharin alternative', Stalin's brutal 'revolution from above' became an 'aberration'.[20] The hard revisionists, on the other hand, rejected the NEP 'retreat' to the market and instead claimed that Stalin's First Five-Year Plan was October's real culmination and Lenin's authentic heritage. This 'second October', moreover, allegedly developed from below through a 'Cultural Revolution' (1928–31) of workers and party activists. The essence of the Stalin era consequently was the proletariat's massive upward 'social mobility' – into the party nomenklatura, that is.[21]

As for the Great Terror of 1936–39, it was swept under the rug with the claim that it was only 'a monstrous postscript' to the Revolution, while the number of deaths by execution was modestly placed in the 'low hundreds of thousands'.[22] Another revisionist classic recognized only that 'many thousands of innocent victims were arrested, imprisoned and sent to labor camps. Thousands were executed.'[23] Even granted that until the opening of the Soviet archives after 1991 our knowledge of the system was incomplete, at no time were these figures anything less than prima facie absurd. It is inconceivable that anyone could get away with similar claims in German history. Yet the hard revisionists at most encountered polite collegial chiding – except from the soft revisionists, who were enraged at their whitewashing of Stalin.

The reason for this internecine passion, of course, is that, as the two schools squared off in the 1970s and early 1980s, they were in fact arguing over what to hope for under the next General Secretary: Bukharinite 'socialism with a human face', or a refining of Brezhnev's existing 'authoritarian welfare state' with its 'institutional pluralism'. The reason for these ideological contortions, of course, was that Stalin was indeed the culmination of the Soviet story and at the same time, in the eyes of his own heirs, a criminal.

It should be transparent to any neutral observer that we are not dealing here with rival emphases in social history but with a sectarian dispute between two species of ideologues: neo-Bukharinists and para-Stalinists, to be precise. Indeed, Western revisionism overall developed within what was basically a Soviet, or at least a Marxist, perspective. Putting matters this bluntly, however, was until recently impossible in academic discourse, especially in the USA. Down through the failure of Gorbachev's perestroika, any allusion to these obvious facts would be met with protestation from the revisionists that they were merely positivists, not Marxists, and that their 'social science', unlike that of the Cold War 'totalitarians', was a strictly non-political, 'value-free' enterprise. Or they might revert to the countercharge of 'McCarthyism'.

But bluntness is at present a therapeutic necessity; for, though the time is long past when the revisionist master narrative was plausible, the time has not arrived when this is adequately reflected in the historiography. Yet where now are revisionism's 'conquests': October as a 'social revolution' rather then a party coup d'état; the 'Bukharin alternative' of market socialism as true Marxism-Leninism; and the 'Cultural Revolution' of 1928–32 as the democratic crowning of the Soviet edifice? All are no more than fantasy chapters of an epic culminating in a socialism that turned out to be a mirage. All the same, though revisionism itself ended along with the Soviet regime, the revisionists themselves are still very much in place, and the debris of their narrative still frames our historical discourse, and so furnishes the basis for our comparisons with Nazism.[24] Since the parties concerned will not say this, it is necessary to say it in their place. And if they protest their positivist purity, one would imagine that this should carry no more weight than the protestations of Holocaust deniers that they are not partial to Nazism.

Why, however, did the Nazi revisionists fail so utterly, while the Communist revisionists' perspective was so long triumphant? The first reason, of course, is that the latter wrote before anyone knew how the Communist adventure would turn out. As Croce's mentor Hegel famously put it, 'the owl of Minerva flies only as the shades of night are falling'. So it was only after Communism, in 1991, at last ended up in the disaster column, as Nazism had 50 years earlier, that it became possible to have a 'normal', post-mortem Soviet historiography.

The transformation has already begun: in the 1990s a new generation has been actively rethinking the Soviet experience – though as yet no new paradigm has emerged to orient what one commentator has called 'a creative disorder'.[25] Indeed, given the 30-year accumulation of revisionist literature it will take a full generation to dig out 'from under the rubble', to borrow Solzhenitsyn's phrase about the Soviet legacy itself.[26] One thing, however, is already clear: a valid new historiography can be built only by reversing revisionism's explanatory priorities, that is, by treating the Soviet system in the first instance not as a society, but as a regime.

The reason why Minerva's owl was so slow to fly in the Russian case (contrary to its performance after the French events which inspired Hegel's maxim) is that October, unlike 1789, never knew a Thermidor. To be sure, ideological zeal abated after Stalin's death in 1953, but the structures of Party, Plan and Police that he and Lenin had between them built remained in place until 1991. Nineteen-seventeen therefore ossified into the historically unprecedented phenomenon of an 'institutional revolution' (to borrow a label from later Mexican history); and its only Thermidor was its demise. Not until the historiographical consequences have been drawn from such a paradoxical outcome can we hope to have symmetrical 'databases' for comparing Nazism and Communism.

Yet, the comparison itself will always be clouded by their contrasting ideological auras; and these derive from their relationship to that greatest of modern utopias, socialism. Both movements after all claimed that name, and both pretended to speak with a single voice for all the 'people'. Hence both strove to transcend liberal democracy by submerging the individual in the 'collective' or the 'communal', whether a fraternal internationalism or a particularistic Volksgemeinschaft. And this aspiration – presciently diagnosed by Elie Halévy – is surely the lowest common denominator of generic totalitarianism. This concept, therefore, is best considered both as a historical benchmark and as an ideal type, not a literal description of either dictatorship's 'monolithic' control of society.

Over and above this bond, however, socialism is relevant to the Nazi–Communist comparison for a still more basic reason: the pervasiveness of its mystique in the moral economy of modern politics. Generic socialism, after all, was the pre-eminent theoretical project of the nineteenth century, and its maximal version was the Marxist program of leaping to an egalitarian society through the suppression of private property and the market. This ambition then became the great practical endeavor of the twentieth century, whether its adherents settled for the diluted democratic variant of a welfare state or sought complete triumph through a Leninist party-state.

We have just spent a near century finding out that Marxism's perfect egalitarian society does not exist, and that on the far side of capitalism there is only a Soviet-type regime. Thus the Great Collapse of 1989–91 brought not only Communism's fall but that of generic socialism as well. To be sure, there are still numerous socialist parties and governments in the world, but none proposes to make the world-historical leap out of capitalism. (It is noteworthy, for example, that the anti-globalization movement of 1999–2001 never called itself 'socialist'.) Still, this second fact has not yet penetrated the contemporary consciousness; and until it does, the specter of socialism will haunt the Hitler–Stalin debate.

For that specter brings with it all the passion of the left–right polarity introduced into history by 1789. In the nineteenth century, this polarity focused on the universal-suffrage republic versus monarchy and aristocracy, and in the twentieth it graduated to the antithesis socialism versus capitalism. Yet, though the nineteenth-century political republic could in fact be achieved, the twentieth-century social republic proved to be a far more elusive goal. Most modern societies have therefore been governed in an alternation of left-center reformism and right-center prudence, and so rarely faced the stark choice: either capitalism or socialism. In the great crises of 1914–45, however, this centrist equilibrium broke down, and both 'Fascism' and Communism attempted the impossible millenarian leap. Ever since, in the modern political dynamic, Communism has functioned as the absolute left and Nazism as the absolute right.

This absolutizing of extremes clearly favors the former – and at the expense of the center. In the nineteenth century the outer limit of the right had been the Bourbons, and the first principle of progressive politics was 'no enemies to the left'. In the twentieth century the outer limit of the right became Hitler, and the Golden Rule received the ironclad corollary of 'no friends to the right'. In consequence, the thesis that Hitler was incomparably evil places moderate conservatives on permanent warning against all 'unsavory' allies to their right, and indeed against their own dark demons.

Conversely, comparing Stalin with Hitler only 'plays into the hands of the right'; for the real target of the comparison, of course, is the social-democratic left.

It is because of this dynamic that The Black Book met with the chilly reception it did – beginning with France's most prestigious newspaper, Le Monde. For did it not deflect attention from the far-right racist, Le Pen? And of course, in the light of twentieth-century experience, racism must always be denounced and combated. Yet, in strict logic, it hardly follows that this means refraining from honest (if belated) recognition of Soviet crime, any more than the scholarly 'historicizing' of Nazism entails its moral 'trivialization'.

Clearly, such passionate reactions cannot be explained by the economic and institutional differences between 'capitalism' and 'socialism'; only the moral and philosophical values grounding those differences provide an answer. At this basic level, what the left is about is equality and universality, or the fraternal unity of the human species; the right, on the other hand, is about hierarchy and particularity, or the functional differentiation indispensable to making any society work – and this inevitably means inequality. By extension, moreover, the right, which in the nineteenth century defended the Old Regime cause of 'altar and throne', in the democratic twentieth century came to defend both capitalism and the various national particularities defining competing societies.[27] In American usage the shorthand contrast for the left–right difference is 'compassionate' versus 'mean-spirited'. (In France, it is the presence versus the lack of 'générosité'.) In modern political rhetoric, therefore, it has always been easier to make a vibrant plea for equality and fraternity than for hierarchy, distinction and privilege, or even for individual liberty. So the moral economy of modern politics gives the left a permanent, built-in advantage.

This fact grounds what is perhaps the most frequently drawn moral distinction between the two regimes. And this is the claim that no matter how criminal Communism became, it was initially inspired by 'good intentions' and humanistic universalism (in Le Monde's high style: the contrast is between la face lumineuse of Communism and its face ténébreuse). Nazism, on the other hand, was never motivated by anything but national egotism, racism, and conquest. (Of course, it is these associations that explain the already noted double standard for judging crimes that are in effect comparable.) Thus such a strong anti-Communist as Raymond Aron has advanced what is now a standard argument: Nazism must be judged worse than Communism, since it practiced extermination as an end in itself while the latter did so as a means to some other, political or economic, end.[28]

This very real Western distinction, however, may be contrasted with the opinion of East Europeans such as Vasily Grossman, Aleksander Wat and Aleksandr Solzhenitsyn, all of whom had direct experience of both

Nazism and Communism and who all held the two to be comparably criminal.[29] The crux of their judgment is that Communist mass murder remains mass murder whatever its ideological inspiration; indeed, crimes against humanity committed in the name of humanity are in a sense more perverse than the blatant criminality of Nazism. This view arises from the insidious nature of the Soviet 'Lie'. A colloquial Soviet term for 'the system' made famous by Solzhenitsyn, the Lie denotes the fatal contradiction of a universalism driven, not by charity, fellow feeling or natural Reason, but by the ideological principle of 'class war', or more exactly pseudo-class war. Indeed, the Soviet 'building of socialism' was not a genuine social contest but a political struggle in which the redeemer class (in fact, its ideological substitute, the party) was destined to eliminate all exploiting classes (in fact, anyone resisting party policies). So 'in the twentieth century ideology made possible evil on a scale of millions'.[30]

These two antithetical moral judgments point to a moral of their own. And this is that our efforts to frame value distinctions between Nazism and Communism will certainly continue to seesaw back and forth with the contrasting magnetisms of the right–left polarity. Nor will this cease to be true even as the historiographies of the two movements approach each other in sophistication.

Nevertheless, achieving that empirical rapprochement remains the precondition for all serious comparison. And for this, the first priority is to overcome the pitiful lag a half-century has put between the historiography of Stalinism and Nazism. Consider the distance the latter has traveled. No one talks any longer about 'finance capital' or 'proletarianized lower middle classes' as basic causes of Nazism. Instead, among our most recent authorities, Ian Kershaw highlights Hitler's 'charismatic' Führerprinzip (leader principle) and Michael Burleigh the 'political religion' of Aryan racial supremacy. Nor is anyone allowed to be value-free; rather, moral judgment is de rigueur and crime is called by its proper name. For moral judgments are indeed intrinsic to all historical understanding.

So how to narrow the discursive gap? A solution might well be for historians of the Soviet phenomenon to read each other less and their Germanist colleagues more. This, in turn, could give the latter a worthy incentive to close the literacy gap on their Eastern flank.

NOTES

[1] Solzhenitsyn's expression, in The Gulag Archipelago, 3 vols, trans. Thomas P. Witney (New York: Harper & Row, 1973–74).
[2] Notably, Stanley G. Payne, A History of Fascism, 1914–1945 (Madison, WI: University of Wisconsin Press, 1995). Significantly, Payne is a historian of Franco's Spain.

[3] The position, notably, of Dan Diner, Das Jahrhundert Verstehen (Munich: Luchterhand, 1999).

[4] The most useful exercises in comparison are, Henry Rousso et al., eds, Nazisme et stalinisme: histoire et memoire comparées (Brussels: Complexe, 1999); and Marc Ferro, ed., Nazisme et communisme: deux régimes dans le siècle (Paris: Hachette, 1993), especially the article by Krzysztof Pomian. A disappointing effort is Ian Kershaw and Moshe Lewin, eds, Stalinism and Nazism: Dictatorships in Comparison (Cambridge/New York: Cambridge University Press, 1997), a volume that never comes to focus. Although Kershaw and some Russianist contributors are aware of the disparity between the two central historiographies, they fail to understand how deep it cuts or the factors that produced it. See Kershaw and Lewin, Stalinism and Nazism, pp. 9, 22, 296 and 343.

[5] Hannah Arendt, The Origins of Totalitarianism (New York: Harcourt, Brace, 1951); Carl J. Friedrich and Zbigniew Brzezinski, Totalitarianism Dictatorship and Autocracy (Cambridge, MA: Harvard University Press, 1956). The best overview of the totalitarianism debate is Enzo Traverso, Le Totalitarisme: le XXe siècle en débat (Paris: Le Seuil, 2001).

[6] Elie Halévy, The Era of Tyrannies: Essays on Socialism and War, trans. R. K. Webb (New York: New York University Press, 1966; first published 1938 from lectures given in 1937).

[7] The intellectual history of the concept is given in Abbot Gleason, Totalitarianism: The Inner History of the Cold War (New York: Oxford University Press, 1995).

[8] Stéphane Courtois, Nicolas Werth and Jean-Louis Margolin, The Black Book of Communism: Crimes, Terror, Repression, trans. Jonathan Murphy and Mark Kramer (Cambridge, MA: Harvard University Press, 1999).

[9] Serge Wolikow, Michel Dreyfus et al., eds, Le Siècle des communismes (Paris: Les Editions de l'atelier, 2000). Colloquially known in Paris as 'The White Book of Communism', this collective endeavor answers The Black Book by breaking Communism down into a series of discrete movements, with mixed positive and negative results.

[10] See, for example, J. Arch Getty's review of The Black Book in The Atlantic Monthly March 2000.

[11] For an academic work treating generic Communism favorably see, William G. Rosenberg and Marilyn B. Young, Transforming Russia and China: Revolutionary Struggle in the Twentieth Century (New York: Oxford University Press, 1982).

[12] Paul Hollander, Political Pilgrims: Western Intellectuals in Search of the Good Society (New Brunswick, NJ: Transaction Publishers, 1998).

[13] This tradition is summed up in Seymour Martin Lipset, Political Man: The Social Bases of Politics (Garden City, NY: Doubleday, 1960).

[14] Ian Kershaw, The Nazi Dictatorship: Problems and Perspectives of Interpretation (London: Arnold, 2000).

[15] For example, Kershaw, ibid., Charles S. Maier, The Unmasterable Past: History, Holocaust, and German National Identity (Cambridge, MA: Harvard University Press, 1988), and Peter Baldwin, Reworking the Past: Hitler, the Holocaust, and the Historians' Debate (New York: Pantheon Books, 1981).

[16] Omer Bartov, review of Michael Burleigh's The Third Reich, in The New Republic (March 2001).

[17] Kershaw at least recognizes this disparity, though he hardly appreciates its depth. Kershaw, Nazi Dictatorship, p. 35, note 35.

[18] To my knowledge there exist only two brief essays on this subject, both in my name: 'L'histoire soviétique', in S. Bernstein and P. Milza, eds, Axes et méthodes

de l'histoire politique (Paris: PUF, 1998), and 'Clio and Tauris', in Anthony Molho and Gordon S. Wood, eds, Imagined Histories: American Historians Interpret the Past (Princeton: Princeton University Press, 1998).

[19] Ronald Suny, 'Towards a Social History of the October Revolution', American Historical Review, 88 (1983), pp. 31–52.

[20] Stephen F. Cohen, Bukharin and the Bolshevik Revolution: A Political Biography, 1888–1938 (New York: Knopf, 1973) and Moshe Lewin, The Political Undercurrents of Soviet Economic Debates: From Bukharin to the Modern Reformers (Princeton, NJ: Princeton University Press, 1974).

[21] Sheila Fitzpatrick, Cultural Revolution in Russia, 1928–1931 (Bloomington, IN: Indiana University Press, 1988).

[22] Sheila Fitzpatrick, The Russian Revolution (Oxford/New York: Oxford University Press, 1982), pp. 3, 157.

[23] J. Arch Getty, Origins of the Great Purges: The Soviet Communist Party Reconsidered, 1933–1938 (Cambridge/New York: Cambridge University Press, 1985), p. 8.

[24] On the level of the general survey see, for example, John M. Thompson, A Vision Unfulfilled: Russia and the Soviet Union in the Twentieth Century (Lexington, MA/Toronto: D. C. Heath, 1996), and the section on the 1930s in Gregory L. Freeze, ed., Russia: A History (Oxford/New York: Oxford University Press, 1997). On the level of new scholarship, see the Yale University Press series, Annals of Communism, the volumes on the 1930s: J. Arch Getty and Oleg V. Naumov, eds, The Road to Terror: Stalin and the Self-Destruction of the Bolsheviks, 1932–1939 (New Haven, CT: Yale University Press, 1999); William J. Chase, ed., Enemies within the Gates?: The Comintern and the Stalinist Repression, 1934–1939 (New Haven, CT: Yale University Press, 2001); and, to a lesser extent, Lewis Siegelbaum and Andrei K. Sokolov, eds, Stalinism as a Way of Life: A Narrative in Documents (New Haven, CT: Yale University Press, 2000).

[25] David Shearer, 'From Divided Consensus to Creative Disorder: Soviet History in Britain and North America', Cahiers du monde russe, Vol. 39 (4) (1998).

[26] Aleksandr Solzhenitsyn, From under the Rubble, trans. A. M. Brock (Boston, MA: Little, Brown, 1975). For an earlier version of the argument given here see Martin Malia, 'From under the Rubble, What?', Problems of Communism, 41 (1992), pp. 89–106.

[27] For a probing analysis, see the Crocean treatment of Norberto Bobbio, Left and Right: The Significance of a Political Distinction (Chicago, IL: University of Chicago Press, (1996).

[28] Aron expressed this view in Democracy and Totalitarianism (Ann Arbor, MI: Michigan Press, 1968). Tzvetan Todorov, in Mémoire du mal, tentation du bien (Paris: Robert Laffont, 2000), pp. 44–7, criticized that book as conceding too much to Communism. In fact, in his last work – Mémoires (Paris: Julliard, 1983) – Aron himself said that such an abstract formulation of Communist intentions is useless.

[29] See Vasilii Semenovich Grossman, Life and Fate: A Novel, trans. Robert Chandler (New York: Harper & Row, 1986) and Aleksander Wat, My Century: The Odyssey of a Polish Intellectual, ed. and trans. Richard Lourie (Berkeley, CA: University of California Press, 1988).

[30] Solzhenitsyn, The Gulag Archipelago, Vol. I, p. 174.

2

The Uses and Abuses of Comparison

Tzvetan Todorov

Nowadays, as everyone knows, the simple fact of comparing and thereby linking Nazism and Communism encounters stiff resistance. There are several reasons why this is so. The first has nothing to do with political analysis; rather, it emerges from the displeasure people naturally feel when reduced to one of many examples marshaled in the service of historical generalization. This displeasure becomes a wound when painful experiences are involved, and those related to totalitarian regimes are always painful. From such a perspective, clearly, what at first seems an inappropriate comparison soon becomes offensive to the individual. One would not go as far as to tell someone who just lost a child that her pain was identical to that of many other unhappy parents. It is important to emphasize this from the outset, so as not to lose sight of – and neglect – the subjective point of view. For each of us, experience, in whatever forms it comes, is of necessity singular. Moreover, singular experiences are the most intense. When reason dispossesses an individual of his past and of the meaning attached to it, in the name of the need to compare and generalize, its arrogance seems insufferable. What is more, it is easy to understand how anyone involved in a mystical experience will refuse as a matter of principle any and all comparisons, and even the very use of words to describe it. For such an experience is and must remain ineffable and beyond representation, incomprehensible and unknowable, because it is sacred.

Such attitudes certainly deserve respect in and of themselves, but they belong in principle in the private sphere, and thus do not concern us here. Unless we take comparison to mean identity or equivalence, it is hard to see on what generally acknowledged principles of public debate the comparison of one event with another could be excluded out of hand.

The second reason for rejecting comparison is no less understandable and yet has no more of a place here. This is that the German form of

Fascism that we know as Nazism, with its particularly macabre institution of the death camp, has become for a majority among us the perfect embodiment of evil. This dismal privilege means that any other event compared with it is framed by the notion of absolute evil. In consequence, since the end of World War II, the comparison of these two ideologies, Communism and Nazism, assumes antithetical meaning, depending on one's point of view. For those who acknowledge a relationship to Nazism, it is an excuse. For those who feel close to Communism, it is an accusation.

In fact, things are a bit more complicated than that, for on each side we must distinguish the victims from their executioners. More exactly, given the amount of time that has passed, we have less and less to do with the actual protagonists, and thus must, by necessity, deal with groups who for either national or ideological reasons see themselves – consciously or not – in one or the other role. This leads to four, typical responses to the comparison between Auschwitz and Kolyma, as the victims of the one find themselves in the company of the executioners of the other:

1. The Nazi executioners are for the comparison, which serves as an excuse for them.
2. The Nazi victims are against it, for they see it as an excuse.
3. The Communist executioners are against the comparison, for they see in it an accusation.
4. The Communist victims are for it, for they can use it as an accusation.

Of course, there are exceptions to this kind of psycho-political determinism, and I shall return to them shortly. Suffice it to say, as a first approximation, that we have a pretty good chance of guessing a person's opinion on this subject if we know to which group he or she belongs.

The situation is further complicated by the fact that it is precisely the Soviet Union, the fatherland of Communism, which assumed the greatest responsibility, and also incurred the greatest losses, in the victory over the Nazis. So it is easy to understand the sense of an historic mutation. Right after the war, the comparison surprised people, and met with indignation, but during the 1930s it was an obvious one, as the commentary of practically all non-aligned observers testifies. The 1939–41 Nazi–Soviet Pact seemed to them to make manifest a complicity that had been disguised by the verbal attacks these warring brothers had earlier directed against one another.

But the resistance to comparing, even if perfectly understandable and even acceptable on a private, individual level (after all, who wants to admit to belonging to the family of the Devil?), must on no account stand in the way of the historian of the twentieth century, nor the political theorist.

Comparison is an indispensable tool of knowledge in those fields; it produces, of course, similarities and differences. Science is always sacrilegious. It refuses to isolate each event, where those who had lived the event personally are tempted to do so. Moral judgement, on the other hand, should follow the acquisition of knowledge, not precede it. Such, I believe, is the consensus among historians and sociologists today, who have studied the question in all its detail; more emphatically still, the consensus of society as a whole, in France as well as in other European countries. To claim that comparison is a legitimate methodology, however, does not imply that its results will be illuminating. For once we allow comparison, two new questions arise concerning how it can be used and what results it can bring when invoked.

How can it be used? To understand our practices better, I would like to propose the introduction of two limits here, two complementary reefs between which all comparisons must navigate. The first is that kind of sacralization that rejects all relationships of similarity or contiguity between an event under consideration and all other historical events. The second is a reflexive trivialization, which assimilates events to one another mechanically.

Let me start by saying that the sacralization of a past event must not be confused with the affirmation of its singularity, specificity or uniqueness. If we ask in what sense such an affirmation has any meaning, it certainly does not refer to the facts themselves: all events are unique, and that is a given which needs no further argument. Nor, it seems to me, can it be situated on some scale of values. All human beings are precious, each as precious as any other. When the victims of a regime are counted in the millions, it is otiose at best to attempt to establish a hierarchy of martyrdom. Beyond a specific threshold, crimes of this nature can no longer be considered specific. They merge in the horror without the distinction that they provoke, and in the absolute condemnation they deserve. We also take risks in assigning superlatives to the acts that touch us most directly. Each of us inhabits the center of selfhood, and we therefore judge what touches us as more important than anything else. If we change contexts for a moment, and consider the example of the Hiroshima atomic bomb: Kenzaburo Oe, Nobel Prize winner in literature, describes it as 'the most cruel experience known to man in our time', 'the worst madness of the twentieth century', and so on.[1]

What is specific, then, and what deserves interrogation, is of course the meaning of events. I will come back to this in a moment, but specificity does not mean sacralization. Let us take the central example of the destruction of European Jewry by the Nazis. Its specificity is established by multiple examples that inscribe it as a precise historical fact. Sacralization, on the other hand, is a retrenchment, a form of withdrawal, a taboo forbidding us to touch an object, or even to use terms like 'genocide' or 'totalitarian' to describe it. Specificity does not separate events from one another; it links them together. The greater the number of relationships, the more a fact becomes specific or particular. God is sacred, absolute and omnipresent, but not particular; indeed, the exact opposite of a fact occupying a unique time and place.

It is not because past events are unique, each having a specific meaning, that we must refrain from relating them to one another. On the contrary: far from excluding uniqueness, comparison alone establishes it. How can one affirm that something is unique without having compared it with anything else? We must not be like the wife of Uzbek, in Montesquieu's Persian Letters, who tells him in the same breath that he is the handsomest man in the world, even as she admits that she has never seen any other men.[2]

Sacralization has a terrible disadvantage: it makes us insensitive to the rest of the world, even as it cuts us off from the present by locking us in the past. The past then screens out the present, instead of leading up to it, and becomes an excuse for inaction. In his book on Rwandan genocide, Philip Gourevitch recounts how, in the spring of 1994, he went to Washington to attend press conferences at the White House.[3] There was a great deal of beating about the bush, because the US government had decided not to intervene in Rwanda. Because of the proximity in space, he found himself at the Holocaust museum one day, where he saw an abundance of badges claiming 'Never Again', 'Remember' and 'Never Forget'. But this appeal to memory hardly contributed to the struggle against what was happening at that very moment in Rwanda. In a way, it contributed to the failure to act.

The symmetrical risk is that of banality, whereby present events lose all specificity by being assimilated to those of the past. The extreme evil of the twentieth century can easily be transformed into a rhetorical weapon. Every time this occurs, however, we renounce the very link to its identity; worse, we run the risk of completely misunderstanding the meaning of new facts. The evil of the concentration camps, according to David Rousset, one of the first great theorists of what he named l'univers concentrationnaire, is not only more intensely evil than others, its very meaning is other.[4] The human charnel houses of Auschwitz and Kolyma reveal the presence of a radically new ideology and political structure.

To use the term 'Nazi' as a simple synonym for 'filthy bastard' is to miss every lesson about Auschwitz. The character of Hitler, in particular, is dressed to suit any and every occasion. He is everywhere, despite the fact that the genocide of the Jews is supposed to be unique. By 1956, Western governments had already found his reincarnation in Nasser, who had the impudence to nationalize the Suez Canal. Ever since, new avatars

28

of the Nazi dictator proliferate. The US government likes to designate its enemies in this way, so as to ensure the unconditional support of the international community. Saddam Hussein has been called another Hitler, and so was Slobodan Milosevic.

In the Middle East it seems like the comparison is invoked on a daily basis. Sometimes it is the Arab neighbor, from Nasser to Arafat, who is presented with the corporal's moustache. Sometimes it is the press that describes a hawkish Israeli statesman as Hitler in action. The insult can be recycled even from within each camp. An American internet site shows Ehud Barak with Hitler's features, in a Nazi uniform, deploying the Palestinian flag. The caption reads: 'I'll finish the job, Mein Führer!' Sometimes, sacralization and banality even function in concert, as when administration at the Holocaust Museum refused entrance to Yasir Arafat on the pretext that he was 'Hitler reincarnated'.[5]

Let us suppose for a moment, then, that we can manage to escape the dual reefs of sacralization and banality, that we have been able to use comparison advisedly. What light does it shed on the phenomena of Nazism and Communism that we have under scrutiny? I do not intend to put myself in the place of analysts whose arguments are often contradictory, nor set myself up as a judge to settle their disagreements. I wish simply to help to define a field based on the reflections of my predecessors, in particular the great Soviet writer Vasily Grossman. So I find myself back not at the question of the comparable or incomparable value of events, but of their respective meanings, and I have claimed that comparison reveals similarities and differences. So, which ones?

If we look at the similarities first, a question immediately arises. Should we not assimilate democracy with Nazism and Communism, or with their common denominator totalitarianism, in recognition of their common relationship to modernity?

As we know, this is the position of those who, in a doctrinal rather than strictly political sense, could be called conservatives. They see in liberalism and totalitarianism just two versions, one moderate, one extreme – soft-core and hard-core, if you will – of the same phenomenon. I have to decline to follow them here. It is true that scientism, the doctrine that subtends totalitarian thought, does indeed belong to modernity, if by that word we mean the ensemble of doctrines that claims a human rather than a divine or traditional origin for the laws of society. Modernity also implies the existence of a science, of a body of knowledge, which has been won by human reason alone, rather than by mechanical transmission down many generations. But in spite of these facts, and no matter what many armchair philosophers stubbornly believe, totalitarianism is not the inevitable outcome, nor the hidden truth of our modernity. Nor is totalitarianism the fatal, slippery slope of democracy. Modernity possesses more than one school of thought and neither free will as such, nor egalitarian ideals, nor the demand for autonomy, nor rationalism lead automatically to totalitarianism. There is a danger here of trivialization, where the comparison becomes diluted for the sake of a universal analogy in which six of one becomes half a dozen of another.

What is specific to totalitarianism (and thus what connects Nazism and Communism) appears clearly when we set those regimes against the liberal democracies. Comparing them is justified first from the perspective of a general typology of political regimes. Both differ significantly from democracy and no less clearly from despotic regimes of the past. Their common features involve the need for a revolutionary phase; the transformation of popular sovereignty into a pure façade; the rejection of all individual freedoms and autonomy; a systematic preference for monism over pluralism; the perception of conflict as the implacable law of existence; the radical elimination of difference as a social goal, leading to the systematic destruction of a part of the population; the general spread of terror; and a programmatic collectivism. Such are their common, essential features.

Their similarity can next be justified in a strictly historical sense. Indeed, the history of the first half of the twentieth century can hardly be understood without taking into account their complex interweaving. There is no need to go so far as to claim that Nazism is nothing more than a reaction to Bolshevism. To do so would be to deny the impact of local conditions. Still it is hard to miss how narrowly they interacted with one another, whether in imitation or in conflict, whether clandestinely, as in the adoption of the Soviet model of camps in Germany, or overtly, as during the Nazi–Soviet Pact. Both movements are, moreover, rooted in a common critique of liberal democracy and individual autonomy; each finds parallel impetus in the carnage of World War I.

These similarities are significant, and far from excluding distinctions, they make them all the easier to perceive. To see them clearly, we need not oppose these regimes to democracy, but simply confront them with one another. The surface distinctions are many, and easy to observe, and we need not bother with them. Instead, I would like to focus on two characteristic differences in the very structure of these regimes. The first involves the ideology each promotes. Scholars have emphasized the differences in content, making it easy to find that theoretical oppositions mask practical similarities, to conclude that the former are mere camouflage, an illusory masquerade without much import. Let me give two examples. If we compare the discourse sponsored by each regime, it would be easy to believe, in the terms of Soviet propaganda, that the Communists chose peace while the Nazis opted for war. In fact, the goal of Soviet politics was always the same imperialist expansion as the Nazis sought.

Communism staked its claim not just to international peace but to equality as well, yet Communism is anything but egalitarian. In the first place, as in a democracy, some individuals are richer, more successful, or more powerful than others. Next, and far more important, at its core, Communist society generates a system of privileges and castes that in some ways recalls the ancien régime. Communist ideology does not openly promote the cult of the superman, yet everything in the Soviet Union was geared to the veneration of the powerful. One caste in particular, the 'new class' of party dignitaries, the army and the political police, enjoyed a freedom and a power beyond the reach of mere mortals. Similarly, the cult of the Vozhd', or guide, was far more distant from the egalitarian program than the Führer was in relation to the openly hierarchical slogans of the Nazi regime.

It is often claimed that Communism is founded on a universalist ideology; accordingly, it becomes very difficult to group Nazism and Communism under the same totalitarian label, for Nazism is explicitly anti-universalist. Despite Communism's internationalist claims, however, the absence of universalism is obvious for both, for international does not mean universal. In reality, Communism is just as 'particularist' as Nazism, since it too explicitly affirms that its ideals do not extend to humanity in its entirety. 'Transnational' does not, for example, extend to social classes: the elimination of some part of humanity is always necessary. A perhaps apocryphal saying of Kaganovich, one of Stalin's close collaborators, expresses this best: 'You must think of humanity as one great body, but one that requires constant surgery. Need I remind you that surgery cannot be performed without cutting membranes, without destroying tissues, without spilling blood?'[6] Simply put, the divisions are not just territorial or 'horizontal' (i.e. defined by national boundaries); they are also 'vertical', cutting across social strata in the same society. Whereas one regime calls for war between nations or races, the other calls for class warfare.

Similarities in content are more numerous than the language used by each side might lead us to suspect. But the different status accorded the very place of ideology itself would seem to constitute an irreducible fact. Communism is a far more ideological project, in which the political program plays a distinctly more important role than in Nazism. Communism's place in the family of utopian projects is certainly more obvious, and the devaluation of the present in favor of the future is stronger. Communist ideology, then, offers a representation of the world more distant from its goals than does Nazism. Beginning with a particular moment in history, it therefore provokes an intense effort to disguise the abyss that separates the world from the representation ideology confers upon it. The Soviet regime is thus far more dishonest, illusionist and theatrical than its Nazi counterpart. The regime's discourse never has the aim of designating the world, nor of working for its transformation; its sole

31

purpose is dissimulation. All that can be viewed at any time is 'a colossal staging' in which the whole world becomes the set: electors pretend to vote, directors to direct; unions mimic the actions of real unions, writers claim to express feelings, peasants pretend to work like dogs. Indeed, only in actual theaters are performances what they seem to be.

The second major distinction involves the attitude taken towards those 'enemies' who are responsible for 'our' misfortunes. It is not that Communism presents itself as a more merciful regime than Nazism. Who can forget Lenin's demand for the 'merciless extermination of the enemies of freedom', for a 'bloody war of extermination', for the 'putting down of counterrevolutionary riff-raff'?[7] All totalitarian systems adopt the Manichaean division of the world into two mutually exclusive good and evil halves, and promote the goal of the annihilation of the evil half. And still the massacres of which Nazis and Communists are guilty do not have the same meaning.

The singular meaning of the genocide of the Jews does not reside in the numbers of the dead, since Stalin intentionally provoked the deaths of as many people between 1932 and 1933 by starving the Ukrainian peasantry. Nor, contrary to an often repeated adage, does it reside in the fact that the Jews were targeted for what they were, and not for anything they did, that they were 'guilty' only of having been born into a specific group. For this has also been true, at certain points in time, for members of the bourgeoisie, for the 'kulaks' and even for the peasants in the Soviet Union, when men, women and children and the elderly died side by side not for anything they had done, but precisely because they belonged to groups deemed unfit to live. The existence of an overriding project, of a plan sanctioned at the highest levels of state, is a fact of both regimes, not just for the Nazis. Finally, the meaning of the Holocaust does not reside in the idea that the Germans were a highly cultured central European people. This is occasionally suggested, even though ever since Rousseau we have known that culture does not automatically produce virtue, and that the immorality of cultivated people should not really surprise us any more.

The specificity of these crimes resides, then, not exclusively but principally in the Nazi project of systematic murder. Even if the idea of eliminating one part of humanity to ensure an eventual harmony can be discerned in both regimes, in reality the scales tip in one direction. In spite of the comparable number of victims, no real parallel can be found for the systematic destruction of the Jews and of the other groups the Nazis deemed unworthy of existence. For if Kolyma and the Solovki Islands were the Soviet version of Buchenwald and Dachau, there was no Treblinka in the Soviet Union: in the extermination camps, murder was the only goal, a goal unto itself.

There were, surely, comparable exterminations on the Soviet side, but they were not the greatest source of mortality. The mass of Soviet victims was engendered by a different logic. The deprivation of life was not an objective: it was a punishment, a means of terror, or an accidental loss considered meaningless. After three months, inhabitants of the Gulag perished from exhaustion, cold or illness. This was of no consequence: they were negligible and would be replaced by others. If the peasants died of hunger, that was the necessary condition for the collectivization of agriculture, for the Ukraine's submission to Russia, for the submission of the countryside to the city. Death, in other words, did not have any particular meaning. It was life that no longer had any value.

In fact, a paradoxical reversal emerges when we consider that the Soviets, who claim an historical and social framework for their global theories, practiced 'natural selection' in the sense that the weak died of hunger, cold or pestilence. The Nazis, on the other hand, despite their emphasis on biological principles, practiced 'artificial selection' both in Auschwitz and in other camps. They, their doctors and camp guards, were the ones who decided who among the prisoners would die, and who would gain a reprieve. So, while one group sacrificed human life as if it were worthless, the other dwelled in what Margarete Buber-Neumann has called an authentic 'frenzy for murder'. From this perspective, despite the apparent similarity of their programs, each regime retains its specificity.

Such is also the lesson Buber-Neumann drew from the painful experience of someone who had the fearsome privilege to pass without any transition from imprisonment in the Soviet camp at Karaganda to Ravensbruck over a period of seven long years.[8] The distinction she emphasizes most consists in the fact that the Soviets treated prisoners as slaves, while for the Nazis they were sub-human, untermenschen.

Both camps served the purposes of terror, but for the Soviets prisoners provided free and obedient manpower for the mines, factories and fields. In the German camps, by comparison, humiliation and degradation took place as if the very goal of the system were to reduce men and women to less than animals. 'The principal role was not played by the work of slaves but rather by torture and systematic degradation', she writes. Similarly, it is striking that the Nazis but not the Communists used human beings as guinea pigs for medical experimentation, because they were 'under-men', incomplete men, and because Jews, Gypsies, slaves, the infirm and the elderly had to die without regard for any possible economic benefit their lives might have.

By way of conclusion, I would like to call upon the example of an artist, the great painter Zoran Music, who spent the last year of World War II in Dachau. When he emerged from that factory of death, he felt unable to depict what he had witnessed. His experience was unique, it could not be communicated. Then, in the 1950s, wars started up again, in Korea, in Algeria, and elsewhere, and with them all the cruelty men know how to inflict upon one another. Surely different, that present was yet similar enough to inspire Music to produce a new series of paintings representing cadavers in the camps. He named it 'We Are Not the Last'. The new-found relationship between past and present, in no way trivial, allowed this painter to produce a shattering, moving work, a work that is both and at once right and true.

NOTES

[1] Kenzaburo Oe, Hiroshima Notes (New York: Marion Boyars, 1995), pp. 79, 16, 29.

[2] Montesquieu, Persian Letters (New York: Penguin, 1981 edn), letter 7, p. 46.

[3] Philip Gourevitch, We Wish to Inform You that Tomorrow We Will Be Killed with Our Families (New York: Farrar, Strauss, Giroux, 1998).

[4] David Rousset et al., Pour la vérité sur les camps concentrationnaires (Paris: Ramsay, 1990), p. 244.

[5] As reported in Le Monde, 16–17 July 2000.

[6] Kaganovich in Stuart Kahane, The Wolf of the Kremlin (New York: Morrow, 1987), p. 309.

[7] V. I. Lenin, Oeuvres choisies en deux volumes (Moscow: GIIJ, 1948), Vol. I, pp. 457, 545. Margarete Buber-Neumann, 'Wie verhält sich der Mensch in extremen Situationen', in idem., Plädoyer für Freiheit und Menschlichkeit (Berlin: Hentrich, 2000), p. 2.

[8] Margarete Buber-Neumann, Under Two Dictators (London: Victor Gollancz, 1949).

3

Worstward Ho: On Comparing Totalitarianisms

Irving Wohlfarth

LEFT FIELD

To forestall misunderstanding: this essay does not contest the need for comparative research on totalitarianisms. Quite the contrary. Its author, who received his training in comparative literature, belongs to a research group whose efforts to pursue such work have in recent years met with considerable ostracism on the French intellectual scene.[1] We have been accused of comparing the incomparable, of trivializing (banaliser), and thereby of denying, the Shoah – a charge which leaves itself open in turn to that of marginalizing other genocides.[2] There is presumably no longer any need to rehearse that sterile debate, or to argue that the 'uniqueness of the Shoah', indisputable though it is, has also served as an untenable and intolerable ideology,[3] or that 'uniqueness' and 'comparison', far from being mutually exclusive, presuppose one another. At this point in the ongoing discussion of the mass atrocities of the twentieth century, the necessity of making cognitive distinctions between totalitarianisms, and the accompanying unavoidability of making moral distinctions between them, can surely be taken for granted.

What is needed, however, is an internal critique of the way in which the comparative study of totalitarianism and genocide is usually undertaken. The target of the following argument is not comparison as such but a peculiarly self-limiting practice of the comparative method. Its claim is that more comparison is needed – boundless comparative activity, which, instead of placing its own position out of bounds, tries to consider its own implication in the objects of its scrutiny. Who really still thinks (s)he is in a position to contemplate history from the serene, free-floating position of nineteenth-century historicism and the typical survey course? To pore over it – se pencher sur, as French positivists used to say – as if it were a book or dossier to be opened and closed at will? Our blind spot is surely the one we occupy – the mote in our own eye. 'From where do you speak?' While all too ritually asked in the wake of 1968, this question has lost none of its virulence.

One may, on this basis, voice reservations about the idea of being asked to decide whether Stalinism or Nazism was the 'lesser evil' without necessarily evading the momentous issues that this question raises. It has come up at a particular moment in a series of ongoing parallel discussions and controversies around the singularity of the Shoah and the evils of twentieth-century Communist regimes. Universal and atemporal though the phrase sounds, the question of 'the lesser evil' is a conjunctural and strategic one, to which in turn only short-lived, conjunctural responses can be made.

While the following remarks draw more heavily on literature than on political science, they are not intended as a provocative literary barb – which is how they were conveniently misheard when delivered at the conference which gave rise to the present volume – but as a sober political one (Stachel: a metaphor of Kafka's to which they will return). They do not snipe from some safe, 'objective' vantage-point. That positionless position is, on the contrary, the cover at which they aim. They do so from the left – a much-vacated area these days – and, needless to say, from within the material security that all Western scholars enjoy.

IN LINGUA VERITAS: ODRADEK

In his study of the emerging Nazi regimentation of the German language, LTI, the Romance philologist Victor Klemperer proposed the above variation on the saying In vino veritas.[4] Theodor Adorno would, significantly enough, extend this statement to our best insights: 'Only those thoughts are true that do not understand themselves.'

The truth will out. One doesn't need wine to elicit it. One need merely observe language at work and at play. Given its inextricable relations with the unconscious, is not indeed all language a more or less arrested slip of the tongue? A pervasive dimension of the 'psychopathology of everyday life'? 'Normality' – the 'everyday language' in which some analytic philosophers blindly placed their trust – would then simply be the most-used frequency on the spectrum. This is perhaps why Franz Kafka and Walter Benjamin traced the Fall to a momentary impatience, a lapse of attention, and why Benjamin saw in that lapse the Fall of language itself.

More than a century earlier, in 1778, the philosopher-scientist Georg Christoph Lichtenberg had jotted down the following observation:

Servants have their turns of phrase:
1. The garrison was cleared, instead of the fortification.
2. A total battle, a total campaign, a total war.[5]

The phrase 'total war' thus antedates Goebbels's 'Do you want total war?' by at least a century and a half. It does so, however, as a slip or misnomer. To a rational eighteenth-century mind, it was self-evident that a war, no matter how devastating, can no more be 'total' than any other single aspect of the world around us; and that language, reason and ethics accordingly require us to avoid such loose habits of speech.[6]

But if the phrase 'total war' was one of those 'subtle confusions'[7] characteristic of an uneducated mind, why did Lichtenberg single out this particular one for special attention? The following jotting suggests a possible answer.

It would surely be possible that our chemists should one day stumble on a means of suddenly dissolving the air we breathe ... That could mean the end of the world. (1795)[8]

As an imaginative and far-ranging man of the Enlightenment, Lichtenberg perhaps sensed that the illiterate phrase 'total war' nevertheless had the potential to come true. Just how true we today sadly know.

At the beginning of World War I, Karl Kraus observed that the language of the present was that of the wordless runaway deed.[9] The 'Great' War brutally realized both the servants' uneducated talk of 'total war' and Lichtenberg's educated guess that the chemists would one day invent a gas that might mean the end of the world. To speak of clearing the garrison instead of the fortifications was to perpetrate verbal and moral confusion. It would, however, prove possible to wreak such confusion with the invention of modern technological and bio-chemical warfare.

Happy was the age to whose ears 'total war' sounded like a contradiction in terms. But it is only because total wars, like totalitarian states, remain inherently contradictory projects – contradictory precisely by virtue of their desire to eliminate all traces of contradiction – that the human species has so far managed to survive them. Despite the untold destruction that total wars have unleashed upon the world, they constitute unreal assaults upon the real. A lie come true remains a lie.

In lingua veritas. The truth that lurks in language can be that of a truth or a lie. Thus, while 'total war' gives itself away in the eighteenth century as servants' talk (and, in the twentieth, as organized propaganda, unprecedented monstrosity, and finally advertising hype), the term 'totalitarianism' is a quite different case. Turning Mussolini's neologism stato totalitario against itself, it points to the contradictoriness inherent in any effort to achieve absolute control. As one -ism among others, the word partakes of the plurality that the thing it designates wants to eradicate. In principle, therefore, none of its adherents should invoke that term.

In lingua veritas. Kafka's fragment The Cares of the House Father describes an elusive, enigmatic entity – small, mobile, untidy, precise, 'of no fixed address', and with a rustling laugh perhaps not unlike the smile of Lewis Carroll's Cheshire cat. No-one will ever be able to pin it down. Its name cannot be traced, nor can it – or he (but not she) – be categorized. It is, for example, neither Kant's 'thing in itself' nor there 'for us'. Unable to come to terms with it, the father of the house has to live with this intermittent reminder of his limits and the 'almost painful' knowledge that it will outlive both him and his descendants.

But isn't Odradek also his close and distant bastard, the illegitimate late child that Law and Order had with Chaos? Could it have been conceived of prior to the age of bureaucracy and the autumn of the patriarch – Freud's worried, compulsive 'ego' that is no longer 'master in its own house'?

But perhaps Odradek also takes us back to the beginning of human time. Another text of Kafka's, A Report to an Academy, speaks of the immemorial 'draught' that cools men's heels – their 'Achilles' heel'. A 'storm' blows from our long-forgotten animal past through the 'hole' out of which mankind once emerged. The hole has meanwhile shrunk behind us – which is why there can be no return and why the storm is now only a draught. This storm nevertheless strangely resembles the gale-force wind that, according to the ninth of Walter Benjamin's Theses on the Philosophy of History, we nowadays call 'Progress'.[10] It is, in Benjamin's version, 'blowing from Paradise'. It dates, in other words, from the Fall. For, just as Kafka attributes the Fall to a momentary 'impatience',[11] so Benjamin traces the Fall of language to 'diversion' (Abkehr), distraction, a lapse of attention.[12] It was, in short, nothing other than our first slip of the tongue.

Progress would thus be the Progress of the Fall. The storm, for Kafka as for Benjamin, 'blows from oblivion [aus dem Vergessen]'.[13] Against this great immemorial storm of forgetting they both range the laughable but indomitable force of the forgotten – be it Odradek or the shrunken mischievous 'little hunchback' of the German nursery rhyme.[14]

In lingua veritas. For example, Odradek. Odradek is what eludes and plays tricks on us: the shrunken but unclosable hole of oblivion, tricks of memory, the Achilles' heel, slips of the tongue. The word Odradek is 'itself' – but is it an 'it' or a 'self'? – such a slip and, like Odradek 'himself', a canny, uncanny one.

Language here anticipates the failure of the totalitarian project, or at least resists it. One definition of the indefinable Odradek would in effect be: 'that which not even an all-controlling, totalitarian Father could ever control – for example, his tongue'.

Perhaps, then, resistance to total domination does not (only) lie in our common 'humanity'. Or, if it does, then in its inhuman part.[15] What escapes totalitarian grasp would be equally, but differently, inhuman. Or rather neither human nor inhuman – like Odradek.

The Apparatus in Kafka's Penal Colony falls apart, as if under the pressure of 'some great force'. Could the weakness of its strength – its Achilles' heel – be inversely correlated to the strength of Odradek's weak-ness? And also to the 'weak Messianic power'[16] – fragile but ineradicable – of which Benjamin spoke in 1940 in the face of the massive totalitarian threat represented by the Nazi Soviet pact?

'THE LESSER EVIL'

To entitle a book devoted to the 'moral comparison' between the two deadliest totalitarianisms of the twentieth century 'The Lesser Evil' is to perpetrate another 'subtle confusion'. Properly used, that phrase refers to the necessity of choosing between two bad alternatives, one of which is considered less unacceptable than the other. At this particular historical juncture, however, we mercifully – that is, by the 'grace of late birth' (Helmut Kohl's Gnade der späten Geburt) – do not need to choose between Nazism and Communism, as we might have thought we did if we had been in our fathers' or grandfathers' shoes. We are confronted with other choices. It goes without saying that these nevertheless require us to try to come to terms with the two worst evils of our 'unmastered past'.

In their wake, Churchill observed that Western democracy, for all its shortcomings, still remains the better, the only viable political alternative. Political utopianism leads in practice to far messier results than do the politics of compromise, relativity and muddling through. Such is, at least, the Anglo-American wisdom that currently prevails in our disenchanted post-totalitarian democracies. Compared with totalitarianism, democracy amounts to the lesser evil. That is, at least, a correct use of the phrase. What, however, does it mean to say that one totalitarianism represents a lesser evil than another?

Another use of the phrase may serve to gauge the present mood: 'From Homer to modern times the dominant spirit wishes to steer between the Scylla of a return to mere reproduction and the Charybdis of unfettered fulfilment: it has always mistrusted any star other than that of the lesser evil.'[17] So far – as Adorno and Horkheimer are arguing here – mankind has thought (it necessary) to opt for the lesser evil. The choice has always been between the pleasure- and the reality-principle, the lethal enchantment of the Sirens' song and the safety of disenchantment. Tertium non datur. Seen, however, from the utopian perspective of that excluded third, the option for the lesser evil is synonymous with an archaic logic of sacrifice. While the logic of the lesser evil was once essential to self-preservation, it has meanwhile – on this argument – been mobilized against the utopian, but increasingly real, possibility of an altogether different alternative.

During recent decades, the politico-ideological mood of the West has been characterized by an 'exhaustion of utopian energies'.[18] The hope that capitalism might one day wither away has itself withered away. The logic of the lesser evil has accordingly reasserted itself. Its corollary is the widely held suspicion that the best is synonymous with the worst and that the utopian dream has in practice engendered – must perhaps inevitably engender – totalitarianism. Abandoning the search for alternatives, the erstwhile left has belatedly caught up with E.M. Forster's 'two cheers for democracy' and Churchill's lesser evil.

Why, then, at this particular juncture, transpose the notion of the lesser evil to the comparison between totalitarianisms? Two reasons suggest themselves. First, recent debates have been entangled in a false alternative between two camps: 'particularist', judeocentric partisans of the 'uniqueness of the Shoah' versus 'universalist' advocates of research into 'comparative genocide'. In the name of uniqueness, the former have thus far refused comparison, even though their case rests on it; the latter (or so the former think) refuse uniqueness in the name of comparison. Introducing into this blocked discussion the notion of the lesser evil appears to open up the possibility of ending the futile polemic between the (real or alleged) 'trivialization' and the (real or alleged) 'sacralization' of the Shoah. The categories of 'singularity' and 'radical evil' can now be pluralized into a differentiated comparison between singularities and evils. Second, the notion of the lesser evil promises to prevent the generic notion of totalitarianism from obscuring the moral differences between totalitarianisms. A case has thus been made for extending to the study of totalitarianism the 'gradations' that law and custom have always made between varying types of murder and execution.[19]

The idea of making moral discriminations between evils of this order of magnitude is nevertheless problematic. Comparative studies do not necessarily entail grammatico-moral comparatives: lesser, worse, etc. True, 'comparative totalitarianism' is hardly comparable with comparative literature or comparative anatomy, neither of which require their students to make comparative moral evaluations of the objects they compare. Moralizing the differences between genocides may nevertheless prove both superfluous and counter-productive. Does morality really need to be injected into this material? Is 'The lesser evil' a promising research agenda? The present volume may provide some answers.

ON COMPARING TOTALITARIANISMS

It is neither possible nor desirable to avoid making moral comparisons between totalitarianisms. But even as one continues, unavoidably, to make them one should also not avoid interrupting that activity. Critical as it is to distinguish between the different shades of black in order to see in the dark, it is no less necessary to ignore these distinctions in order to see the dark itself. To be blinded in one eye, unblinking in the other: is not this what it would take in order to get 'what happened' (Celan) into any kind of focus?

The true witnesses are those who did not survive, observed Primo Levi, one of the truest witnesses to have survived Auschwitz.

'Where a chain of events appear before us, he sees one single catastrophe', wrote Benjamin in 1940 – he being the 'Angel of History'.[20] We, it is true, are no angels, and cannot see through his eyes, cannot see that spectacle 'steadily and whole'. Nor would the spectacle of a single catastrophe be immediately useful for comparative purposes. But can we see two or more without glimpsing the one – by proxy, through shielded, averted eyes?

Is not Arendt's work on totalitarianism somehow informed by the following diary entry of Kafka's, which she cites in her essay on Benjamin?

> Anyone who cannot cope with life while he is alive needs one hand to ward off a little his despair over his fate ... but with his other he can jot down what he sees among the ruins, for he sees different and more things than the others; after all, he is dead in his own lifetime and the real survivor.[21]

Two pairs of eyes in one head, an Angel's and a man's – two lives, one dead, one alive – two hands – literature and political science – to be and not to be – survive and not survive – cope and not cope ...

'How was he able to survive in this air?', asks Benjamin of Kafka.[22] 'Who knows', asked Baudelaire in the mid-nineteenth century, 'whether the coarsening of our nature is not the only obstacle that prevents us from appreciating the environment in which we breathe?' Long before the wars and camps of the twentieth century, nineteenth-century city-dwellers developed a psychic callus in order to survive their daily experience. In order not to experience it. Not to live it – in order not to die from it – and thus to die from it. But those who, like Kafka, have no callus die from that. Nothing is more vulnerable than the capacity for vulnerability. Without it, one dies; with it, one dies; one survives, that is, one way or another.

Dealing with the worst, as deal one must, one gets inured. Such deformation attends many professions. To a non-professional ear, the phrase 'the lesser evil', valid though it may be for its prescribed purposes, may also sound like an embarrassed, embarrassing euphemism disconnected from the incommensurable experience of the camps.[23] When Wilfred Owen or Conrad's Kurtz invoked the 'horror' and 'the pity of it all', they weren't merely expressing emotion or seeking catharsis. 'The heart has its reasons that reason does not know': the literature of the camps has a knowledge that the professional literature ignores at its peril. Should it not rather try to translate that knowledge into its own?[24]

Under the pressure of an abnormal world, normal comparisons sooner or later reach the limits of grammar and sense. A text of Samuel Beckett's entitled Worstward Ho holds out at that limit for 47 pages. Its language records the disintegration of the ready-made phrases we exchange when we talk of good, better and worse:

> Try again. Fail again better again. Or better worse. Fail worse again. Still worse again. Till sick for good. Throw up for good. Go for good. [...]. Good and all.
> All of old. Nothing else ever. But never so failed. Worse failed. With care never worse failed.[25]

Could an expression like 'the lesser evil' have passed Beckett's ear unscathed – an ear that refuses the language of comparative optimism in the name of a superlative pessimism? In cannibalizing Charles Kingsley's Westward Ho, his title gives us to understand – but how understand it? – that it is the West that 'never so failed', 'with care never worse failed' and that there was 'nothing else ever'.

In his essay on Surrealism (1929), Walter Benjamin denounced the bourgeois belief in progress vested in a certain telltale use of the comparative. Its unreal optimism masked a no less unreal pessimism, to which the only response could be an active, organized pessimism (not unrelated to Nietzsche's 'active nihilism' and Gramsci's 'pessimism of the intellect, optimism of the will'):

> For what is the program of the bourgeois parties? A bad poem about springtime, filled to bursting with comparisons. The socialist visualizes the 'finer future of our children and grandchildren' as a matter of their all acting 'as if they were angels' ... . These are mere images. And the stock-in-trade of this social-democratic association? The gradus ad parnassum of these poets? Optimism. ... nowhere do ... metaphor and image ... collide so drastically and irreconcilably as in politics. For to organize pessimism means nothing other than to expel moral metaphors from politics and to discover in political action a sphere given over one hundred percent to images [den hundertprozentigen Bildraum].[26]

In lingua veritas. The quality of the moral comparisons between present and future so characteristic of social-democratic programs gave itself away in would-be poetic metaphors that transform action into acting as if. What they expressed was not a real, illusionless belief in progress,[27] but the resigned, hopeless, phantasmagorical faith of the kind anatomized in Baudelaire's prose poem Les Chimères ('Chimeras'): belief in whatever – against all better knowledge.

The road to totalitarianism was paved with false optimisms and false pessimisms. Nor did these disappear in the aftermath.[28] Comparative meliorism still persists in duly chastened form. Today it takes the form of refusing false optimism and false pessimism. What, then, of a moral comparison of totalitarianisms from some such position?[29] It would probably be judged unduly pessimistic by the editors of the present volume if one were – not, perhaps, to counter – but at least to counterpoint their title with the one that Zoran Music gave his haunting sketches of fellow-inmates in Auschwitz: 'We Are Not the Last.'

IN THE PENAL COLONY: APPARATUS, SPIKE, EMBARRASSMENT

It was an important moment. The old partners of the spectacle of punishment, the body and the blood, gave way. A new character came on the scene, masked. It was the end of a certain kind of tragedy; comedy began, with shadow play, faceless voices, impalpable entities. The apparatus of punitive justice must now bite into this bodiless reality.

Regard punishment as a political tactic. ... make the technology of power the very principle both of the humanization of the penal system and of the knowledge of man. ... in our societies, systems of punishment are to be situated in a certain 'political economy' of the body ... .

These 'power-knowlege relations' are to be analysed, therefore, not on the basis of a subject of knowledge who is or is not free in relation to the power system, but, on the contrary, the subject who knows, the objects to be known and the modalities of knowledge must all be regarded as so many effects of these fundamental implications of power-knowledge and their historical transformations.

The carceral network does not cast the unassimilable into a confused hell; there is no outside.

I am not saying that the human sciences emerged from the prison. ... The carceral network constituted one of the armatures of this power-knowledge that has made the human sciences historically possible.[30]

Another work of literature may serve here as a parable for the dilemma facing the comparative study of totalitarianism. Kafka's In the Penal Colony[31] is an allegory without explicit moral acted out by nameless character-masks; these will be capitalized in the following pages in order to accentuate their allegorical status. The narrative voice, too, is strikingly impersonal:[32] that of 'an individual (by the name of Franz Kafka)'.[33] The story was written at a turning-point in Western history – only weeks after the outbreak of World War I. A war machine of unprecedented destructiveness had been almost accidentally set in motion. It was perhaps this shock that precipitated some of Kafka's central images.[34]

Unlike Kafka's animal stories, this narrative takes place within the human realm, albeit at its outer rim. Its protagonist is a 'travelling scholar' (Forschungsreisender),[35] generally abbreviated to 'the Traveller', whom the unseen 'New Commandant' of an unidentified penal colony has invited to witness an execution. A 'peculiar Apparatus' invented by the 'Old Commandant', and now lovingly maintained by his surviving lieutenant, 'the Officer', engraves on each Prisoner's back the rule he has transgressed. The rule in the present instance – 'Honor your superior' – combines echoes of bureaucratic regulations, a military command and the ten command-ments. It entails its own sentence (in both senses of both words) inasmuch as the Law seems almost calculated to induce its transgression. It exists, like God, for its own greater glory, and its executive Apparatus operates more or less 'on its own' (für sich), like an automat. Hence the Officer's quasi-religious, fetishistic veneration for all aspects of his inheritance, notaby for the Old Commandant's handwritten manuscripts, whose contents are programmed into the machine and thence applied to the guilty man's back. By a further refinement, the writing is rendered almost illegible by a proliferation of flourishes which serve to prolong the dying man's agony. 'Ornament is crime', said Adolf Loos: here it is gratuitous punishment, as purposefully purposeless as a modern work of art.[36] Like the crucifixion of Christ, the whole process lasts twelve hours. From the sixth hour on, so the Officer claims, the condemned begin to decipher their wounds and finally die transfigured by the justice that they have experienced in the flesh.

The Prisoner is thus as much an appendage of the machinery of justice as the workers portrayed in Capital and Modern Times are of the industrial machine. They give it work and get back socially redeeming meaning. Many seemingly incompatible motifs – among them, the cold logic of the modern judicial machine, the 'poetics' (Vico)[37] of the old jurisprudence, the fetishism of technology, the 'metaphysics of crime',[38] redemption through religion and/or art and the 'total state' as a 'total work of art'[39] – seem to have gone into this composite, 'overdetermined' machine. It has the ambiguity of those 'dialectical images' in which 'the new is intermingled with the old'.[40] The Old Commandant and his Apparat are 'historicist' combinations of age-old and ultra-modern elements – home-spun prototypes of sinister things to come.[41]

The Traveller, too, is part of a larger Apparatus: Althusser's 'ideological state apparatus', Foucault's 'power–knowledge relations'. As such, he is enlisted into the strategy of the New Commandant, who has a stake in doing away with an apparatus that represents the last barbaric relic of the old order. To this end, he wants to be able to produce the outside opinion of a recognized expert. After all, what else can an accredited scholar do but condemn an institution that defies the most elementary modern European notions of criminal justice? The Officer cannot therefore but fail in his bid to win the Traveller to his side. He thereupon takes the Prisoner's place and prepares to martyr himself to his cause. The Traveller, respecting his decision, refrains from intervening. No sooner, however, has the apparatus gone into motion than it begins to fall apart. In the process, it butchers the Officer, who dies transfixed, but not transfigured, before the Traveller's now frantic eyes. His 'calm and convinced' expression betrays 'no sign of the promised redemption'; his forehead is traversed by 'the tip of the [disintegrating machine's] great iron spike [Stachel]'.[42] In their respective ways, both are spiked.

In a brief epilogue, the Traveller visits the Old Commandant's grave before rejoining his ship. We last see him raising a heavy, knotted rope against the Prisoner and the Soldier, who are seeking to escape with him.[43]

The public reading of Kafka's text was advertised by its sponsors under the title Tropische Münchhausiade: this association with the fabled Baron Münchhausen, who was best known for having pulled himself up out of a swamp by his own boot-straps, was as strange as it was apt. Not for nothing, however, did Kafka entitle the story In der Strafkolonie. There is no way out, no safe passage back, not even for a returning Traveller. Just as, according to Freud, a certain 'discomfort' (Unbehagen) is endemic to all 'culture', 'psychopathology' being inherent in 'everyday life', and just as, according to Nietzsche, morals, religion and the whole civilizing process have their origins in 'systems of cruelties', so the outlandish sequence of events that occurs at Kafka's colonial outpost points to the darkness at the heart of all Empire and Enlightenment.

The historical evidence condensed in this literary insight continues to accumulate. Three randomly selected items may stand here for the global archipelago.

1. 'Concentration camps' were first invented by the British in South Africa before being imported back to Europe.

2. It is currently reported that Fuertaventura, a Spanish island internationally known mainly to tourists from northern Europe, will soon house a technologically sophisticated holding camp for refugees caught trying to cross by boat from Africa to Europe.
3. Terrorist suspects from Afghanistan are currently being held by the United States Army at its military base in Cuba in order to prevent civil justice from having jurisdiction over them.

The post-colonial Empire has, in short, still not done away with the old Apparatus; it has merely overhauled it. The dialectic of old and new is indeed the underlying thrust of Kafka's story. The fact that the Traveller does not leave the colony before having visited the Old Commandant's half-buried burial place suggests that the prophecy he finds inscribed 'in very small letters' on the latter's tomb – the promise to return after a 'certain number of years' to 'lead' his followers to victory – is not to be dismissed.[44] It was not long before Leaders did indeed emerge.

But could it not be that the mythical Old Commandant has already returned in the guise of the New? And that (as Freud argued in Totem and Taboo) the Primal Father forever keeps returning? In which case, the Old Commandant would not merely be the object of a marginalized sectarian cult but rather the Weltgeist in all its reincarnations – the guiding spirit of a brave new world that no longer believes in ghosts.

The enclosed world over which he rules is thus not easily periodized in historical terms.[45] It is – in Freudian and Marxian terms – at once trans- and prehistorical. While it loosely shares certain traits both with colonial rule[46] and the ancien régime, these terms should be understood here in a larger sense. Kafka's fictional world is, needless to say, freely invented. But its freedom has all the rigor of 'free association'. In this sense, his narrative is a 'historical' one – just as, conversely, the historical record is always also a 'literary' one.

At the public reading of the story in 1916, some people fainted and many left before the end. When Kafka's habitual publisher nervously termed it peinlich, Kafka readily agreed. But the way he did so subtly cast his correspondent in the ambiguous role of the 'impresario' that he portrays – now as a tyrant, now as a valet – in his own stories. The word peinlich, he wrote, applied to almost almost everything he had published, to the times in general, and to his own times in particular.[47] Kafka is playing here on the connotations of a peculiarly untranslatable word. Etymologically cognate with pain, penalty and punishment (as in the Latin pena, the French peine and the German hochnotpeinliches Gericht), it most commonly means 'embarrassing' or, as in the phrase peinlich genau, 'painstaking' or 'exact(ing)'. The latter phrase occurs, significantly in the German translation of F. Winslow Taylor's Principles of Scientific

Management, published in 1913, which aimed to turn workers into more efficient cogs of capitalist production through an increased division of labor, time and motion studies, etc.[48] In these various connotations, the word peinlich occurs three times within the story itself.[49] It also occurs in others. And it is perhaps not unrelated to the worried house-father's 'almost painful' knowledge that Odradek will outlive him and his children. In this case, Odradek would be the story, and the house-father the artist and/or his impresario.

Something peinlich took place, in effect, both in and around this story. An eye-witness described Kafka's 'embarrassment' at his one public reading of his text, during which 'every new word was a new spike that etched the slow execution into [the hearer's] back'.[50] The text is thus itself a writing-machine akin to the one at its center. It, too, is ingeniously put together from disparate materials; it, too, works implacably; and if its last pages are indeed, as Kafka claimed, a 'botched piece of work' (Machwerk) which point to something rotten in the whole,[51] this too has its counterpart in the final breakdown of the machine. Likewise, Kafka's style is itself a Stachel, a painfully exact stylus, a precision instrument that writes in blood. While conspicuously lacking in all superfluous ornament, it nevertheless resembles the Old Commandant's handwriting inasmuch as it is hard to read the underlying message. Here too the multiplication of other lines serves to prolong the agony.

In hindsight, it is difficult not to hear in the coupling of the word peinlich with a lethal Apparat forebodings of the most bureaucratic administration of torture and death ever to have occurred on a mass scale – namely, the Nazi death-machine. Such retro-projection cannot be ruled out a priori as tautologous or unfaithful to the original text. All interpretation moves within a 'hermeneutic circle' that is potentially a vicious one. This circle may also be described as an ellipse inasmuch as it revolves around two foci: the time of the writing and that of the reading. For better or for worse, the connections made between them will always be, in every sense, elliptical. The critical difference lies in how well a given reading succeeds in negotiating its two foci. In short, a double fidelity is required.[52]

At this point, a brief word should be interjected concerning Lawrence Langer's argument that Kafka's work in general, and In the Penal Colony in particular, is not the prophetic allegory of the Holocaust that too many commentators have read into it.[53] As a specialist of Holocaust literature and testimony, Langer is eminently qualified to make this case. The elaborate treatment administered in Kafka's story to a single prisoner is, he observes, worlds apart from the apparatus of the later death-factories. This accurate line of argument is a necessary corrective to sloppy analogies and, more generally, to facile notions of the 'kafkaesque' (most recently typified in 2002 by the exhibit 'Kafka in Prague' at the Jewish Museum in New York, where another story of Kafka's, The Burrow, was grotesquely misrepresented by a multi-media scenario vaguely evocative of the camps). Langer's own reading of Kafka's story is, however, perfunctory. He sees in it little more than a counterpart to Veblen's account of the impact of the machine on modern culture. Unchecked by a stronger reading, his strong polemic seduces him into concluding that Kafka's story has no inkling of what is to come. The present reading aims to show otherwise.

Langer's point of departure is Jean Améry's insight: 'No bridge led from death in Auschwitz to Death in Venice.' He might also have cited the following paragraph from Hannah Arendt's Origins of Totalitarianism:

> There are no parallels to the life of the concentration camp. All seeming parallels create confusion and distract attention from what is essential. Forced labor in prison and penal colonies, banishment, slavery, all seem for a moment to offer helpful comparisons, but on closer inspection lead nowhere.[54]

But while Arendt's study shows in detail that an unprecedented breakdown of 'nearly three thousand years of Western civilization' took place between 1914 and 1945,[55] its concern is nevertheless to elucidate its origins, the prehistory that made that break with history possible.

Langer accuses, among others, Theodor Adorno, Günter Anders, George Steiner and, with noticeably more circumspection, Walter Benjamin of having read Kafka as a 'holocaust prophet'. In so doing, he implicitly equates prophecy with vision: pre-vision, foreseeing, seeing ahead in a literal sense. Clairvoyance is, however, precisely what Biblical prophecy was not.[56] It is in this sense that Benjamin calls Kafka's work prophetic: prophetic because non-visionary, unseeing, blind to the present,[57] a mirror which reflects the future in the far-distant past.[58] This is what Friedrich Schlegel meant by calling the historian a 'backward-turned prophet'. Benjamin glosses the latter phrase as follows: 'He turns his back on his own time; his seer's gaze [Seherblick] is ignited by the ever dimmer tips of earlier events. His own age is more clearly present to this seer's gaze than to the contemporaries who "keep pace" with it.'[59] Benjamin's 'angel of history' and 'materialist historian'[60] are in this sense backward-turned prophets: seers into the past. He thus brings to Kafka's work the optic that he finds within it. This is also the optic within which the present reading of In the Penal Colony seeks to work.

'In the factory', noted Kafka in his diary on 31 July 1914, the year of In the Penal Colony: 'the girls, their clothes intolerably dirty and loosened, their hair all awry as if they had just awoken, their facial expressions arrested by the ceaseless din of the transmissions and by machines that, though automatic, break down unpredictably, are not human beings'.[61] This empirically observed dialectic of order and disorder – of humans painfully reduced to predictable automatons, but thereby to regressive disarray, by painfully exact yet unpredictable machines – is almost out of Kafka.

Georg Lukacs's History and Class Consciousness, written nine years later (1923), in the wake of Marx and Max Weber, develops the interconnections between the various sub-divisions of the capitalist apparatus. According to Weber, the capitalist business (Betrieb), based as it is on principles of rational calculation, especially in the area of law, could arise only in a bureaucratic state where 'the judge is more or less an automatic statute-dispensing machine'.[62] Lukacs suggestively develops this argument in the chapter entitled 'Reification and the Consciousness of the Proletariat', which explores the extension of such reification throughout all sections of the apparatus:

> There arises a rational systematization of all statutes regulating life, which represents, or at least tends towards, a closed system applicable to all possible and imaginable cases. ... The formal standardization of justice, the state, the civil service, etc., signifies objectively and factually a comparable reduction of all social functions to their elements, a comparable search for the rational formal laws of these carefully segregated partial systems. ... all issues are subjected to an increasingly formal and standardized treatment in which there is an ever-increasing remoteness from the qualitative and material essence of the 'things' to which bureaucratic activity pertains. ... The specific type of bureaucratic 'conscientiousness' and impartiality, the individual bureaucrat's inevitable total subjection to a system of relations between the things to which he is exposed, the idea that it is precisely his 'honor' and his 'sense of responsibility' that exact this total submission, all this points to the fact that the division of labour which, in the case of taylorism, invaded the psyche here invades the realm of ethics.[63]

There are evident homologies between the Betrieb, as here described, and Kafka's judicial Apparat; between Weber's bureaucrat and Kafka's Officer; and between the correlative knowledge-business (Wissenschaftsbetrieb) and the 'ethics' and 'psyche' of Kafka's Traveller, all of whose actual or potential traits ('impartiality', 'sense of responsibility', 'honor', etc.) are strictly synonymous with their opposites (conformism, irresponsibility 'treason of the clerks'). We have here the 'metaphysics of officialdom' – a term of Max Weber's cited fours years before Kafka's story by Alfred Weber, Max Weber's brother and Kafka's doctoral promotor, in his essay 'Der Beamte' ('The Civil Servant') in connection with the gigantic 'apparatus' of modern bureaucracy and the peculiar mystique of self-sacrifice that it breeds in German officialdom. The relevant pages of this essay[64] likewise provide an apt commentary on Kafka's Officer and the Fascist potential of the German Beamtentum.[65]

Moreover, in retro-projective hindsight, Lukacs's Marxo-Weberian account of a system of formal, rational calculability divided into autonomous sub-systems, unfettered by qualitative, material reason, and staffed by bureaucrats with compartmentalized minds and Taylorized ethics also reads like an uncanny anticipation of the Nazi death-machine and the 'Kantian' ethics of an Eichmann. A disturbing set of correlations thus begins to emerge between In the Penal Colony, the structure of bourgeois society, and the anatomy of National Socialism. Mercifully, the capitalist system that Lukacs analyzed in 1923 in the name of proletarian revolution survived National Socialism and Soviet Marxism. Disturbingly, it is now taking on ever more global proportions.

In the late nineteenth century, travel was rapidly turning into tourism. In the twentieth century, the tourist boom even spilled over into ethnography.[66] It is as a tourist idler that Nietzsche, in The Uses and Abuses of History, and Benjamin, in his Theses on the Philosophy of History, portray the academic ('historicist') historian, indeed the academic tout court.

Kafka's Traveller is likewise only passing through. He wants merely to act as an observer and to stay out of trouble. He is not without conscience, human and professional, nor is he lacking in respectable reasons for not speaking out. Are not penal colonies, de facto and de jure, governed by martial law? What right does a non-citizen have to intervene, except possibly in a private capacity? And so on. Such alibis were to prove terrifyingly familiar in the age of totalitarianism.

Kafka's Traveller thus exemplifies the illusory freedom of academic research, whose agents inhabit the grey zone between good and bad faith, unshakeable principles and shaky character. Exteriority to the tentacular colonial system rests here not with this 'stranger' but with the enigmatic narrative perspective from which he is in turn observed. For while the narrator's exterior position is even more powerless and free-floating than that of the Traveller, there is nevertheless a world of difference between them. It is the narrator, and he alone, who is the true 'stranger' in Georg Simmel's sense of the term.

Within the world of the penal colony, no-one – neither the refined upper class nor the loutish lower class, neither the old nor the new order – comprehends the Peinlichkeit of the whole situation. No-one except the disembodied narrator: the self-effacing no-one who makes no comment. For that too would merely be peinlich. He thereby makes the only possible comment on a story that exceeds all comment. 'Let him who has something to say', wrote Karl Kraus two months after the outbreak of World War I, 'step forward and hold his peace.'[67]

What is so peinlich about Kafka's story when read today is less the exquisite detail with which the Officer describes the workings of his machine than the Traveller's wishy-washiness – and by extension the reader's too, especially if the latter happens to be a member of the same profession. Whatever the Traveller does, there is no way out, least of all that of going 'home' and 'telling' on the Officer.[68] Reforms are, after all, underway; the Traveller is indeed playing a minor role in getting them implemented. They serve, however, to modernize the colonial system, not to abolish it. What emerges from Kafka's story is thus not so much the break between old and new as the unbroken continuity between them: the changing of the guard. Not for nothing does the epilogue leave the Traveller physically enforcing the separation between the haves and the have-nots. However 'indeterminate'[69] his gestures may be, this final image fixes once and for all which side he is on.

Like a prison visitor, he too goes 'home' at the end of the day. He returns to one of those 'northern' countries from which a hardier breed of discoverers had once set out to colonize the world. After the conquerors and missionaries (observed Lévi-Strauss), the ethnographers come to glean what is left of the indigenous cultures. Kafka's Traveller is neither: neither a Columbus nor a Humboldt, neither a Cook nor a Lévi-Strauss. What exactly he is supposed to be researching is left deliberately unclear. The Officer assumes that he was 'sent out to inspect criminal procedure in all countries'; he evasively replies that he is 'no expert in criminal procedure'; and is, so he tells himself, 'travelling only as an observer, with no intention at all of altering other people's judicial systems'. This much is clear: prior to all active collusion, he is a fellow traveller of the powers that be.

'The two or three pages before the end', wrote Kafka to his editor, Kurt Wolff, on 4 September 1917, 'are botched, the fact that they exist points to a deeper failing, there is a worm somewhere that makes even the full part [das Volle] of the story hollow.'[70] We have no direct knowledge of the revisions he planned or made to these closing pages. Evidence of some such process exists, however, in ten diary entries dated 8 and 9 August 1917, which briefly sketch new scenes and raise the possibility of an alternative ending.[71] Three nights later, Kafka suffered the first attack of his terminal tuberculosis. He went back over the manuscript in November 1918, and sent it to the publisher in 'slightly shortened' form. Neither the manuscript nor any variants from this second revision have been preserved.

What was the problem with the closing pages? Was it that of how to end the story? And was that the whole point – the precise and painful Stachel – namely, that there was no closure, no end in sight – no end, that is, to the 'positively endless traffic' on which another story, The Verdict, ends?[72] But how did this reflect back on the rest – the 'full part' – of the story? Did the intractable nature of the tale – as a faithful reflection of a peinlich age – somehow carry over to its own telling? Thus cutting off the possibility of any purely literary resolution of the difficulty? The possibility of redemption through literature?

Be this as it may, Kafka seems to have decided in the end to let his protagonist get away seemingly unscathed. This final version is, however, counterpointed by the left-over scenarios, which tell a somewhat different story. Under the combined pressure of his moral predicament and the tropical climate, on which he blames his woes ('My judgment stayed home in the North'), the Traveller betrays increasing signs of mental and physical collapse. Belied by his deeds, his words promptly take their revenge. Hand on heart, he swears: '"I will be a son of a bitch [Hundsfott: 'cur', 'dog', 'coward'] if I let this happen". But then he took it literally, and began to crawl about on all fours. Only sometimes did he leap up, tear himself away, hang on one of the [Commandant's] men's necks, wail tearfully "Why is all this happening to me?", and hurry back to his post.'[73] A pantomimic succession of gestures – the expression of honorable intentions, their prompt betrayal, flights into hysteria, regression and self-pity – culminates here in dutiful compliance with the existing order. This can, however, vary at any moment. Thus, in another fragment, the Prisoner and Soldier take advantage of the Officer's death to force the now power-less Traveller into a new alliance, 'All three now belonged together'.[74] In these finally discarded scenes, it is no longer always clear whether the Traveller will finally make it back to Europe. They all nevertheless represent so many variations on a single theme. They bring out, and put to the test, a failing for which Kafka likewise blamed himself and which made it so difficult to end the story: irresolution. The Traveller, however, is bereft of all psychology; his indecisiveness can only be a matter of professional deformation. It is this inability to make up his mind that probably explains why he should not only be repelled but also fascinated by the Officer's fanatical single-mindedness. This virtual alliance with the Officer, like that with the Prisoner and the Soldier, bodes nothing good for future relations between the functionaries of knowledge and the powers that be.

The Officer and the Traveller represent two antithetical versions of the 'authoritarian personality' that will soon staff the totalitarian apparatuses. Both respectively exemplify what Anna Freud will, in a different context, diagnose as an 'identification with the aggressor'. According to one aban-doned scenario, the Officer survives – but under his hair his forehead is still pierced by the spike. The question remains what hidden marks the Traveller carries away under his brow – or on his back.

This question is brought up by another scenario in which he is the one to be transfixed, as if by a metaphorical Stachel. A sudden insight crosses his mind:

'How come?', said the Traveller suddenly. Had something been forgotten? A word? A motion? A gesture? Very possible. Highly likely. A gross miscalculation [Fehler in der Rechnung], a basic misconception, a screeching, ink-squirting stroke [Strich] all through the whole. But who will set it right? Where is the man to set it right? Where is the good old country-loving [landsmännisch] miller from the North who will stuff that grinning pair over there [i.e. the Prisoner and the Soldier] between the mill-stones?[75]

For a brief moment, the Traveller dimly perceives that his own particular guilt is part of a larger impersonal scheme of things, before lapsing back into an ominous invocation of the strong man who will know how to deal with the villains. He seems to be reflecting here not only on the workings of the Officer's machine, which was indeed impaired by a screeching cog and bespattered with the ink of human blood and vomit, but above all on the Apparatus within which he himself is trapped. Something seems to be irreparably wrong with it. There is a play here on the German expression ein Strich durch die Rechnung and a tacit comment on what Max Weber was at that time singling out as the hallmark of Western civilization: 'rationalization'. The 'stroke through the reckoning' of modernity seems to be integral to its calculus. It is a gross, built-in, all-pervasive error. Yet it appears to derive from the slight inattention, the forgotten word or gesture, the forgotten act of forgetting that he elsewhere equates with the Fall. In addition, the expression Fehler in der Rechnung also strangely parallels Kafka's reference to the 'deeper failing' with which he was struggling at that very moment – the 'worm' eating away at his story. Something was rotten on many levels at once.

'The time is out of joint: O cursed spite./That ever I was born to set it right.'[76] For a brief moment, Kafka's Traveller senses that something is rotten far beyond the confines of the penal colony. But he also knows that he is not the man to 'set it right'. Far from it. 'Why is this happening to me?', he wails. It is the mentality of the modern individual, an apparatchik who feels overburdened by anything beyond his job-description. Unlike the Officer, the Traveller has no dead Father to avenge and has thus inherited no mission. He is heir only to Hamlet's doubts. 'The scholar', said Nietzsche, 'a décadent!'

The turning-point sketched by Kafka between the old and new orders corresponds in certain respects to the transition analyzed by Michel Foucault from the penal system of the ancien régime to the 'liberal', 'humanitarian' code that supplanted it.[77] A roughly similar redistribution of power, knowledge and commerce underlies the reforms introduced by the New Commandant, who is doing away with an eccentric, barbaric system on behalf of a normal, civilized, but hardly less punitive one. The function of penal colonies had been to settle uninhabited territories, keep subjugated peoples down, and otherwise contribute to the economic, political and social needs of the colonial nations. The New Commandant is engaged in modernizing that program. He is adapting the modern European model of sub- and superstructure to backward colonial conditions. The upshot is a division of labor between two areas of reform: hard economic liberalism and 'mild' philanthropic liberality. It is also a division of roles between male and female domains and a combination of carrot and stick (in German: Zuckerbrot und Peitsche). On the one hand, we have the sweets (Zuckersachen) and handkerchieves distributed to the Prisoner by the New Commandant's Ladies.[78] On the other, there is his own exclusive focus on commerce ('dock construction, dock construction over and over again!', the Officer sighs) – the 'endless traffic' on which The Verdict closes – and the discipline he imposes on his workers.[79] Such utilitarianism stands in marked contrast to the futility of the hyperbolic military code enforced by the Old Commandant. But it presumably benefits from its rigor.

The barbed question that hangs over Kafka's story is thus whether the ancien régime, with its echoes of an immemorial barbarity, doesn't also extend forward to the brave new world that carries the future before it. Old or New, Commandants are above all Commandants, 'All rulers', writes Benjamin, 'are the heirs of those who conquered before them.'[80]

The office at which Kafka served his time[81] – the Bureau for Workers' Accident Insurance (Arbeiter-Unfall-Versicherungsanstalt) – was a particularly good post from which to observe the stabilizing function of social reform. Wagenbach describes it as a Zuckerbrot.[82] It was, in effect, primarily the Wilhelmine State that such welfare measures were intended to insure – to protect, that is, against an altogether different type of industrial accident: the 'danger to public order [gemeingefährliche Bestrebungen] represented by social democracy'.[83]

'How modest these people are', Kafka remarked to Max Brod of the injured workers who came to his office for redress. 'Instead of storming the premises and destroying everything in sight, they come with a request.'[84] Within his limited sphere of action, he did what he could. He treated their claims, evaluated factory conditions and made specific proposals for redesigning dangerous machinery.[85] From within the Apparatus, he helped protect workers from its worst damage. He dreamt of revolutionary anarchy and meanwhile helped implement minimal social reform.

A Reformist Age was indeed dawning. One of the sources for Kafka's story was a report commissioned by the German Colonial Office (Kolonialamt) and the Imperial Ministry of Justice (Reichsjustizamt) from a young lawyer, Robert Heindl: 'My Journey [Reise] to the Penal Colonies' (1912).[86] Partly as a result of this report, penal colonies were coming to be considered inappropriate. 'The "old" system of combining punitive deportation with colonization', notes Wagenbach, 'was being replaced by the "new" system of emigration and dependency on trade (and it seemed more practicable to use the military to conquer and defend trading posts and harbors than to waste them on guarding prisoners).'[87]

In the Penal Colony does more than reflect this transition. It shows how the old and new systems, from their respective sides of the divide, (mis)interpret the change, each other and themselves. Marx did something roughly analogous in his Economic and Philosophical Manuscripts. The silence of Kafka's narrator is that of the Revolution.

Heindl had spoken out against deportation, unable though he was to suppress a certain fascination for the executions and executioners he had observed – a trait that Kafka partially lends his Traveller. What makes all the difference between Heindl's and Kafka's reports is that the latter includes the reporter and his discourse within its purview, perhaps indeed within the penal colony.[88] There is a sense in which Heindl's is the 'fictional' and Kafka's the 'non-fictional' account.

One of the central political insights implicit in Kafka's story lies in its juxtaposition of two liberalisms: reformist, humanist discourse and renewed economic enterprise. Foucault likewise shows how a new humanist discourse served to rationalize the historical shift to a penal system that was not only more 'humane' but also differently inhuman. His analysis of that shift provides a genealogy of the totalitarian potential that lurks not only in right- or left-wing utopias but also in the functioning of their middle-of-the-road antidote: modern Western democracy. 'Big Brother' is not exclusive to the Soviet system (or to European TV). Foucault shows, in effect, how the system of surveillance first practiced in nineteenth-century prisons – those 'complete and austere institutions', as Baltard called them[89] – has increasingly spread throughout modern Westernized societies. This dynamic is terminologically reflected in the shift from what Jürgen Habermas originally called the 'structural transformation of public space' to what he came to call the 'colonization of the life-world'. Colonization has returned home, equipped with appropriate technology. A new, and no less 'peculiar', Apparatus is central to Foucault's account: Bentham's Panopticum.[90] Already Kafka's New Commandant – a shadowy figure whom the reader, at least, never sees – oversees the penal colony without unnecessary recourse to public executions. Bentham's prison, where every cell can be observed from a central command-post, marks a new stage in this process of invisible surveillance. And meanwhile today's New Commandants have so sophisticated an apparatus at their disposal that they do not even need to exist.

The far-reaching parallel between In the Penal Colony and Discipline and Punish should be completed by a further one between Kafka's narrative and Hannah Arendt's Origins of Totalitarianism, the second section of which demonstrates that the period of imperialism (1881–1914) constituted a 'preparatory stage' for the coming totalitarian catastrophes.[91] Arendt cites from Kipling (Kim and The Tomb of his Ancestor), T.E. Lawrence (The Seven Pillars of Wisdom) and Conrad's Heart of Darkness ('Exterminate all the brutes'), motifs from which were to find their way into Francis Ford Coppola's Vietnam film Apocalypse Now. She might also have extrapolated one of her central theses from Kafka's story: namely, that what Europe did in its colonies would return to plague its inventors.[92] It was not only in the heart of Africa but at the core of the Enlightenment that darkness lay.

IMPLICATIONS

The first of the following passages dates from 1938, the second from 1951:

> ... Kafka's world ... is the exact complement of an era which is preparing to abolish [abschaffen] the inhabitants of this planet in considerable quantities (Massen). The experience that corresponds to that of Kafka as a private individual will probably be acquired by the masses only on the occasion of such abolition.[93]

> We do not know the full implications of totalitarian rule and the chances are that we never will. Its potentialities can be realized only if it has conquered the earth ... . Unable ... to build from small achievements, to be content with temporary successes, able only to think in centuries and continents, totalitarianism has only one chance of eventual victory, and that is global catastrophe which would have to occur, so to speak, at a moment's notice.
>
> All this seems to indicate that totalitarianism will one day simply disappear, leaving no other trace in the history of mankind than exhausted peoples, economic and social chaos, political vacuum, and a spiritual tabula rasa. It may well be that even our generation will live to see a time when it is permitted to forget the holes of oblivion, the mass manufacture of corpses, and that sins greater than murder ever existed. The futility of totalitarianism in the long run is as essential an aspect of the phenomenon as the offensive ludicrousness of the tenets for which it is prepared to commit its monstrosities. The tragedy, however, is that this futility and this ludicrousness are more deeply connected with the crisis of this century and more significant for its true perplexities than the well-meaning efforts of the nontotalitarian world to safeguard the status quo. ... the fact is that the true problems of our time cannot be understood, let alone

solved, without the acknowledgment that totalitarianism became this century's curse only because it so terrifyingly took care of its problems. ... The totalitarian attempt to make men superfluous reflects the experience of modern masses of their superfluity on an overcrowded earth. ... Political, social and economic events everywhere are in a silent conspiracy with totalitarian instruments devised for making men superfluous. ...; The Nazis and Bolsheviks can be sure that their factories of annihilation which demonstrate the swiftest solution to the problem of overpopulation, of economically superfluous and socially rootless human masses, are as much of an attraction as a warning. Totalitarian solutions may well survive the fall of totalitarian regimes in the form of strong temptations which will come up whenever it seems impossible to alleviate political, social or economic misery in a manner worthy of man. ... No divine command ... and no natural law ... are sufficient for the establishment of a new law on earth, for rights spring from human plurality, and divine command or natural law would be true even if there existed only a single human being. ... The greatness of this task is crushing and without precedent. Only a supreme calamity could have forced us to face it. Unfortunately, to take any other course would lead us auto-matically into the wilderness where right is that which is 'good for' – the individual, or the family, or the people. Such a definition, even if the unit to which the 'good for' applies is as large as mankind itself, will never prevent murder. For it is quite conceivable that one beautiful day a highly organized, mechanized, and centralized humanity may decide that it would be better for the whole to do without a certain part. ... In the meantime, it may have been useful to find the origin, and to contemplate the forms, of those new movements which pretend to have discovered the solution to our problems, and whose fantastic claims to having founded thousand-year realms and Messianic ages are believed, despite all evidence to the contrary, because they respond, albeit in a radically destructive way, to the terrible challenge of the century.[94]

These concluding remarks of Arendt's study of totalitarianism are poised between two possibilities. On the one hand, the contradictory nature of the totalitarian project helps explain its instability and the likelihood of its disappearance.[95] On the other, what totalitarianism has shockingly shown is that 'everything is possible'.[96] 'The tragic fallacy ... was to suppose ... that the idea of total domination was not only inhuman but also unreal-istic.'[97] But even if this idea were realized, its success would be its failure. For man would then no longer be man. 'He can be fully dominated only when he becomes a specimen of the animal-species man.'[98] Perhaps, then, the totalitarian idea is indeed inherently unrealizable, because it is at odds with the human condition. Or can the human condition indeed be abrogated?

('Everything is possible.' This formula loosely sums up both totalitarian and utopian hopes. As the last lines of the above-cited passage intimate, the former feed on the latter. This seems to lead Arendt to renounce all Messianism:

> ... we shall have to create – not merely discover – a new foundation for human community as such.
>
> In historical terms this would mean not the end of history but its first consciously planned beginning, together with the bitter realization that nothing has been promised us, no Messianic age, no classless society, no paradise after death.[99]

But what is the consciously planned creation of a human community if not a Messianic idea – the project, in Marx's phrase, of ending 'prehistory'? Today's fundamentalisms continue to entangle totalitarian and Messianic elements. This is still no reason to lump the two together. The task is rather to disentangle them.)

Totalitarianism would thus seem, on Arendt's account, to be both impossible and all too possible – then as now. For while the bulk of her study shows that totalitarianism is an outgrowth of modern Western society, her concluding remarks raise the specter of its survival into the post-totalitarian world. Her foreboding that this world may one day resort to totalitarian methods of population control may, for the time being, seem dated or exaggerated. But a closely related claim reads like a backward-turned prophecy:

> For the first disastrous result of men's coming of age is that modern man has come to resent everything given, even his own existence – to resent the very fact that he is not the creator of the universe and himself. ... In his resentment of all laws merely given to him, he proclaims openly that everything is permitted and believes secretly that everything is possible. And ... he resents even his nihilistic convictions, as though they were forced on him by some cruel joke of the devil.[100]

These sentences – which implicitly root totalitarian logic in Enlightenment thinking and in what Nietzsche called the history of 'European nihilism' and the 'psychology of resentment' – are strangely premonitory. Reading them today, one cannot but think of the moral issues meanwhile forced on us by advances in biological and medical research (cloning, reproductive technology, pre-natal diagnostics, etc.), and the traffic and expectations that they breed. They suggest disturbing continuities between the 'bio-politics'[101] of the totalitarian and the post-totalitarian era – that is, between various versions of the conviction that 'everything is possible'.

At this point, a question arises which puts the issue of the 'lesser evil' in a different perspective. In what sense does the West constitute not merely the pre-history of totalitarianism but its post-history as well? Its unmastered future? Its present? This is surely the only cognitive and moral perspective within which totalitarianism should be studied. It is the one from which – in their respective ways – Benjamin, Arendt and Foucault work. 'Make an effort not to be under your times.'[102] Is not this the most urgent priority?

The foregoing reading of Kafka as a 'backward-turned prophet' claimed to find in In The Penal Colony pointers to the factual and moral implication of the West (Enlightenment, modernity, capitalism, colonialism, Imperialism) in its totalitarian 'other'. As long as the postwar 'open society' confronted that 'other' in a bi-polar world, it could claim – with real, if limited, plausibility – to be opposed to an outside 'enemy'. This is no longer possible today in any simple sense. It is, now more than ever, confronted by a more insidious enemy: itself. What does this mean for writing the history of the present? And the comparative study of totalitarianism?

Kafka's scholar found himself momentarily trapped between two eras of colonial rule. Nothing (we may extrapolate) then stood in greater need of comparative research than that historical shift. Fieldwork of this kind would, however, no longer have been be safely exotic. It would have confronted the ethnographer with his own ethnography. Kafka's scholar studiously avoided the subject and was therefore reduced to acting it out. Were he to face it, there would have been little point in deciding which of the two régimes – unenlightened or enlightened colonialism – was the lesser evil. (The ways in which much Kafka criticism has found it necessary to choose between the old and new order are embarrassing.) They mark two phases of an unfolding historical dialectic.

The contributors to the present volume have been asked to make 'the moral comparison' between the two major totalitarianisms of the twentieth century and to do so from a non-totalitarian vantage-point called 'democracy'. The question is whether this implicit claim to a position of non-implicated enlightenment does not correspond, mutatis mutandis, to the compromised stance of Kafka's scholar. Like him, we go home to capitalism; like him, we never left it behind. But is not capitalism, early and late, one of the most ramified roots of the problems we are addressing?

Why, then, doesn't the open, democratic society that we inhabit figure among the terms of comparison as well as being their supposedly neutral ground? What new New Commandant may be enlisting our scholarly testimony, and to what ends? Does not our system, too, have its 'black book'? What complicities historically obtain between the Western democracies – Churchill's lesser evil – and the incomparably worse, worst possible evils, the Nazi and Soviet totalitarianisms? Why are these entanglements, which enmesh us all, not a major area of academic research? Is it because such work wouldn't get funded? Because it would go too close to home – the home of ongoing collaboration with the worst as well as the best? Given the present relation of forces, however, the system can easily afford to subsidize its academic critics and can, in so doing, plausibly claim to prove them wrong.

No-one in his right mind would place our lesser evil – Western democracy – on a par with the worst. (The fact that England saved my family from extermination is part of this particular scholar's embarrassed indebtedness to a bloody old empire.) Military and economic considerations aside, it was perhaps the evident moral difference between them that made all the difference – that enabled the West to triumph successively over two totalitarianisms.

But was not totalitarianism a monster engendered by the sleep of reason (Goya)? Is not the belly still fertile from which it crept (Brecht)? The plague dormant but not dead (Camus)? In Syberberg's film, Hitler, a Career, Hitler, having died, lives on in his victors. This is, of course, a melodramatic conceit (on a par with, say, the closing scene of Roman Polanski's Dance of the Vampires, where Dracula's daughter escapes out into the world on a sled behind the unsuspecting hero and is about to sink her fangs into his neck). But here as elsewhere wild suspicions grow where scholarship will not or cannot not go.

We are living through an unprecedented world-historical and geopolitical conjuncture. The capitalist democracies, having triumphed over their totalitarian enemies, constitute the sole surviving system. Globalization has acquired an irreversible, relatively unchecked momentum. The bourgeoisie, wrote Marx, 'creates a world in its own image'. That phrase has proved involuntarily prophetic – at the expense of his consciously willed predictions. The blasphemous program it names – that of man usurping God's position – has an undeniably totalitarian potential. Arendt sums it up as the nihilistic belief, common to both the Enlightenment and the totalitarian mind, that 'everything is possible'. But it is no less undeniable that the world created by the bourgeoisie cannot be called totalitarian in any hitherto accepted sense.[103] For this very reason, however, capitalism seems well equipped to succeed where the totalitarian systems failed. They finally foundered on their contradictory bid for total control. It has so far thrived on its contradictions and ambivalences. That is the genius of democracy.

Looking back on Dialectic of Enlightenment (1944) in 1969, in the thick of the Cold War, Horkheimer and Adorno hazarded the following prognosis:

ON COMPARING TOTALITARIANISMS

In a period of political division into immense power-blocks, set objectively on collision, the horror continues. The conflicts in the Third World and the renewed growth of totalitarianism are just as little mere historical episodes as ... was Fascism at the time. ... The trend [Zug] towards total integration is interrupted, but not cancelled out. It threatens to realize itself through dictatorships and wars.[104]

More than a decade after the fall of the Berlin Wall, the trend towards total integration continues to accelerate – Zug also means 'train' – and to take in its stride the abolition of human beings, not to mention other forms of life on this planet, in considerable quantities. It is unclear to what extent this controlling dynamic can be controlled and where it is going. So far it has contained all contradictions and interruptions. Is a 'cunning of reason' (Hegel) at work? Or a 'gross miscalculation' (Kafka)? Reason as its own miscalculation? What is clear is that today's crimes against humanity cannot take place without the surveillance, the complicity or at least the acquiescence of commanders-in-chief who possess a perfect alibi: they act in the name of the people.

How to ignore our implication in this nightmare? Don't we risk resembling Kafka's hapless scholar as long as we fail to reckon with a system that includes us in its calculations, that made the old totalitarianisms possible and impossible, that fostered and defeated them, and that now – westward ho! – seems to have the wind in its sails?[105]

NOTES

1 Association Internationale de Recherche sur les Crimes contre l'Humanité et les Génocides, based in Paris.
2 On the need for such comparative studies, see Catherine Coquio's and Irving Wohlfarth's Preface to C. Coquio, ed., Parler des Camps, Penser les Génocides (Albin Michel, Paris, 1999), pp. 11–15; and on the misunderstandings to which they have given rise Coquio's essay 'Le malentendu' in the same volume. The volume was based on a conference held in 1997, which was violently denounced by Claude Lanzmann in Le Monde on the grounds that it is obscene to want to understand the Shoah, let alone to compare it with any other atrocity.
3 On this issue see Jean Michel Chaumont's pioneering study La Concurrence des Victimes (La Découverte, Paris, 1997).
4 Victor Klemperer, LTI (= Lingua Tertii Imperii) (Reclam, Halle, 1957). See my 'In lingua veritas. LTI mit und gegen Klemperer gelesen', Mittelweg, 36 (April/May 1999), pp. 73–90 (published in a fuller version in 'Identités/Existences/Résistances, Réflexions autour des Journaux 1933–1945 de Victor Klemperer', Germanica, 27 (2000), pp. 103–46).
5 Georg Christoph Lichtenberg, Schriften und Briefe (hereafter SB), ed. Wolfgang Promies (Hanser, Munich, 1992), vol. II, p. 569.

6 Around the same time, Faust's wild desire for all-embracing totality meets its limits in his humbling encounter with the Erdgeist.

7 See SB, vol. III, p. 387.

8 SB, vol. II, p. 460. Hannah Arendt is thus mistaken in assuming that no man of the Enlightenment could have foreseen that 'man's mastery of nature would reach a point where he could conceive the possibility of destroying the earth by man-made instruments' (The Origins of Totalitarianism [hereafter Origins] (Harcourt Brace, New York, 1951), p. 435). The Enlightenment is Janus-faced: the same mind that imagines discoveries that could mean the end of mankind visualizes other, related ones that would bring it no less immeasurable benefit: 'One of the greatest discoveries for the economy would be the invention of some cheap material with which to dissolve the nitrogen in the atmosphere and thus to liberate its warmth' (SB, vol. II, p. 504).

9 'In dieser grossen Zeit, die ich noch gekannt habe, wie sie so klein war ...; in dieser Zeit, in der eben das geschieht, was man sich nicht vorstellen konnte und in der geschehen muss, was man sich nicht mehr vorstellen kann, und könnte man es, es geschähe nicht ...' (Karl Kraus, Weltgericht (Fischer, Frankfurt am Main, 1968), p. 7).

10 Walter Benjamin, Illuminations, ed. Hannah Arendt (Schocken, New York, 1969), p. 258.

11 'Because of impatience they were driven out of Paradise, because of carelessness [lässigkeit] they didn't return' (Franz Kafka, Betrachtungen über Sünde, Leid, Hoffnung und den wahren Weg, no. 3, in Er (Suhrkamp, Frankfurt, 1964), p. 195).

12 Walter Benjamin, Reflections, ed. Peter Demetz (Harcourt Brace, New York, 1979), pp. 326ff. The Fall of language also marks for Benjamin the beginning of the 'arbitrary': both the arbitrary sign and arbitrary violence. Cf. my essay, 'Die Willkür der Zeichen. Zu einem sprachphilosophischen Motiv Walter Benjamins', in Perspektiven kritischer Theorie. Festschrift für Hermann Schweppenhäuser, ed. C. Türcke (zu Klampen, Lüneburg 1988), pp. 124–73.

13 Benjamin, Illuminations, p. 138.

14 On Odradek and the (hunch)back as the site of Entstellung – forgetting, misplacement, displacement, distortion, guilt – see Benjamin's essay on Kafka (Illuminations, pp. 111–45, especially 131–4); and on the hunchback as the forgotten, shrunken, (un)canny embodiment of theology see Illuminations, p. 253.

15 In this connection see my analysis of the extraordinary letter written by Robert Antelme on his return from a German labor camp: 'L'espèce humaine à l'épreuve des camps. Réflexions sur Robert Antelme', in Coquio, ed., Parler des Camps, Penser les Génocides, pp. 569–608.

16 Benjamin, Illuminations, pp. 253–4.

17 Theodor W. Adorno and Max Horkheimer, Dialectic of Enlightenment, trans. John Cumming (Continuum, New York, 1972), p. 31.

18 See Jürgen Habermas's essay of 1984, 'Die Krise des Wohlfahrtsstaates und die Erschöpfung utopischer Energien', reprinted in Die Moderne – ein unvollendetes Projekt. Philosophisch-politische Aufsätze 1977–1990 (Reclam, Leipzig, 1990).

19 See Micha Brumlik's article 'Die Graduierung des Grauens', Frankfurter Rundschau, 20 February 2001; also Sonia Combe's comparison between the commandants of Auschwitz and Ozerlag, 'S.K. Evstigneev, roi d'Ozerlag', in Ozerlag 1937–1964. Le Système du Gouloag: Traces perdues, Mémoires réveillées d'un Camp sibérien, ed. Alain Brossat (Paris, 1991).

20 Benjamin, Illuminations, p. 257. Translation modified.

21 Diary entry of 19 October 1921, cited in ibid., p. 19.

22 Ibid., p. 126.
23 In this context, 'experience' is another euphemism. Robert Antelme, a survivor
    of a Nazi labor camp, placed inverted commas around the word. See my essay
    on Antelme cited in note 15. 'For never', wrote Benjamin, 'has experience been
    belied more thoroughly than strategic experience by positional warfare, economic
    experience by inflation, bodily experience by mechanical warfare, moral experience
    by those in power' (Illuminations, p. 84; translation modified).
24 In an essay entitled 'Homage to the Extreme: The Shoah and the Rhetoric of
    Catastrophe (Times Literary Supplement, 6 March 1998, pp. 6–8), Michael Bern-
    stein has challenged the type of argument advanced here. It is typified in his eyes
    by Jean-François Lyotard's claim that the Shoah produced a shock so powerful
    as to have destroyed the instruments by which to measure it. Would he also fault
    Arendt for claiming that totalitarianism has ruined all inherited philosophical
    concepts – a claim that she does not perhaps argue radically enough (Origins, pp
    vii–ix, 434–9)? True, we cannot speak with the mute staring eyes of Benjamin's
    Angel. But what is our language worth if it is uninformed by that silence? True,
    'that claim cannot be settled cheaply' (Illuminations, p. 254). If it is, the result
    will indeed be a 'rhetoric of catastrophe'. There remains, however, the catastrophe
    itself and the problem of how 'to fail again better again' – that is, 'better worse'
    – to address it. No-one's rhetoric is safe from that demand.
25 Samuel Beckett, Worstward Ho (John Calder, London, 1999), pp. 7–8.
26 Benjamin, Reflections, pp. 190–1. Translation modified. In his Theses on the
    Philosophy of History, Benjamin – in Nietzsche's wake – describes historicism as
    combining progressism, conformism and 'indolence of the heart'.
27 'Belief in progress does not mean that progress already happened. That would be
    no belief' (Kafka, Betrachtungen über Sünde, Leid, Hoffnung und den wahren
    Weg, no. 48, p. 200).
28 'The central events of our time', writes Arendt in the Preface to her study of
    totalitarianism, 'are not less effectively forgotten by those committed to a belief
    in unavoidable doom than by those who have given thmeselves to a reckless
    optimism. ... [This book] holds that Progress and Doom are two sides of the same
    medal; that both are articles of superstition, not faith' (Origins, pp. vii–viii). True,
    Benjamin's 'weak' Messianism and strong pessimism are also two sides of the
    same coin. But the pessimism is directed against Progress, and the Messianism
    against Doom.
29 The following extract from a pre-conference statement made by Helmut Dubiel
    representatively illustrates the link between the prevailing intellectual climate and
    the rhetoric of the 'lesser evil': 'The awareness of this critical point at which civic
    virtues are not able any more to contain the destructive potential inherent in
    any modern society is informed by a distinct philosophical perception. In this
    perception, the present state of our society appears neither as the "not yet" of a
    distinct future nor as the "no more" of a Golden Age lost forever, but as a
    precarious balancing of a civilization, always threatened by the danger of
    relapsing into barbarism. Walter Benjamin used in this context the biblical image
    of the angels who immediately vanish the very moment they stop singing. In the
    second half of the twentieth century, the utopian dream of an anti-traditional
    society based on an association of free citizens was fatally damaged by the trauma
    of state-organized genocide, mass expulsions and systematic rape to a degree
    heretofore unknown in the history of mankind. Although at the beginning of the
    twenty-first century there are reasons for more optimism than existed fifty years
    before, there can be no unambivalent joy over the global spreading of democracy

so far, because one postwar argument for democracy seems to be the avoidance of genocide.' According to this 'distinct philosophical perception', Marx's utopianism [sic!] is a historically ruined 'dream'. Some tattered remnants of – a wiser, sadder, ambivalent, far from reckless – progressivism nevertheless survive. There are – appropriately qualified – reasons for 'more optimism' than 50 years ago. This certainly isn't what Arendt said about the preceding 30 years in her 1968 essay on Benjamin (Illuminations, p. 38). Nor is Benjamin Dubiel's man: Benjamin's angels are all Messianic. Nor does civilization threaten to 'relapse' into barbarism; it constantly reproduces it. And if 'one postwar argument for democracy' has been 'the avoidance of genocide', what grounds for optimism – however cautious – does the postwar record of the foreign actions and inactions undertaken by the Western powers afford? Is it not only a matter of time until, in our collective name, UN troops act as helpless bystanders at the next genocide? In short, the above statement contains what, it says, cannot be contained. In his closing statement at the conference, Dubiel claimed that globalization holds the promise of an internationalization of human rights. This is indeed the only hope presently available for improving the treatment that international politics continues to reserve for millions of human beings. But the call for betterment and 'humanization' has accompanied modernity from the start. There are grounds for fearing that the 'uncompleted project' of modernity, as Habermas calls it, is structurally incapable of completion and that its best institutions will continue to condone its worst practices. The best explanation, and the most substantial argument, that I can see for Dubiel's position is the experience of his generation: the establishment of Western democracy on the ruins of Nazi Germany.

30 Michel Foucault, Discipline and Punish: The Birth of the Prison (hereafter Discipline) (Random House, New York, 1979), pp. 16–17, 23, 25, 27–8, 301, 305.

31 The Penguin Complete Short Stories of Franz Kafka (Penguin, New York, 1983), pp. 140–67.

32 'Since Michael Kohlhaas, no German novella has been written that seemingly suppresses all inner sympathy with such controlled force', wrote Kurt Tucholsky in his review (cited in Klaus Wagenbach In der Strafkolonie. Eine Geschichte aus dem Jahre 1914, Wagenbach, Berlin, 1998, p. 68).

33 Benjamin, Illuminations, p. 140.

34 'When thinking suddenly stops in a configuration pregnant with tensions, it gives that configuration a shock, by which it crystallizes into a monad' (ibid., pp. 262–3).

35 Edwin and Willa Muir's translation of the travelling scholar as 'explorer' mistakes Forschungsreisender with Entdeckungsreisender.

36 Flaubert dreamt of a 'work of art about nothing', liberated from petit-bourgeois content; Nietzsche dreamt of hewing the Superman from human, all-too-human stone; according to the Officer, the only imperfection of the Apparatus is that it should be too easily dirtied by human fluids; and, according to Arendt, the totalitarian rulers – were they capable of telling the truth – would say: 'The apparatus seems superfluous to you only because it serves to make men superfluous' (Arendt, Origins, p. 428).

37 Cited in Foucault, Discipline, p. 45. See the following jotting of Baudelaire. 'The death penalty is the result of an idea that is completely misunderstood nowadays. It does not aim to save society, at least materially. Its aim is to save society and the guilty man (spiritually). For the sacrifice be perfect, there must be assent and joy on the victim's part. To give chloroform to a condemned man would be impious, for it would be to take away his consciousness of his grandeur as a victim

and to eliminate his chances of reaching Paradise' (Charles Baudelaire, Oeuvres Complètes, Gallimard, Paris, 1968, p. 1278). This argument, which goes back to Joseph de Maistre's defense of the ancien régime against the French Revolution, marks a reactive defense of the old penal system against the new. Kafka's Old Commandant, who devises new means to achieve the old spiritual ends, is a far-flung cousin of Baudelaire's preferred authors: de Maistre and Sade.

[38] A term often associated with Lacenaire, the nineteenth-century gentleman delin-quent who held up a mirror to the illegality of the privileged classes (cf. Foucault, Discipline, pp. 283–5). The 'metaphysics' of evil – considered as the dark secret of the world – goes hand in hand here with the 'aesthetics of crime' exemplified by De Quincey's Murder Considered as One of the Fine Arts. At the end of the nineteenth century, the same double frisson is prompted by a novel with which Kafka was familiar: Octave Mirbeau's Le Jardin des Supplices ('The Garden of Torments'). A traveller who has come to compare the various systems of admin-istering penal colonies finds himself confronted by the contrast between the lost art of murder preserved in China and the vulgarly administrative mass murder practiced in the West. 'Administrative murders' – a term coined by a British civil servant in India – were in fact first visualized, though not yet realized, in the colonial context (cf. Arendt, Origins, pp. 186, 216, 221). What is new about Kafka's New Commandant is that he seems potentially capable of administering murder out of existence on behalf of more humane and, above all, more efficient modes of control.

[39] Less than 20 years later, Benjamin diagnoses Fascism as the 'consummation of l'art pour l'art' and the 'aestheticization of politics' (Illuminations, p. 242).

[40] Benjamin, Reflections, p. 148.

[41] Both fit Arendt's account of totalitarianism as the evacuation of common sense combined with the imposition of a super-sense: 'The insanity of such systems lies not only in their first premise but in the very logicality with which they are constructed. The curious logicality of all isms, their simple-minded trust in the salvation value of stubborn devotion without regard for specific, varying factors, already harbors the first germs of totalitarian contempt for reality and factuality' (Origins, p. 432). Such total systems are headed by similarly total men. The Traveller asks the Officer whether the Old Commandant was everything in one: 'Soldier, judge, constructor, chemist, draughtsman?' Stalin and Hitler were likewise to cast themselves as leader, general, linguist, architect, etc.

[42] Stachel (cognate with 'stake') means 'prickle', 'barb', 'thorn' (as in 'a thorn in one's flesh'), 'sting' (as in 'Death, where is your sting?'), etc., and is not usually associated with anything mechanical. Just as the Apparatus is made up of a 'Bed', a 'Harrow' and a 'Drawer', its Spike seems poised between plant or animal life (Stachelschwein: 'porcupine') and modern mass production (Stacheldraht: 'barbed wire', the material of modern animal pens and human camps).

[43] Since Kafka's story leaves essential questions cunningly unresolved, any brief plot-summary is bound to distort it. Such indeterminacy is in itself an effective strategy of resistance to all final, total constructions of meaning and in this sense to the totalitarian project. The enigmatically calm expression on the dead Officer's face is a case in point. Betraying no sign that he has been redeemed, it belies his own narrative of redeeming torture. His pierced forehead does not exhibit the holy stigma of a crucified martyr. It is, if anything, a sign that the Officer remains in death what he was in life: not erlöst ('redeemed', 'released') but verbohrt ('stubborn', 'bored-through', from bohren, 'to drill'). The image combines resistance to the totalitarian with forebodings of it. For it is totalitarianism that

makes 'martyrdom, for the first time in history, impossible' (Arendt, Origins, p. 423).

44 The closing words of the prophecy – 'Believe and wait' ('Glaubet und wartet') – echo the traditional Messianic promise of Zion. (See Wagenbach, In der Strafkolonie (p. 119) on Kafka's familiarity with Yiddish plays which turned on the conflict between orthodox Judaism and the Enlightenment – the matrix of 'Reform' Judaism). While the ancient Messianic promise is adopted here to the Old Commandant's followers, later history was to show that any New Commandant or totalitarian Leader can adapt remnants of Messianism to his purposes. Kafka's text also raises the question whether such perversions of the Messianic promise say something about the original belief – and if so, what.

45 Like Octave Mirbeau's 'Garden of Torments', Kafka's story alludes obliquely to the Dreyfus Affair, the case of a Jewish officer of the French General Staff who was falsely convicted of espionage and deported to a penal colony known as Devil's Island. A well-known print had shown an officer ceremonially breaking Dreyfus's dagger: Kafka has his Officer break his own. The Officer speaks French; unlike the Prisoner and the Soldier, the Traveller understands him, but French does not seem to be his native tongue. Where, then, is this penal colony located? As in the case of the Apparatus, Kafka seems to have deliberately scrambled the clues. The cumulative impression is that of an interchangeable, sketchily identified, vaguely foreign, yet all-too-familiar colonial outpost somewhere in the South Seas. As such, it is sufficiently far away to allow the author the freedom to reinvent it. Therein, he paradoxically resembles the Old Commandant. The Apparatus is, in effect, their joint invention. The Old Commandant is furthermore not without a certain resemblance to Nietzsche's Zarathustra (and vice versa). In his own way, he too is a 'poet' out to 'redeem' 'all-too-human' material by 'creating' an anti-humanist utopia/dystopia out of an eclectic collection of religious, historical and anthropological motifs. Therein, however, the worlds that they create seem to constitute escapist, all too 'reactive' counter-models to modernity. In which case, they would be reactionary (anti-)modernists and, as such, Fascist prototypes; and their worlds would be far-flung counterparts to the sectarian 'house-chapel' denounced by Max Weber a few years later in 'Science as Vocation'.

46 'When ... the English conqueror in India became an administrator who no longer believed in the universal validity of law, but was convinced of his own innate capacity to rule and dominate ..., the stage seemed to be set for all possible horrors' (Arendt, Origins, p. 221). The Old Commandant, for his part, takes the law into his own hands by inventing a hyperbolic version of universal law.

47 Letter to Kurt Wolff of 1 October 1916. Similarly, when his father reproached him for supporting 'the abnormal', he replied that this wasn't 'the worst since the normal is, for example, the World War'. Both statements are cited by Wagenbach, In der Strafkolonie, pp. 63–4.

48 Cited in Wagenbach, In der Strafkolonie, p. 94.

49 The motions of the machine have to be 'exactly calculated' (pp. 143–4); the Officer is 'embarrassed' (p. 146) when asked whether the New Commandant will attend the execution; and so too is the Traveller by the lack of respect shown by the Prisoner and the Soldier towards the Officer's heroic act of self-sacrifice (p. 164).

50 'Shadowy, dark-haired, pallid, a figure that didn't really know how to dispel its embarrassment (Verlegenheit) at its own appearance' (Max Pulver, quoted in Wagenbach, In der Strafkolonie, p. 65).

51 Letter to Kurt Wolff of 4 September 1917 (cited Wagenbach, In der Strafkolonie, p. 60).

52 Cf. on the two foci of the ellipse described by Kafka's own work and on the critical constellation between 'then' and 'now', Benjamin, Illuminations, pp. 141–3 and 253–64.

53 Lawrence Langer, 'Kafka as Holocaust Prophet: A Dissenting View', in Admitting the Holocaust (New York, Oxford University Press, 1995), pp. 109–24. Cf. also Michael Bernstein on the insidious vice of 'foreshadowing' prevalent among critics who, in the aftermath of the Shoah, have become prophets-after-the-fact and have found themselves unable to read stories like "The Penal Colony" without thinking of the concentration camps' (Foregone Conclusions: Against Apocalyptic History, Berkeley, CA, and London, 1994, p. 21).

54 Arendt, Origins, p. 416. Thus, in the imperialist phase, 'even horrors were still marked by a certain moderation and controlled by respectability' (p. 123).

55 Arendt, Origins, p. 434.

56 'We know that the Jews were prohibited from prying into the future. The Torah and prayers, on the other hand, instructed them in remembrance. This stripped the future of the magic to which all those succumb who get their information from soothsayers' (Benjamin, Illuminations, p. 264; translation slightly modified).

57 Kafka 'registered [gewahrte] what was to come without registering what surrounded him. ... there was here no far-sightedness or "visionary talent" ["Sehergabe"]. Kafka listened to tradition, and he who listens hard does not see' (Benjamin, Illuminations, p. 143; translation modified).

58 Cf. Walter Benjamin, Gesammelte Schriften, ed. Rolf Tiedemann and Hermann Schweppenhäuser (Suhrkamp, Frankfurt, 1972–89), vol. II, p. 678.

59 Ibid., vol. I, p. 1235.

60 Benjamin, Illuminations, pp. 257–8 and 254ff.

61 Cited by Wagenbach, In der Strafkolonie, pp. 23–5.

62 Cited in George Lukacs, History and Class Consciousness (1923), p. 96.

63 Lukacs, History and Class Consciousness, pp. 96–9. Wagenbach cites a contemporary review of Taylor's Principles of Scientific Management (1913). Its author, Kurt Eisner, grimly claims that Taylorism is a religion in which management has assumed the role of Providence: it develops each worker's special abilities and amortizes them like the machines to which they too have meanwhile been reduced. This combination of pseudo-Messianism and pseudo-science is not without echoes of Charles Fourier, Auguste Comte and Saint-Simon. It has its fictional counterpart in the Old Commandant's Apparat – a technical invention that is also the object of a sectarian cult.

64 Cited by Wagenbach, In der Strafkolonie, pp. 100–2.

65 See likewise Arendt on Kafka as the 'humorist and critic' of the 'pseudomysticism that is the stamp of bureaucracy when it becomes a form of government': 'Since the people it dominates never know why something is happening, and a rational interpretation of laws does not exist, there remains only one thing that counts, the brute naked event itself. ... Deification of accidents serves ... as rationalization. ... "And Accident ... in the language of religion is called Providence"' (Arendt, Origins, pp. 245–6). This holds even for Kafka's Prisoner, whose futile attempts to understand the brute events assailing him are crowned by the absurd assumption that he owes his release to the higher authority of the 'foreign [fremder] Traveller'. He nevertheless gets the basic message. In his very incomprehension, he understands the Old Commandant's justice ['Sei gerecht'] as vengeance ['Rache', 'gerächt'] – echoes of this Nietzschean word-play are scattered in the text – and refuses to be denied the sweet spectacle of the Officer's execution. Thus, the brutalized victim is no better than his executioner. The

disintegrating Apparatus no longer produces guilt and reconciliation but the makings of Arendt's guilt-free, avenging 'Mob'.

[66] See the first chapter of Claude Lévi-Strauss's Tristes Tropiques (Plon, Paris, 1995), 'La fin des voyages' ('The end of travelling'), which begins as follows: 'I hate voyages and explorers. And here I am about to narrate my expeditions' (p. 13).

[67] Cited in Benjamin, Reflections, p. 243.

[68] 'I'll tell it back home', one of the unpublished variants has the Traveller imagine himself warning the Officer (Franz Kafka, Tagebücher, ed. H-G. Koch, M. Müller and M. Pasley, Frankfurt, 1990, p. 826).

[69] For a further occurence of this telltale word in one of the variants, see ibid., p. 825.

[70] Cited in Wagenbach, In der Strafkolonie, p. 60.

[71] See Kafka, Tagebücher, pp. 822–7; also Wagenbach, In der Strafkolonie, pp. 60–2. One breathtaking fragment sketches the emerging times with a few bold strokes.

> 'Prepare the way for the serpent!', came the cry. 'Prepare the way for the great Madam!' 'We are ready', came the answering cry, 'we are ready!' And we preparers of the way, we much-vaunted stone-smashers, marched out of the bush. 'To work!', cried our ever-cheerful commandant, 'to work, you snake-fodder!' Thereupon we raised our hammers, and there began the busiest of hammering for miles around. No pause was allowed, only hand-shakes. The arrival of our serpent was already announced for that evening; by then everything had to be hammered to dust; our serpent cannot tolerate the smallest stone. Where else is so sensitive a serpent to be found? She is, moreover, a unique serpent, she's incomparably spoilt by our work, and for that reason alone incomparably constituted [daher auch bereits unvergleichlich geartet]. We fail to understand, indeed we regret, that she should still call herself serpent. She should at least call herself Madam, although as Madam she is of course also incomparable. But that's not our worry, our business is to make dust. (Kafka, Tagebücher, pp. 376–7)

This dream-like sequence might in retrospect be entitled 'Arbeit macht frei' or 'The Soviet Five-Year Plan'. It is also comparable with the following account of a Chicago stockyard in a book which left its traces on Kafka's image of America: 'From seven in the morning till seven in the evening, everyone has to perform the same small but crucial movement; he has to be sure to succeed, because the chain knows no rest. How could he speak, wipe away the sweat from his forehead or the blood that squirts from the cadavers …?' (Arthur Holitscher, Amerika. Heute und Morgen, Berlin, 1912, cited in Wagenbach, In der Strafkolonie, pp. 117–18). The difference is that the Commandant's workers love their work and know nothing of alienation. Not unlike the cannon-fodder that was during those months happily setting out for the front, the individual machine-fodder of the old order has become the mass snake-fodder of the new. One finds here not a revolutionary master–slave dialectic, but an immobilized dialectic between a sub- and superhuman species, in which the former not merely creates but maintains the latter in place. The self-castrating mass flattens itself and the way before its fetish, a transcendent being of its own making, a female phallus so ineffable and incomparable as to be, so they want to believe, beyond all species-name. One may recall here Benjamin's claim that Kafka's work is an unseeing reflector in which the coming world and the immemorial past obliquely mirror one another and the upshot is a dialectical image of the unseen present. It is some such past that is reflected here in the eager identification of the proto-totalitarian masses with their totemistic leader. The disenchanted world which grinds everything – notably myth – to dust thereby reverts to a mythic, indeed a pre-mythic stage. The New Commandant, who combines the despotism of an ancient slave-driver with an all-American optimism – Kafka wrote In the Penal Colony in the same weeks as the chapter 'The Nature Theater in Oklahoma' – turns out to be second in command to a pre patriarchal Serpent, a pre monotheistic One, a Prima Donna in every sense. It is as if the bush were being civilized by drones on behalf of a Queen Bee. 'Kafka did not consider the age in which he lived to be an advance over the beginnings of time. His novels are set in a swamp world … the stage which Bachofen called hetaeric' (Benjamin, Illuminations, p. 130). This precisely wild image of an incomparable, archaic Madam seems to know something about totalitarianism that specialized comparative work – work! – on it does not.

[72] 'But precisely the open end of the story remains as much a Stachel for the reader as the one in the Officer's burst forehead and the traveller's threatening gestures at those who remain behind' (Wagenbach, In der Strafkolonie, p. 126).

[73] Kafka, Tagebücher, pp. 822–3. The British Empire was acquired, according to an unnamed author cited by Arendt, 'in a fit of absent-mindedness' (Origins, p. 207).

[74] On the 'temporary alliance between the Mob and the Elite' in the (pre)history of totalitarianism, see Arendt, Origins, pp. 318–21. It too was prepared for in the colonies. 'The perfect gentleman and the perfect scoundrel came to know each other well in the "great wild jungle without law", and they found themselves "well-matched in their enormous similarity, identical souls in different disguises". … what, after all, took decades to achieve in Europe, because of the delaying effect of social ethical values, exploded with the suddenness of a short circuit in the phantom world of colonial adventure' (Origins, p. 190; quotations are from Conrad).

[75] Kafka, Tagebücher, pp. 823–4.

[76] On the actuality of this passage from Hamlet in the contemporary philosophico-political context see Jacques Derrida, Spectres de Marx (Galilée, Paris, 1993), pp. 46ff.

[77] Parallels exist notably between Foucault's account of the theatrical spectacle of public execution under the Ancien Régime, in which the tortured body renders the truth of the sentence legible for all, thus confirming the avenging sovereign's omnipotence, and the literalization of this process in the Officer's account of his 'peculiar Apparatus'; and between the contrast on which Kafka's story turns between the grandiose performance of redemptive justice and the far less visible workings of the 'mild' new régime and, on the other hand, Foucault's analysis of the replacement of torture by a new economy of the power to punish in which an 'enigmatic leniency' coincides with the ubiquitous extension of the punitive apparatus. Under the new régime, old-style execution takes place 'without public participation' and is being phased out. As if in its place, the New Commandant makes a 'show' (Schaustellung) of the advisory sessions at which he assembles all the ladies and administrative officials who once attended the executions; he plays to the gallery which he has had built for that purpose. The Old Commandant had consulted no-one; the only transparent aspect of his governance was the glass construction that enabled everyone to watch the execution of the verdict. Is, then, the new show of democracy the new spectacle, the showcase of a peculiar new Apparatus? Are these executive sessions the new, bloodless executions?

[78] Philanthropy adds insult – if not indeed injury – to injury. No sooner has the Prisoner been placed in the Apparatus than he vomits up the sweets, thereby further dirtying the Officer's beautiful machine. As for the ladies' handkerchieves,

they pass from hand to hand. First they are confiscated by the Officer, who squashes them behind the collar of his uniform – how interpret that? Then he returns them to the Prisoner when he decides to take his place. Finally, the Prisoner and the Soldier struggle half playfully for their possession. In the same spirit of philanthropy, a corrosive liquid may no longer be used on prisoners' backs to prepare them for fresh incisions. Water will have to do. Such is reform. The new order does not get off men's backs or wipe them clean. It merely smudges the old writing. Foucault sums up its message as follows: 'We punish, but this is a way of saying that we wish to obtain a cure'. He adds: 'Today criminal justice functions and justifies itself only by this perpetual reference to something other than itself, by this unceasing reinscription in non-juridical systems' (Foucault, Discipline, p. 22). Penal 'reform' aims 'not to punish less, but to punish better; to punish with an attenuated severity perhaps, but in order to punish with more universality and necessity; to insert the power to punish more deeply into the social body' (p. 82). 'Prison "reform" is virtually contemporary with the prison itself; it constitutes, as it were, its programme' (p. 234).

79 Cf. on the quasi-military regimentation of the work-force the fragment cited in note 71. Although 'the industrial system requires a free market and, in the nineteenth century, the role of forced labor in the mechanisms of punishment diminishes accordingly' (Foucault, Discipline, p. 25), this does not apply to the penal colonies. Kafka is, no doubt deliberately, vague on this subject. His narrator knows no more than the Traveller about the men whom the latter finds at the tea-house where the Old Commandant lies ingloriously buried: 'They were probably dock-workers, strong men with short, black, glistening beards. All were coatless, their shirts torn, poor humiliated folk [Volk].' One cannot tell whether these men are free or forced labor, European convicts or an indigenous population. How, above all, interpret the smile on their faces when the Traveller has finished reading the inscription on the Old Commandant's tomb? It is, we are told, 'as if' they had read it along with him and were now encouraging him not to take it seriously. But the Officer had told him that on days when executions are carried out many covert adherents of the Old Commandant frequent the tea-house. Are, then, the men he now finds there the adherents mentioned in the inscription ('who may at present bear no name')? And is their smile the incognito of a conspiratorial assembly whose members believe in the announced resurrection of the Old Commandant and are waiting for him to lead them to victory? But the latter was surely no friend of the oppressed. What, then, can 'poor humiliated folk' expect from a restoration of the old order other than a chimerical release from their present oppression? Such a scenario would confirm Zarathustra's prediction that the best service one can render the old order is to overturn its statues, because they will then arise again with more 'god-like', 'seductively suffering' features (Friedrich Nietzsche, Also Sprach Zarathustra, Book II, Von grossen Ereignissen (Of Great Events)). Or should we rather associate the scene at the tea-house with the hidden revolutionary activity of, say, freemasons' lodges or Chinese secret societies? One of the alternative scenarios that Kafka sketched in his diary evokes such a conspiracy: 'Hold up the lamp, you in front! You others quietly behind me! All in a row. And silent. That was nothing. No fear. I bear the responsibility. I will lead you out' (Kafka, Tagebücher, p. 825). Who is speaking here? The Old Commandant? The Officer? Is he addressing the nameless Volk? Is it conceivable that the Traveller has switched sides and is now leading the workers out?! If socialism seems as remote a prospect in Kafka's penal colony as it is in his America, this is perhaps because the shadowy new régime against which the adherents of

the old order conspire is the more effective conspiracy. 'The totalitarian move-ments', writes Arendt, 'have been called 'secret societies in broad daylight' (Arendt, Origins, p. 363). Something analogous holds for Kafka's world.

[80] Benjamin, Illuminations, p. 256.

[81] In a diary entry of 24 January 1914, Kafka compares his work at the office to the penalties (Strafarbeiten) imposed on schoolchildren: that of repeating the same senseless sentence ten or a hundred times, according to their degree of guilt. The difference, Kafka adds, is that he has to go on until he drops (cited in Wagen-bach, In der Strafkolonie, p. 19). Here too, then, there is no end to the penal colony. A related note of Benjamin's reads like a commentary on this story: 'The basic idea of myth is the world as punishment – punishment that itself produces the guilty party. In [Nietzsche's doctrine of] the eternal return, the punishment of having to stay behind at school is projected onto the cosmos: humanity has to copy its text over and over again' (Gesammelte Schriften, vol. 1, p. 1234).

[82] Wagenbach, In der Strafkolonie, p. 83.

[83] Cited by Wagenbach (ibid., p. 83). The inauguration of workers' insurance had been proclaimed in 1881 at the end of a religious service in the Berlin Schlosskapelle by 'Imperial Decree' (Kaiserliche Botschaft). Could the latter be one possible context for Kafka's fragment of that name? There the Emperor is dying; his whispered message may never reach its addressee at the outermost confines of his Empire; the latter may indeed have dreamt the whole story up.

[84] Cited in ibid., p. 84.

[85] See the documentation of Kafka's professional activities in ibid., pp. 84–91.

[86] An extract is published by Wagenbach, In der Strafkolonie, pp. 103–5.

[87] Ibid., pp. 71–2.

[88] In the Penal Colony has its counterpart in A Report to an Academy, where an ape tells an unseen assembly of scholars how he was shot and captured by hunters from Hagenbeck's zoo and transferred to Europe under cruel, though economically rational, conditions reminiscent of those that had prevailed during the slave trade. Freedom, from his perspective, lies back in the African jungle, not in European civilization. All that he can now hope for is to find a 'way out' – that is, to exchange his cage for a better one – the one that Max Weber called the 'iron cage' of modern Western civilization. To that end, he completes the process of colonization, subjects himself to the apparatus of subjectivation, miraculously assimilates the skills of an average European, and finds his niche as a performing ape in a variety show. In the civilized world, as in the jungle, mimesis is synonymous with survival. The ape accordingly apes humanity for a living. The only way out thus lies in becoming a certain kind of artist. This is also, but differently, implied by the narrative stance of the Penal Colony. Neither version has anything in common with the Romantic cult of the artist.

[89] Cited in Foucault, Discipline, p. 235.

[90] See ibid., pp. 201ff.

[91] Arendt, Origins, p. 123.

[92] The House of Commons, said Burke, will preserve its greatness 'as long as it can keep the breaker of the law in India from becoming the maker of the law for England' (cited in Arendt, Origins, p. 183). 'There was no trial by jury in India and the judges were all paid servants of the Crown, many of them removable at pleasure ... Some of the men of formal law felt rather uneasy at the success of the Indian experiment. 'If', they said, 'despotism and bureaucracy work so well in India, may not that be perhaps at some time used as an argument for introducing something of the same system here' (A. Carthill, The Lost Dominion [1924], cited in Origins, p. 216).

93 Benjamin, Illuminations, p. 142. Translation modified.

94 Arendt, Origins, pp. 429–39.

95 On the inherently contradictory nature of the totalitarian project see my essay on Robert Antelme cited in note 15.

96 David Rousset, cited in Arendt, Origins, p. 299.

97 Arendt, Origins, p. 427.

98 Ibid., p. 428.

99 Ibid., p. 436.

100 Ibid., p. 438.

101 This term is introduced by Michel Foucault toward the end of La Volonté de savoir (Gallimard, Paris, 1976, p. 188) and developed by Giorgio Agamben in Homo sacer (Einaudi, Turin, 1995). Agamben extrapolates from it the claim that 'the camp is the hidden paradigm of modern political space'. That is not the position argued here.

102 Lichtenberg, SB, vol. I, p. 302.

103 'Enlightenment', wrote Theodor W. Adorno and Max Horkeimer in 1944, 'is totalitarian' (Dialectic of Enlightenment, p. 6). This is, needless to say, an exaggeration, but it also happens to be profoundly true. The only truths to be found in psychoanalysis are, Adorno elsewhere writes, its exaggerations.

104 'Preface to the New Edition', Dialectic of Enlightenment (pp. ix–x). Translation modified.

105 The present essay was written for a conference in March 2001 and revised in February–March 2003. It does not attempt to take 11 September 2001 – an unprecedented terrorist attack from outside and inside the dominant world-system – into account. To do so would be to grapple with the following question: How does the ensuing sequence of events 'fit' into the larger (post-)totalitarian aftermath sketched in the above-quoted sentence: 'The trend toward total integration is interrupted but not cancelled out'?

4

Imagining the Absolute: Mapping Western Conceptions of Evil

Steven E. Aschheim

The themes of this volume – the problem of comparative victimization, the issues associated with the hierarchizing of genocide into greater and 'lesser evils' – are thoroughly charged, over-determined, and, for some, even a tasteless enterprise: how does one presume to grade evils? Perhaps a further source of disquiet arises from the point made by Martin Malia in his controversial article that has occasioned the proceedings of this book: 'Nazism's unique status as "absolute evil"' he writes, 'is now so entrenched that any comparison with it easily appears suspect.'[1] One may (or may not) find such entrenchment normatively problematic or unwarranted but few, I think, would question the empirical accuracy of Malia's assertion that Nazism has indeed come to occupy a unique demonic status within our moral economy, symbol of the deepest incarnation of barbarism and inhumanity. Perhaps Malia should have added an important rider to this statement: the model of Nazism as radical evil applies peculiarly and particularly to Anglo-American spheres of influence and western and central European societies (and to an increasing degree, certain countries in eastern Europe).

To be sure, 11 September now threatens either to erode or displace this paradigm – an issue to which we shall return later – but even prior to the bombing of the Twin Towers, this privileged position had increasingly came under attack on a number of fronts and from a variety of more or less persuasive perspectives.[2] These contestations did not go without effect. There is by now broad agreement that such a paradigmatic emplacement (especially concerning the Holocaust's putative radical incommensurability) has all too often been accompanied by a variety of crude instrumentalizations and vacuous, ideologically motivated 'lesson-drawing' (often of an internally contradictory kind). But these exposés are far better at undermining the paradigm than they are in accounting for its initial emergence and later persistence. To argue, as has Peter Novick in his otherwise insightful work, that this figuration is above all a matter of strategic decisions and choices taken by American Jewish communal leaders who, from the 1970s on, discovered a 'workable' identity-strengthening commodity in an age of waning Jewish identification, is surely not to take the phenomenon sufficiently seriously. Its far-flung flowering over the last few decades – well beyond the boundaries of the United States and in societies where the Jewish presence is negligible – suggests that the roots go deeper than this and that the required explanation be a little more rounded.[3] Not all commodities 'work' (as Saul Friedlander somewhere pointed out). Something in the event itself, its state-sanctioned criminality, its taboo-breaking aims, industrial methods and mammoth, transgressive scale clearly rendered such an absolutizing discourse both possible and plausible.[4]

Yet, on its own, this cannot fully account for the centrality of Nazism and the Holocaust within European and American discourse. Perceptual and normative hierarchies are seldom unmediated; representations are not built exclusively upon purely immanent or 'objective' considerations. In this chapter I want to explore another important, though insufficiently remarked and rather subliminal, component of this figuration. That it will prove to be both psychologically ambiguous and ethically problematic should come as no surprise.

What, at least in Western consciousness, is the 'something' that lifts this case above others? For Michael Andre Bernstein the Shoah has become what he calls 'the decisive evidentiary event' not simply as a result of its extremity (there are, after all, many other examples of extreme human cruelty) but because of our need for a 'monotheistic ideology of catastrophe', for a single 'exemplary model of the darkness at the heart of the modern world' and because of the Holocaust's singular 'figural plasticity', its amenability 'to almost every imaginable, ideological, philosophical and moral construction'.[5] For Tony Judt, the Holocaust has attained its iconic stature 'because it captures succinctly and forcibly, at the end of our terrible century, something for which we lack a modern vocabulary, but which lies at the heart of our recent past and thus our present inheritance. That something is the idea of evil.'

But, to some extent, these accounts (while on their own merits quite correct) beg the main question. We need still to probe into what within Western sensibility has, particularly and concretely, allowed Nazism and the Shoah to perform this exemplary and incarnatory role. Judt, indeed, does provide a hint when he writes that:

> The Holocaust is not an irreplaceable reminder of human nastiness; for such knowledge we can look in many places. But it is a rather distinctive reminder – or a distinctive warning – of what happens

74

when the patina cracks ... civil society, public life, open political systems and the forms of behavior they encourage and on which they depend, are all paper-thin constructions. They are all more fragile than it suits us to believe.[6]

This insight – that the special scandal resides in the fact that it is our own, recognisably civil society that is implicated – gets us an important part of the way. But it is only part of the way. I want here to suggest another delicate dimension of this emplacement. The special, enduring fascination with National Socialism and the atrocities it committed, the very deep drive to account for its horrors and transgressions (far greater than that of the Gulag or Cambodia or Rwanda or other genocides and mass murders of the twentieth century), the rich multiplicity of ruminations it has produced and its accumulative imprint on our political and intellectual discourse (including, one must add, the resulting ubiquitous attempts to relativize or neutralize or elide and displace its significance and impact), resides also in the particular nature and identity of both the victims and the perpetrators themselves. That is to say, an added, potent impetus derives from an inverted kind of Eurocentrism, our rather ethnocentric sense of scandal and riddle, the abiding astonishment that a modern, allegedly cultured and civilised society like Germany – traditionally taken to be the example of the enlightened *Kulturnation* – could thus deport itself.[7] Unlike the barbarities perpetrated by imperial powers in remote parts, these horrors occurred upon the European mainland, and were visited not upon African 'primitives' but the Jews whose literate presence represents a constitutive – albeit problematic – ingredient of Western civilisation itself. We are, I suggest, less likely to be taken aback by atrocities removed from the imagined Western 'core' (including when they are our own) – and even from the Gulag, because this occurred in what we still imagine to be a realm that remains geographically and mentally still 'halb-Asien' (half-Asian).

This system of judgement and expectation applied from the beginning of Nazi rule. For example, commenting on the 1933 boycott, the conservative owner of the Spectator, Sir Evelyn Wrench, wrote: 'I had come across anti-semitism in Eastern Europe before, but I thought racial persecution belonged to another age. Half-civilised peoples might still indulge in it but surely not the Germany I had known.'[8] The following quote, I think, is representative, typical of the substance of our perceptions, the special shock, which Nazism more than any other example of mass cruelty, evokes for us: 'The cry of the murdered sounded in the earshot of the universities; the sadism went on a street away from the theaters and museums ... the high places of literacy, of philosophy, of artistic expression, became the setting for Belsen ... We know now that a man can read Goethe or Rilke in the evening, that he can play Bach and Schubert, and go to his day's work at Auschwitz in the morning.'[9] George Steiner may be rather idiosyncratic but his emphases, it seems to me, articulate and capture a far wider, generalized feeling and predeliction. To be sure, there have been numerous attempts to displace this identificatory impulse onto a peculiar Germanic anthropology, an historical and ontological Sonderweg ('special path'), that distances and separates Germany from the mainstream. But these have not proved to be enduring. The paradigm retains much of its power because the perceived cultural commonalities seem to overwhelm the differences.

The 'blackness'(!) of the atrocities, Steiner adds, 'did not spring up in the Gobi desert or the rain forests of the Amazon'. By extension, if and when it does in places removed from the Enlightened European center – say in Rwanda – one is (tragically) less likely to be appalled, less able to connect empathically. While commemorative and historical interest in Nazism persists, massive imperial crimes remain virtually unkown. The Belgian King Leopold II's slave-labour rule over the Congo, it is generally estimated, took many millions of lives. Yet, as Adam Hochschild comments at the beginning of his superb study of one of the major killing grounds of modern times, 'Why were these deaths not mentioned in the standard litany of our century's horrors? And why had I never heard of them?'[10]

It is true, as Michael Ignatieff has recently pointed out, that ethics typically follows ethnicity, that empathy and moral principles take root within tribal boundaries and are most easily and naturally expressed within its confines.[11] The question of the capacity for empathy is important but my point goes beyond that. It is rather to state that the special status of Nazism within Western sensibility, our almost obsessive wrestling with its ghosts and dynamics, is (amongst other things) generated by our enduring outrage – and fascination – that the barbarous could erupt precisely where culture seemed most entrenched, that fundamental transgressions occurred within, and were visited upon, what we regard as the most advanced of civilizations.

This is a crucial motor for the encoding of Nazism as the measure of absolute inhumanity. This is so even in the face of the worst excesses and brutalities of the Stalinist regime. Contra Novick, I would argue that even at the height of the Cold War, the Gulag was never able to compete with the symbolic resonances – immediately accessible through photographic evidence – first of Buchenwald, and then of Auschwitz. Contemporary scholarship is only now beginning to analyze the role of these iconic images that have became archetypal and which inform and filter into all our subsequent perceptions of atrocity.[12] Such photographic evidence was obviously not available for the Gulags and would, in any case, I hasten to add, probably not have been as palpably dramatic. But, it is worth pointing out that even in cases where such photographic evidence was abundantly available, as in the recent events in Rwanda and Bosnia, the reactions seem to have been somewhat blunted and short-lived.

Various political explanations have been proffered for our inability to empathize with the manifold victims of Bolshevism as we do with those of National Socialism. While Nazism appeals to the lowest instincts, Communist ideology speaks to liberal and universalist ideals – thus we are more appalled by the former. Martin Malia has argued the opposite case. Mass murder 'in the name of a noble ideal', he writes,

> is more perverse than in the name of a base one. The Nazis, after all, never pretended to be virtuous. The Communists, by contrast, trumpeting their humanism, hoodwinked millions around the world for decades, and so got away with murder on the ultimate scale. The Nazis ... simply killed their prey, the Communists compelled their victims to confess their 'guilt', and thus acknowledge Communism's 'correctness'. Nazism, finally was a unique case and it developed no international clientele. By contrast, Communism's universalism permitted it to metastasize around the globe.[13]

Who could imagine a survivor of a Nazi camp describe his or her sentiments in the terms used by a former Gulag inmate: 'The most important factor that secured my survival ... was my unflinching, ineradicable belief in our Leninist party, in its humanist principles.'[14]

At any rate, whatever the intrinsic merits of Malia's argument, it elides a crucial psychological dimension: the ubiquitous nature of the political symbolism evoked by Nazism within Western culture. Michael Bernstein[15] has shrewdly observed that, while the Gulag has usually been invoked by conservative and right-wing political interests, and Hiroshima by left-wing discourses, both camps have been successfully able to buttress their own positions by appealing to and deploying the Shoah. That this should be so is directly related to our present theme. While predicating it upon different, interested political causes and interpretations, all ground their analyses upon common readings of the breakdown of European culture and civilization.

Moreover, from the psycho-dynamic viewpoint of Western perceptions, Communism and its outrages retain a more or less distant Asian and Third World character (Pol Pot, Mao, Ho Chi Minh – these are not exactly European names). At the same time, the incapacity to be equally outraged by Stalin and his inequities derives less, I think, from the fact that the Communists were allies in the struggle against Nazism (after all, Stalin became the bogeyman of the West immediately after the war) but rather because Russia has seldom been considered part of the fully cultivated epicentre but, rather, as significantly remote from (western) Europe's geographical and spiritual core, a still not fully civilized force. As an image this stereotype still pertains.[16]

Atrocities, perhaps especially our own, are more acceptable when performed in distant places and upon 'uncivilized' populations. This has an ancient pedigree. 'The Romans distinguished explicitly between war against civilized peoples, which had to obey certain rules of honor and mercy, and war against barbarians, which could be conducted without restraint of any kind.'[17] European imperialist and racist cruelties were rationalized not only by the patent 'primitiveness' of their subjects but made easier by the fact that, far from home, conventional standards could quickly collapse. Behavioural restraints were not applicable to life in the jungles. Joseph Conrad perceived this moral-geographical factor quite clearly, as did Rudyard Kipling:

> Ship me somewhere east of Suez,
> where the best is like the worst,
> Where there aren't no Ten Commandments,
> an' a man can raise a thirst.[18]

The burden of enlightened expectations are greatest at home. George Steiner has honestly owned up to this predeliction. 'I realize', he writes,

> that barbarism and political savagery are endemic in human affairs ... But I think there is hypocrisy in the imagination that would claim universal immediacy, that would seek impartial appropriation throughout the provocations of all history and all places. My own consciousness is possessed by the eruption of barbarism in modern Europe ... I do not claim for this hideousness any singular privilege; but this is the crisis of rational, humane expectation which has shaped my own life and with which I am most directly concerned.[19]

The Holocaust, as Shiraz Dossa once provocatively put it, is the classic instance of 'the murder of eminently "civilized" victims by equally "civilized" killers'.[20] Much of its paradigmatic power derives from this equation. Our representations of the killers refuse to be entirely severed from images of the greatness of German culture; the full horror of the 'Final Solution' cannot be separated from conceptions of the charged role and status of the victims themselves.

If a powerful, ongoing negative anti-Jewish stereotype permeates Western culture it is also true that the Jews are deeply and familiarly implicated within, indeed, co-constitutive of that history. Indeed, one could argue that the venom and rejection of Gentiles towards Jews derived precisely from the depths of intimacy and dependency, from the complex set of inter-relations that characterize the relationship, the knowledge that at all kinds of levels Jews represent salient, creative forces and figures within that very culture.[19] In his 1961 report on the Eichmann trial, the Dutch author Harry Mulisch asked: 'Had the Jews been a cultureless tribe ... would their death have been any less wrong? ... During the noon recess I pose the question to Public Prosecutor Hausner ... He does think so – I don't.'[22]

This then was no 'meaningless' massacre but rather a historical 'project' saturated with manifold significances. The Jews were not faceless, anonymous atoms. 'Hitler's crimes are particularly poignant', Jason Epstein has written, 'because they occurred so to speak in the house next door ... The victims were ourselves at barely one remove ... The Soviet victims in their faraway country with their unpronounceable names and odd clothes were nothing like us.'[23] Phillip Lopate has caught a crucial aspect of the psycho-dynamics of the lesser evil syndrome. He asks why

> those piles of other victims are not as significant as Jewish corpses ... Is it simply because they are Third World people – black, brown, yellow-skinned ... I sense that I am being asked to feel a particular pathos in the rounding up of gentle, scholarly, middle-class, civilized people who are then packed into cattle cars, as though the liquidation of illiterate peasants would not be as poignant. The now-familiar newsreel shot of Asian populations fleeing a slaughter with their meager possessions in handcarts still reads to us as a catastrophe involving 'masses', while the images of Jews lined up in their fedoras and overcoats tug at our hearts precisely because we see them as individuals.[24]

This Eurocentric figuration brings with it numerous contradictions and ironies that mingle uncomfortably with each other. Scott Montgomery has insightfully formulated one such aspect. The strange purity we have bestowed upon the Nazis as the ultimate in malevolence, 'the horror at Auschwitz [as] supreme by virtue of being fully modern, occurring in the very center of Europe', renders other horrors in Africa, Asia, South America – and, I would add, even eastern Europe – 'no matter how brutal or planned, somehow qualify as more primitive ... In a strange twist of logic, the Holocaust is made to seem more sophisticated, more advanced than any other incident of its kind. The terrible irony here is that Nazism finally becomes, at this elevated symbolic height, a perverted reflection of Eurocentrism.'[25]

But things are in actuality not that simple. For at the same time that we have bestowed this purity and absoluteness upon Auschwitz, it has determined our iconic and moral imaginations, informed what one observer has called our overall 'atrocity aesthetic' – the Holocaust as archetype girds our depictions of East Timor, Rwanda, Bosnia, Somalia and Cambodia.[26] As Martin Jay points out:

Only in Hollywood movies can the Holocaust be contained within the boundaries of an aesthetic frame; in real life, it spills out and mingles with the countless other narratives of our century. Its real horror, we might say, is not confined to the actual genocidal acts it has come to signify. Historicizing the Holocaust need not mean reducing it to the level of the 'normal' massacres of the innocents that punctuate all of recorded history, but rather remembering those quickly forgotten and implicitly forgiven events with the same intransigent refusal to normalize that is the only justifiable response to the Holocaust itself.[27]

This essay was written prior to the events of 11 September 2001. It would be remiss not to reassess these comments in this light for we do not know yet how these attacks will affect future mappings of political atrocity. Certainly the problem of 'evil' has been reawakened, set into a new context, and become a central preoccupation of both political and intellectual discourse.[28] Will Osama Bin Laden and al-Qaeda and the new 'axis of evil' (Iraq, Iran and North Korea) usurp the more home-grown twentieth-century forms of the Gulag and the death camps, Fascism and Communism?

It is, of course, too early to tell. A few possibilities exist. Nazism, Communism and contemporary terrors may merge into one, rather undifferentiated (and confused but easily manipulable) picture of pernicious wrong-doing. To be sure, a complex, plural culture should be more inclusive, able to face and commemorate these different transgressive expressions not by merging, comparing or hierarchizing them but rather by noting the distinctions.[29] But that is more of a normative prescription than a prediction.

My own feeling, given the logic outlined in this chapter, is that Nazism will not easily yield its paradigmatic hold. As Mark Lilla notes the new 'axis of evil' hardly corresponds to the classic totalitarian regimes that produced the great evils of the last century but consist of a diffuse hodge-podge of various degrees of 'tyranny',[30] and as such seem to be less amenable to sustained 'absolutist' discourse (and thus also renders decisions of policy necessarily more complicated and confused). Saddam Hussein was a ruthless tyrant but few would argue that he is on a par with Hitler or Stalin. We should note too that this list is made up not of modern or first-world regimes and is thus easily relegated to a more primitive 'non-European' status. Our own 'enlightened' post-1945 sensibility may still be most fascinated by allegedly civilized sites and regimes where 'evil' was supposed to have been banished and yet was committed on a gargantuan scale (itself part of the fascination).

But what of the terrorist attack on the Twin Towers?[31] As Susan Neiman has noted, the 11 September terrorists (as well as the Taliban) have bypassed our more complex Auschwitz-generated ruminations on mass murder, rendered Hannah Arendt's sophisticated model of Eichmann's bureaucratic 'thoughtlessness' superfluous. No theories of the 'banality of evil' or, for that matter, the dialectic of Enlightenment or bourgeois morality (or its violation) or the Sonderweg are required.[32] Here, instead, was a 'case of single-mindedly thoughtful evil' that serves to reinstate more direct, simpler conceptions of transgression.[33] (Of course, this 'simplicity', as Neiman persuasively demonstrates, in no way detracts from the fundamentally 'evil' character of such actions.)

Yet, I would want to argue, an ambiguity – deriving from the Euro-centric bias discussed here – persists. On the one hand, 11 September allows for a certain self-righteous displacement. 'Evil' has been thrust outward; it exists elsewhere, especially in alien and primitive climes. The geographical, cultural (and perhaps religious) contours of light and darkness have been restored. To all intents and purposes this is a clash between 'our' and 'their' civilizations. Simplicity reigns again. Yet, for all that, I suspect that post-Auschwitz consciousness will continue to instruct us, perhaps maintain its paradigmatic position, precisely because it has enlarged and complicated our horizons of transgression and placed at its center this inverted Eurocentric sense of scandal and sophistication. This peculiarly Western mapping of evil inhibits its own impulses at displacement because it renders, at all possible levels, (our own) modern selves and 'culture' culpable: 'civilization' itself remains in question. At its heart stands a kind of uneasy self-interrogation. That too is its unique, saving grace.

NOTES

[1] Martin Malia, 'The Lesser Evil? Obstacles to Comparing the Holocaust and the Gulag even after the Opening of the Soviet archives', Times Literary Supplement, 27 March 1998, pp. 3–4.

[2] See Peter Novick, The Holocaust in American Life (Boston, MA: Houghton Mifflin, 1999) and Michael Bernstein, 'Homage to the Extreme: The Shoah and the Rhetoric of Catastrophe', Times Literary Supplement, 6 March 1998, pp. 6–8, and his earlier Forgeone Conclusions: Against Apocalyptic History (Berkeley, CA: University of California Press, 1994).

[3] See the insightful critique of Novick by Tony Judt, 'The Morbid Truth', The New Republic (issue date, 16.7.1999 from the internet). Nevertheless, Novick's emphasis on the differential contextual consequences of the absolutist claim is important and needs to be addressed: while in Germany it operates, correctly, as a force demanding confrontation and responsibility, in America and elsewhere it may be an aid to evade one's own crimes. I may add, that in the Israel–Palestine conflict this remains perhaps the most powerful and ubiquitous metaphor though the constant attempts to invoke it – between the two national sides or in domestic Israeli left/right confrontations – is typically depicted as verging on the blasphemous.

[4] I am purposely leaving aside here the question of 'uniqueness' because I believe that the claim has become almost irretrievably ideological. In the present context, it simply assserts or assumes what needs to be explained.

5   Bernstein, 'Homage to the Extreme'.

6   Ibid., p. 14 (of 16) for Judt quotes in this paragraph and one before.

7   I have analyzed some of these themes in my chapter in the book of the same name, Culture and Catastrophe: German and Jewish Confrontations with National Socialism and Other Crises (New York: New York University Press, 1996), although I develop them further here and take them into slightly different directions.

8   Evelyn Wrench, I Loved Germany (London, 1940). Quoted in Michael Burleigh, The Third Reich: A New History (London: Macmillan, 2000), p. 282.

9   See 'Preface' to George Steiner, Language and Silence: Essays on Language, Literature and the Inhuman (New York: Atheneum, 1977), pp. viii, ix.

10 Adam Hochschild, King Leopold's Ghost: A Story of Greed, Terror and Heroism in Colonial Africa (New York: Houghton Mifflin, 1999), p. 3. Perhaps even more stunning is the almost total ignorance – including widespread neglect by historians – of the great famines that took between 30 and 50 million lives throughout the 'Third World' between 1876 and 1899, the time in which European imperialism reached its height and global market forces were unleashed as never before. These mass starvations and deaths (and often murders) were not the inevitable outcome of 'natural disasters' but a result of deliberate political and economic policy. On this 'political ecology of famine' ('the missing pages – the absent defining moments ... – in virtually every overview of the Victorian era') see the revelatory work by Mike Davis, Late Victorian Holocausts: El Niño and the Making of the Third World (London and New York: Verso, 2001).

11 Michael Ignatieff, 'The Danger of a World Without Enemies', The New Republic (Internet, post date 21.02.01/issue date 26.02.01), p. 1.

12 See, for instance, Barbie Zelizer, Remembering to Forget: Holocaust Memory through the Camera's Eye (Chicago, IL, and London: University of Chicago Press, 1998) and, quite controversially, Dagmar Barnouw, Ansichten von Deutschland (1945). Krieg und Gewalt in der zeitgenössischen Photographie (Basel: Stroemfeld Verlag, 1997).

13 Malia, 'The Lesser Evil', p. 4.

14 Quoted in Anne Applebaum, 'After the Gulag', New York Review of Books (24 October 2002), p. 41.

15 Bernstein, 'Homage to the Extreme', p. 7.

16 There is certainly merit in Dan Diner's somewhat different explanation. In Germany, he writes, 'the nation is the focus of perception and judgment for dealing with Nazi crimes. In contrast, the regime serves as the focal point for dealing with Stalinist crimes in the former Soviet Union.' Nazism, he argues, becomes a national or German crime yet one perpetrated on the 'other' thus setting it in 'a zone apart, as it were, from one's own mnemonic collective. Quite different from the task of coming to terms with the mass crimes of the Soviet Union's Stalinist regime ... part of the same historical mnemonic collective, the process of overcoming the evil past naturally becomes a wrestling with oneself.' This argument applies only to the ways in which German and ex-Soviet memory operates. Mine takes in a larger compass. Moreover, while Diner makes a very clear distinction between 'outwardly' and 'inwardly' directed crimes, one burden of my argument is that in the case of the Jews – who are seen as ambivalently integral to Western civilization – such a distinction becomes blurred. See the chapter (11) 'Nazism and Stalinism: On Memory, Arbitrariness, Labor, and Death', in Dan Diner, Beyond the Conceivable: Studies on Germany Nazism and the Holocaust (Berkeley, CA: University of California Press, 2000). The quotes are to be found on pp. 190–1.

[17] Quoted in Ignatieff, 'The Danger of a World without Enemies'.

[18] Rudyard Kipling, 'Mandalay', in Barrack Room Ballads (London: Methuen, 1892). Quoted in Hochschild, King Leopold's Ghost, p. 138.

[19] All the quotes from Steiner are taken from his 'Preface' to Language and Silence, pp. viii–ix.

[20] Shiraz Dossa, 'Human Status and Politics: Hannah Arendt on the Holocaust', Canadian Journal of Political Science, June (1980), see esp. pp. 319–20.

[21] I have explored these dynamics on a smaller canvas in 'German History and German Jewry: Junctions, Boundaries, and Interdependencies', in In Times of Crisis: Essays on European Culture, Germans, and Jews (Madison, WI: University of Wisconsin Press, 2001).

[22] This quote appears in manuscript form from the – as yet unpublished – English translation of the original Dutch by Dederik van Hoogstraten. See Harry Mulisch, Case 40/61: A Report on the Eichmann Trial, p. 65

[23] Jason Epstein, 'A Dissent on Schindler's List', New York Review of Books, 41 (21 April 1994). To be sure, traditional ghetto Jews, 'Ostjuden', were more remote than the modern, assimilated variety. Yet, as representatives of Judaism, they formed an essential part of the European landscape. For all the attempts to depict them as frighteningly alien, their urban, literate presence was an ambivalently familiar part of social life.

[24] Phillip Lopate, 'Resistance to the Holocaust', Tikkun, vol. 4 (May–June 1989), p. 58. Quoted in Novick, The Holocaust in American Life, p. 235.

[25] Scott Montgomery, 'What Kind of Memory? Reflections on Images of the Holocaust', Contention, vol. 5, no. 1 (Fall 1995), pp. 79–103, esp. pp. 100–1. Mark Lilla has recently stated this a little differently: 'This is the paradox of Western political discourse ever since the Second World War: the more sensitive we become to the horrors brought on by the totalitarian tyrannies, the less sensitive we become to tyranny in its more moderate forms.' See his 'The New Age of Tyranny', New York Review of Books, 24 October 2002, pp. 28–9. The quote appears on p. 29.

[26] Zelizer, Remembering to Forget, pp. 204 and 210.

[27] Martin Jay, 'The Manacles of Gavrilo Princip', Salmagundi, vols 106–7 (Spring–Summer 1995), p. 21. Zelizer, Remembering to Forget, however, claims that this normalization of atrocity is indeed what has taken place through iconic familiarization (p. 212). She adds that this may not only be a case of habituation but the very plenitude of cases and images creates what Anthony Lewis calls 'compassion fatigue' (see ibid., p. 218).

[28] As evidenced by a rash of recent publications. See Charles Kimball, When Religion Becomes Evil (San Franciso, CA: Harper, 2002); James Waller, Becoming Evil: How Ordinary People Commit Genocide and Mass Killing (New York: Oxford University Press, 2002); Richard J. Bernstein, Radical Evil: A Philosophical Interrogation (New York: Polity Press, 2002). The work that is attracting the most attention is by Susan Neiman, Evil in Modern Thought: An Alternative History of Philosophy (Princeton, NJ: Princeton University Press, 2002). On this see Edward Rothstein, 'Defining Evil in the Wake of 9/11', The New York Times (Arts and Ideas section), 5 October 2002, pp. A17, A19; and Judith Shulevitz, 'There's Something Wrong with Evil', New York Times Book Review, 6 October 2002, p. 39.

[29] As Neiman puts it, Evil in Modern Thought, p. 286: 'To call something evil is to say that it defies justification and balance. Evils should not be compared, but they should be distinguished.'

30 See the suggestive analysis by Lilla, New Age of Tyranny, pp. 28–9.

31 Post-1945 discussions of political 'evil' have typically revolved around the themes of genocide, mass murder and perhaps imperialism and the dynamics of racist regimes. Now it seems almost certain that the very diffuse notion of 'terrorism' will be included.

32 Jeffrey Herf's term 'reactionary modernism' may come closest to depicting this variety of technologically aware and armed fundamentalism. See his Reactionary Modernism: Technology, Culture and Politics in Weimar and the Third Reich (Cambridge: Cambridge University Press, 1984).

33 Neiman, Evil in Modern Thought, pp. 281–8.

5

Remembrance and Knowledge:
Nationalism and Stalinism in Comparative Discourse

Dan Diner

In recent historiographical approaches, remembrance is increasingly assuming an epistemic importance. What is remembered and preserved, by whom and why? These are vital questions for historical anthropology and the cultural sciences in the broadest sense. After all, memory spins narratives that precede any interrogation of the historical material. Those narratives are not arbitrarily selected: via the narrative mold, they channel the imprint of past historical reality into reconstructions crafted by professional historians. Consequently, it is not just a subjective endeavor to try to determine the various modes of seeing intrinsic to differing perspectives; from their intersections, relevant truths can be extracted that are both objective and universal. In this chapter, I attempt to exemplify the approach that assigns memory an epistemic significance, developing this via an often demanded comparison between National Socialism and Soviet Communism. Indeed, such juxtaposing itself can be understood here as the articulation of a specific structure of memory.

CONVERSION: REGIME INTO NATION

The rituals of remembrance that commemorate the crimes of the Nazi regime differ quite markedly from the passive memorialization of the victims of Stalinist rule in the former Soviet Union. The reasons for that discrepancy are obvious: Hitler's crimes are perceived as atrocities perpetrated by Germany against others. This is how they enter German collective memory; this is how they are preserved in the memory of the others – as German crimes. The Nazi period is perceived as an integral component of German history, indelibly engraved in collective memory. By contrast, it is hard to frame the crimes of Stalin and the Communist regime in the former Soviet Union as Russian crimes. Moreover, a distinctively Soviet memory nowadays is in any event only marginally viable, especially since the peoples and successor states of the former Soviet Union have distanced themselves from the now defunct union that once united them.[1]

While in Germany nationalism succeeded in melding nation and regime, seeking its victims primarily outside the so-called German Volk community, the Soviet population itself was the prime target of victimization by its own regime. And while Hitler directed his war as a German war against adversaries mainly outside Germany's borders, Stalin waged a war that was internecine. That proved an ultimate catastrophe, but was initiated ostensibly as a grand social upheaval, appropriating the discourses of class struggle and civil war. In marked contrast, Hitler's racial ideology fell back on the narrative and terminology of an integrative nationalism. Consequently, National Socialism, in its distinctively German wrapping, was able to contaminate German memory with the crimes of the Nazi regime. They continue to be preserved in German memory and that of the others as German crimes.

There is an inherent problem in the formation of a post-Soviet memory in whose mold the crimes of Stalin and the Communist regime are preserved in their full enormity. How can crimes that elude the armature of an ethnic, and thus long-term, memory be kept alive in collective remembrance? Can crimes perpetrated not in the name of a collective, such as the nation, but in the name of a social construction, such as class, be memorialized in an appropriate form? What narratives that preceded the events have to be tapped so as to open memory's door to those events?

Outside professional historiography, the crimes committed by Soviet Communism and not incorporated into individual long-term memories threaten to fade into a kind of oblivion.[2] It is evident that those nations whose collective memory is marked by a fierce struggle with the old imperial Russia tend to be more successful in keeping alive a remembrance of the things past. Those in the main are peoples whose tales of suffering under Soviet domination coalesced with the narrative of their former resistance to the Russian empire. I am thinking here in particular of the Poles, the Hungarians and even, to a certain extent, the Germans as well. In Germany's former eastern lands, Soviet rule established itself as 'Russian' rule, infusing explosive memories of both world wars.

The Polish example can illustrate the welding of the present with narratives from the past. Like no other nation, the Poles were able to incorporate Soviet presence and domination into a long chain of historical events. Its compressed arsenal of memory reaches back to the partitions in the late eighteenth century and the Polish uprisings in the nineteenth century, extending on back even further, to the Polish–Muscovite clash in the seventeenth century, manifested in its extreme religious form in the dualism Roman Catholicism–Russian Orthodoxy.[3] All these peak, and are collated, in the image of the mass executions of Polish officers by the Soviet NKVD (secret police) in 1940 in the Katyn Forest near Smolensk. Thus, a link is welded between the age-old Polish–Russian conflict and the ideological confrontation in the twentieth century.

In Hungary, there was the historical sounding board of the revolution of 1848/49 and its suppression by Russian troops, coming to Austria's aid.[4] Finland's special position in the Cold War cannot be understood without the country's Russian prehistory and the Finno-Russian War of 1939–40. The former Baltic Soviet republics were also able to join together sufficient historical material to recognize in Soviet domination a Czarist Russia redux.

Other peoples of the Soviet Union also managed in various ways to see in Soviet rule the lurking hulk of old imperial Russia, and the memory of its crimes of colonization and expansion, especially where the empire's expansion had gone hand-in-hand with a process of cultural Russification. In these instances, the 'social', i.e. class, crimes of the Soviet regime were reprocessed into the respective ethnically constituted memories and their narratives, emerging from that alembic as 'Russian' crimes. That is especially true in the case of the 'persecuted peoples',[5] who were subjected by the regime to a policy of mass deportation and resettlement, such as the Tartars, Kalmucks or ethnic Germans.

Aside from the highly urbanized Jewish population, whose intellectual class in the late Stalinist period was accused of 'cosmopolitanism' and thus of high treason, and subjected to anti-Semitic persecution and executions, the regime presented itself to the Orthodox Russian population in a pure form: as a dictatorship and a despotic rule, committed to a massive social experiment that led to catastrophic results. Yet in post-Soviet Russia, past Communist rule, not just on the extreme fringes of the political spectrum, is often ethnically infused and projected as a regime of non-Russian nationalities, dominated by the Jews, the Caucasians, the Baltic peoples and others.

The conversion of phenomena of the grand-scale social experiment of Soviet Communism into national narratives is a process especially salient in the Ukraine. There, the consequences of the forced collectivization of 1929–33, and particularly the terrible famine of 1932, are interpreted as a kind of genocide against the Ukrainian people. That is how collective memory has preserved those ordeals.[6] In the Ukraine, throughout the entire 'black earth' region and other agricultural areas such as Kazakhstan, events during the period of forced collectivization and 'de-kulakization' are transposed into the various antecedent narrative and interpretative structures, and integrated in this way into historical memory. The narrative of the Civil War plays a central role here. After all, the Ukraine, southern Russia and the northern Caucasus were not only especially hard hit by forced collectivization and the subsequent famine, but had also been ravaged by the earlier events of the Civil War and outside intervention.[7] Again and again in the early 1930s, the Soviet authorities, representatives of the Party and of the People's Commissariat for Internal Affairs imagined they were confronted with acts of sabotage by purported members of the White Guard, veterans of the White armies, landowners, NEP (New Economic Policy) profiteers, clerics and other counter-revolutionaries – as though the horrors of forced collectivization were some sort of linear sequel, an encore to the Civil War.

The agricultural areas of southern Russia and the Ukraine were transformed into a battle zone of internal and internecine struggle. With the despotism distinctive to the Soviet regime, each was identified as a purported saboteur and class enemy. Suspicions and accusations spread like an epidemic as scapegoats were sought for the consequences of economic mismanagement, inefficiency and theft in the collective farms established during forced collectivization. The frenzied mood at the time was reminiscent of the hysteria of witch-hunts. National and local conflicts, available as convenient fodder for such fictions, were kneaded into the general mélange of suspicion.[8]

The persecutions, arrests, executions and deportations in the former areas of Civil War were styled as 'class struggle' and took on the character of 'social purging'. Paradoxically, they followed a principle of seizing on social, not ethnic origin – the status and position of a person's ancestors, a kind of social genealogy. This offered an ideological justification for the persecution and punishment of purported delinquents.[9]

Such a 'biologized' class origin was sufficient to accuse the harassed individuals of counter-revolutionary acts – or at least to suspect them of possible malicious intent. Supposedly reactionary fathers and grandfathers had their 'sins' visited upon sons, daughters and other relations. They were crushed as 'objective' 'class enemies' in the mills of social purging.[10] Anyone branded as a 'class enemy' was subject to the caprice of the authorities and the machinations of his or her milieu. In an atmosphere of rank suspicion, every conceivable local conflict was rationalized and legitimized, ranging from personal enmity to rivalries based on social envy, appropriating the terminology and ideology of class struggle.

At times, such resentment and rancor reached back into the pre-Revolutionary period; re-energized during the Civil War, it continued on during the NEP. In any event, enough tinder for conflict had been collected, and it was an easy matter to utilize the dominant codes of legitimization to harm others. The terror kindled from above was further fanned from below. In a climate of fear and mutual distrust, the despotic power so significant for the system and its functioning destroyed the last remnant of social solidarity. The upshot was a total atomization of society.

NATIONALISM AND STALINISM IN COMPARATIVE DISCOURSE
SIMILARITIES AND DIFFERENCES

Contrary to their own self-perception, Communism and National Socialism are linked by striking similarities. Seen from the vantage-point of liberal democracy, with its institutional safeguards for civil rights and separation of powers, and in particular the separation of the public and private spheres, both regimes correspond to the genotype of totalitarian rule. That is heightened in both cases by the distinctive tie to a charismatic leader. Both regimes were driven by historical-ideological worldviews, sources of legitimization for political action that appeared (and still do) highly suspect to Western liberal democracies. While in accordance with Communist conviction, Stalin's regime sought to speed up historical time, ready to sacrifice past and present to a supposedly better future; National Socialism beat against time's current, buoyed by its 'biological' fictions of society and race. The historical-philosophical project of accelerating or stemming time's flow extends beyond the individual, utilizing him or her as mere grist for the sake of a grand project, whether in the name of universal humankind or a superior race yet to be bred. Both projects are utopian and require the exercise of institutional force for their realization. As a result of their horrific crimes, both regimes are engraved in the century's memory as twins of terror. Yet if you leave the plane of the general, common features and look at these regimes more closely, the picture that emerges is far more differentiated.

The parameters of possible juxtaposition are complex. A comparative reckoning of the hecatombs of their respective victims is complicated if only by the fact of duration: the Nazi regime lasted for only 12 years and was smashed from the outside, while the Soviet regime was in power for two generations until it imploded and collapsed. In addition, the crimes of the National Socialists were perpetrated largely during the war, compacted into some 48 months from 1941 to 1945; they did not victimize the German population but 'foreigners', the so-called Fremdvölkische. By contrast, the mass crimes of Stalinism were committed in peacetime, with their terrible twin apogees during forced collectivization and mass famine exacting a toll of many millions of lives.[11]

This social war was waged almost exclusively against the broad agrarian classes. By contrast, the 'purges' in the Party, military leadership, and technocratic class during 1936–39 mainly affected members of the elite, as a kind of prophylactic Civil War.[12] It was not until the beginning of World War II that internal relief was felt. In the 'Great War for the Fatherland', the regime appealed to the patriotic sentiments of the population. Repression was significantly reduced, but not eliminated. After the war, the number of inmates in Gulag surged, declining only in the 'thaw' after Stalin's death.[13]

This salient difference in relation to time and number does not provide much basis for any quantitative comparison. There are also great difficulties in qualifying the victims, which is in any case problematic. But one thing is clear: compared with the Nazi regime, the Stalinist system was notable for its over-reaching surplus of despotic caprice. Not even the top echelons of the regime were spared from periodic, systematic persecution. To participate in power heightened a person's profile, endangered their situation; in any event, it provided no security.[14] The political elites were scapegoated for the constant shortcomings, trials and tribulations, then held up as negative examples and executed. The frequent comparison between the Kirov Affair and the Röhm Putsch is misguided, if simply because the 1934 Blood Purge, the 'night of the long knives', constituted an exception in the short chronicle of the Nazi regime, while similar events were quite commonplace in Stalin's Soviet Union.[15]

In the heyday of Stalinism, despotism and fear had become the veritable elixir of totalitarian rule. Anyone could fall victim – the regime's opponents, its supporters, Stalin's henchmen, sycophants and lackeys, the members of special units involved in mass executions. Not to forget respectable Soviet citizens and comrades who had no idea how they had been sucked into the rotary blades of the 'Red Inquisition'.[16]

Measured by this despotism, Hitler's rule gives the impression of a high degree of order, and even of legal security. After all, the criteria for persecution were, so to speak, 'objective'.[17] Every one could be certain of what fate awaited him or her, one way or the other. In any event, the Volksgenossen who did not oppose the regime were allowed to go about their daily lives basically unmolested. Thus, for members of the Volk community, the regime was far less totalitarian than was the Stalinist Soviet Union for its population. In addition, thanks to its initial successes, the Nazi regime also enjoyed comparatively broad support during the war. It was to a larger degree a system of rule with the people rather than against it. By contrast, those excluded from the Volk community were given to understand in no uncertain terms that they were undesirables. Generally, those targeted were always promptly apprised of the constantly exacerbated restrictions and other oppressive measures.[18] There was nothing capricious and arbitrary here. Of course, about the final act they were kept officially in the dark.

The most striking difference between Stalinist rule and the Nazi regime probably lay in the circumstances surrounding the death of their victims. One key feature of this difference was the use of labor. Apart from the victims who died of starvation, Soviet Communism subjected millions to forced labor on a vast scale. This type of exploitation had developed out of the system of military forced labor introduced by Trotsky. It soon helped supply an array of sectors and enterprises with cheap labor.[19] The relevant office subordinate to the Commissariat for Internal Affairs was able to fall back on a virtually unlimited labor pool, replenished with a constant influx of new 'delinquents'.

Thus, political and legal despotism went hand in hand with the system of forced labor in the Stalinist Soviet Union. Control over such an inexhaustible arsenal of extremely cheap labor had terrible consequences. Owing to the unlimited, constantly replenished supply of slave labor, the system tended to neglect the minimal level of support for the physical survival of its slave laborers, overworking them to the point of exhaustion.[20] In extreme cases, they were forced to meet performance levels that exceeded the limits of their physical capacity for work and sheer survival.

Slave labor was certainly no stranger to the Nazi regime. But such Zwangsarbeit (forced labor) was carried out by others, not by ethnic Germans. The exploitation of forced slave labor under National Socialism was closely bound up with the regime's wars of expansion and conquest.[21] The types of enslavement implemented in the course of that expansion and subjugation can, in conjunction with the Nazi ideology of future utopia, afford some notion of the likely scenario, had Germany emerged victorious from that destructive struggle: a multi-tiered hierarchy of races and labor. In the east, entire peoples would have been reduced to virtual serfdom as slave laborers.[22] For the moment, the regime was satisfied to subjugate foreigners as forced and slave laborers to further the aims of its war economy. Other inmates, in any case doomed to death, were exploited to the absolute limit of their physical endurance, and thus quite literally worked to death. In the system of forced labor under Stalinism, the death of slave laborers was accepted in the dark bargain, but was not a specific ideological aim.[23]

Yet the fundamental difference between the two regimes becomes clear where the goal was to kill human beings, over and beyond the exigencies of a forced labor economy. The Nazis murdered for annihilation's sake. In the extreme case of the Holocaust, they made use of labor, if at all, to create the semblance of a sham objective, an ostensible utility factor. Certainly, the crimes of Stalinism are dwarfed by the death factories of the Nazis. These were production sites for dead bodies, beyond any dictates of exploitation and economic utility – a project that also annulled the universally valid standards for self-preservation. Stalinism had nothing to compare with that distinctive enormity.[24]

Though a comparison between National Socialism and Stalinism is instructive, it is questionable whether it serves to augment real knowledge. After all, these were systems that were basically different. They had arisen in different cultures under strikingly different conditions. The fact that they were locked in a global struggle, however real, partial or only ostensible, can challenge contemporaries and posterity to interrogate their nature. Yet more relevant than any such juxtaposing is an inquiry into their driving motives. The urge to compare is by no means self-evident. Rather, it would appear to spring from specific, culturally determined memories which feel constrained to counterpoise atrocities, to weigh them off scale against scale. To that extent, the modes of comparison are not universally valid: rather, they derive from particularistically motivated collective memories. These wish to convert events such as state crimes – crimes by a vicious regime – into the canon and narrative of a specific ethnos.

GERMAN MEMORIES

This process whereby crimes by a regime are converted into crimes against an ethnic collective becomes strikingly clear in the notorious case of Poland. On the basis of Poland's geopolitical location between Germany and Russia and its associated chronicle of tragic history, two types of suffering meld in Polish memory: suffering caused by regimes perceived as totalitarian, and affliction flowing from the oppression of the Poles as a nation.[25] Thus, the murder of thousands of Polish officers by the Soviet secret police in Katyn is one crime in a chain of sufferings perpetrated over the course of history by Russia against the Polish nation, a 'Christ' among the peoples of the world. The national interpretation of this deed against the backdrop and sounding board of the long Polish collective memory drowns out its significance as a state crime by the Stalinist regime. Its memory has festered down into the present, keeping alert Polish caution toward Russia. That caution does not spring from any fears of a possible resurgence of Communism in Russia, but rather from the depths of a long memory of Polish history, part of its saga of protracted tragic confrontation with the Russian empire.

Why is there in Germany a decided need to engage in a comparison of these two totalitarian systems? The question is complex, primarily because beyond its immediate borders, National Socialism acted as an excessive nationalism, not as a regime comparable with Stalin's rule.[26] The war launched in 1941 against the Soviet Union entered collective memory as the 'Russian campaign', especially since the vaunted anti-Bolshevism of the regime appeared in the guise of national rather than universal-political wrappings. The enmity toward the Soviet Union qua regime receded, and an excessive racist nationalism came to the fore.[27] In Soviet memory during the war as well, elements linked to the Communist self-identity of the regime were downplayed. Instead, emphasis was placed on the patriotic character of the war against the German invaders, coupled with a Russian-centered ethnicizing of Soviet memory. Concepts such as 'Hitlerism' and 'anti-Fascism' were still used, yet increasingly lost their former political meaning. The closer the Red Army came to German territory in its thrust westward in the war's final phase and the atrocities perpetrated by 'the Russians' spread fear and anxiety like wildfire among the population, the more ideological motives retreated into the background, and national and ethnic elements were stressed.[28]

In any case, the flight and expulsion of the German population were driven by ethnic not social reasons. That could not be compared with past crimes of the Communist regime, such as the 'social purges', common during the forced collectivization in the 1930s. Rather, these events in the former German east took on the character of 'ethnic cleansing'; and they were engraved in collective memory as such. This holds both for the expulsion of Germans from the areas incorporated by Poland and for the extradition of Germans from the Sudeten region, once again Czechoslovak. The ethnic homogenizations in central and east-central Europe in the war's direct aftermath were solidly in the tradition of the nationality conflicts during the interwar period, even if they were an immediate reaction to the National Socialist policies of oppression, resettlement and genocide. This was not first and foremost a struggle between two regimes in the sense of the epochal confrontation between Bolshevism and anti-Bolshevism, as some claim. Against the background of the experiences of the interwar period and the war instigated by Hitler, the Western Allies also gave their 'OK' to these population shifts as a justifiable solution to festering problems of nationalities and minorities.[29]

RELIGIOUS DISCOURSES

In postwar Germany, people did not wish to remember what the population had endured, at least not in public memory. There was virtually no talk about the victims of the deportations or the air war. Those lost in battle went largely unmourned, or became integrated as more general victims of the two world wars. There may have been various reasons for this silence. One is undoubtedly pivotal: the collective intuition that the crimes perpetrated by the Germans in the name of Germany were of such a crushing magnitude that they demanded silence – the expression of a sense of enormous injustice beyond any conceivable comparison.

Collective German memory sought to escape this paralyzing impasse.[30] Accusations hurled against the West were taboo. Because of the German question – closely bound up with the now deepening Cold War – the memory of the air war by the British and Americans against the German population and the massive expulsions from the German east were sealed in memory, even though recalled as a projection by a later generation in the face of burning issues in international politics.[31] Memory found a more legitimate terrain for comparison in the Soviet Union. This, as often

93

suggested, may well have been due to the constellations of the Cold War. Especially in a divided Germany, where the regime in the former Democratic Republic viewed its legitimization solely in terms of the element of class – and withdrew from German collective memory, styling itself as an anti-Fascist polity exculpated by dint of its socialist ideology – the comparison between the systems was made on the basis of a confrontation of values and worldviews. The political enmity between the two Germanies evoked images and concepts reminiscent and derivative of the clashes during the Weimar era. In particular, the Communists in the East, in keeping with their unshakable philosophy of history, equated their present adversaries with the bugbear of 'Fascism'.[32] In short, the German past was made serviceable to the ongoing scrimmage between the systems. Nonetheless, traces of collective memory surfaced, especially in the waves of ideological rhetoric that washed over the two states: as, for example, when representatives of the regime in East Berlin were stigmatized as traitors and labeled henchmen of the 'Russians'. Or when West German politicians were denigrated by their East German counterparts as lackeys of the 'Anglo-Americans', who were ultimately to blame for the massive bombing of German population centers during the war.[33]

In German collective memory, the comparison driven by later events is also projected on to the screen of the 'Russian campaign'. This national undertaking, waged as an intense and brutal ideological war, is revamped in memory into a campaign that was exclusively anti-Bolshevik. After all, other European nations had also taken part with their own military units sent east to 'defend the West'. Inscribed in this constellation, it was possible to reframe the German 'Russian campaign' as the decisive front in a global civil war, and employ it in collective memory to weigh the crimes perpetrated during 'Operation Barbarossa' against those of the Soviet regime. The symbolism of Stalingrad was transformed into the emblems of Stalinism. On the one hand, the Cold War seemed to support such an interpretation, of West versus East. On the other hand, this memory was stamped with a special mark: the crimes of Nazi Germany and its regime had been against others, the crimes of the Soviet regime were perpetrated internally, against their own population.

The attempt to convert the crimes committed by Nazi Germany into the crimes of a regime not a people clashes with the memory of the former Soviet population. They were doubly victimized at the hands of both extreme regimes of our century, ravaged by the violence of the Communist utopia and its mammoth experiment and by the violence of Nazi German warfare, with its biological-racist, anti-Bolshevik justification. Both outrages were perceived as directed against the Soviet people, though differing in manner and in keeping with collective memory: crimes based on class and crimes rooted in race.

This comparison corresponds, if at all, more to the modes of German memory in the former Democratic Republic. There, a link was forged between the impact of Nazi rule and the Communist regime that superseded it. In the eyes of ethnic Germans, both regimes certainly can be perceived as variants of totalitarian rule. Yet in the eyes of those excluded by dint of origin from the German Volk community, the Communist regime that supplanted it may have had despicable totalitarian features, but not anything resembling Nazi inhumanity: the destruction of human beings due solely to their ethnic or religious origin. In any case, the cheap conversion of collective crimes into those of a regime invites the denial of other collective memories. This may shed some light on why the crimes of the Stalinist regime are necessarily recalled in a different way in the former Soviet Union than the memory of Hitler's crimes in Germany.

European national cultures seem to be infused with an urge for comparison. In the interwar period in continental Europe, Fascism and Communism stood pitted against each other – the grand ideologies of the twentieth century locked in civil war.[34] Especially in the world of ideas, it was difficult to avoid the dominance of this confrontation, however clearly the history of conflict in this century was driven by other factors as well. Today, the modes of those discourses have lost their interpretive power. They nonetheless exert an impact on attempts to make the past a living present. This applies especially when it comes to interpreting the central events of the twentieth century, namely the huge crimes against humanity perpetrated by German National Socialism and Soviet Communism. To unravel their meaning seems tantamount to reaching a kind of final judgment on the century. Otherwise, it is difficult to comprehend the fervor that has accompanied debates on this question. That passion points to more profound motives that seem to spring from the memory store of religion; and it is so because much in this discourse of comparison corresponds to the modes of final, ultimate reason.[35] Unmistakably religious contours of a secular discourse surface as soon as debate ensues over the status and significance of crimes, especially the Jewish Holocaust. The question of the possible singularity of the Holocaust appears analogous to disputes about the topos of sacred chosenness redux. While the urge to compare and the associated anthropologizing of the crime would seem to follow the modus of the Christian account, insistence on singularity follows those of the Jewish narrative.[36]

The purportedly secular historical discourse is inscribed with diverse distinctive features of religious narrative. It is thus likely that any attempt to arrive at a narrative and an interpretation that does justice to the reality of the mass annihilation and genocide will hardly be able to avoid being pulled into the powerful vortex of precedent narratives – calibrated to the argumentation of final and ultimate reason. That holds both for controversies in historiography on the Nazi mass crimes and for the discourse of any comparison between National Socialism and Communism. To decipher the codes of the respective representations and narrative structures is a challenge for a historical anthropology that interrogates the political history of the past century – and for the humanitarian sciences more generally.

NOTES

This paper was originally published as 'Gedächtnis und Erkenntnis. Nationalismus und Stalinismus im Vergleichsdiskurs', Osteuropa, 6 (2000), pp. 698–708.

[1] D. Yaroshewski, 'Political Participation and Public Memory: The Memorial Movement in the USSR 1987–1989', History & Memory, 2 (1999), pp. 5–31.

[2] Dietrich Geyer, 'Klio in Moskau und die sowjetische Geschichte', Sitzungsberichte der Heidelberger Akademie der Wissenschaften, Philosophisch-historische Klasse, 2 (1985), pp. 36–8.

[3] Ekkehard Klug, 'Das "asiatische" Russland. Über die Entstehung eines europäischen Vorurteils', Historische Zeitschrift, 245 (1987), pp. 256–89.

[4] Karlheinz Mack, ed., Revolutionen in Ostmitteleuropa 1789–1989. Schwerpunkt Ungarn (Vienna and Munich, Oldenbourg, 1995).

[5] Aleksandr M. Nekrich, The Punished Peoples: The Deportations and Fate of Soviet Minorities at the End of the Second World War (New York, Norton, 1978).

[6] Nicolas Werth, 'Ein Staat gegen sein Volk. Gewalt, Unterdrückung und Terror in der Sowjetunion', in Stéphane Courtois et al., eds, Das Schwarzbuch des Kommunismus. Unterdrückung, Verbrechen und Terror (Munich and Zurich, Piper, 1998), pp. 51–298, here 188–9.

[7] Lynee Viola, 'The Second Coming. Class Enemies in the Soviet Countryside 1927–1935', in J. Arch Getty and Roberta T. Manning, eds, Stalinist Terror: New Perspectives (Cambridge, Cambridge University Press, 1993), pp. 65–98, here 75–6.

[8] Ibid., p. 77.

[9] Lynne Viola, 'The Campaign to Eliminate the Kulak as a Class, Winter 1929–1930: A Reevaluation of the Legislation', Slavic Review, 45 (1986), pp. 508–11.

[10] Igal Halfin, 'From Darkness to Light: Student Communist Autobiography during NEP', Jahrbücher für Geschichte Osteuropas, 45 (1997), pp. 210–36.

[11] Alec Nove, 'Victims of Stalinism: How Many', in Getty and Manning, eds, Stalinist Terror, pp. 260–74.

[12] J. Arch Getty, Origins of the Great Purges: The Soviet Communist Party Reconsidered 1918–1938 (Cambridge, Cambridge University Press, 1987).

[13] Werth, 'Ein Staat gegen sein Volk', pp. 257 ff.

[14] Anton Antonov-Ovseenko, The Time of Stalin: Portrait of a Tyranny (New York, Harper & Row, 1981), p. 216.

[15] Hannah Arendt, Elemente und Ursprünge totaler Herrschaft, Vol. III: Elemente totaler Herrschaft (Frankfurt am Main, Ullstein, 1975), p. 145.

[16] Boris Lewytzkyj, Die Rote Inquisition. Die Geschichte der sowjetischen Sicherheitsdienste (Frankfurt am Main, Societäts-Verlag, 1967).

[17] Ernst Nolte, 'A Past that Will Not Pass Away (A Speech It was Possible to Write, But Not to Present)', Yad Vashem Studies, 19 (1988), pp. 65–74.

[18] Uwe Dietrich Adam, Judenpolitik im Dritten Reich (Dusseldorf, Athenäum, 1979).

[19] Ralf Stettner, 'Archipel Gulag'. Stalins Zwangslager – Terrorinstrument und Wirtschaftsgigant. Entstehung, Organisation und Funktion des sowjetischen Lagersystems (Paderborn, Schönigh, 1996), 118

[20] Ibid., pp. 337–8.

[21] Ulrich Herbert, Hitler's Foreign Workers: Enforced Foreign Labor in Germany Under the Third Reich (Cambridge, Cambridge University Press, 1997).

[22] Mechthild Rössler and Sabine Schleiermacher, eds, Der 'Generalplan Ost'. Hauptlinien der nationalsozialistischen Planungs- und Vernichtungspolitik (Berlin, Akademie Verlag, 1993).

[23] David J. Dallin and Boris I. Nicolaevski, Forced Labor in Russia (New Haven, CT, Yale University Press, 1947).

[24] Dan Diner, 'Nationalsozialismus und Stalinismus. Über Gedächtnis, Willkür, Arbeit und Tod', in idem, Kreisläufe. Nationalsozialismus und Gedächtnis (Berlin, Berlin-Verlag, 1995), pp. 47–76.

[25] Andrzej Paczkowski, 'Polen, der "Erbfeind"', in Courtois et al., eds, Das Schwarzbuch, pp. 397–429.

[26] Peter P. Knoch, 'Das Bild des russischen Feindes', in Wolfram Wette and Gerd R. Ueberschär, eds, Stalingrad. Mythos und Wirklichkeit einer Schlacht (Frankfurt am Main, Fischer, 1992), pp. 160–7.

[27] Lutz Niethammer, 'Juden und Russen im Gedächtnis der Deutschen', in Walter H. Pehle, ed., Der historische Ort des Nationalsozialismus (Frankfurt am Main, Fisscher, 1990), pp. 114–34.

[28] Norman M. Naimark, The Russians in Germany: A History of the Zone of Occupation 1945–1949 (Cambridge, MA, Harvard University Press, 1995); Atina Grossmann, 'A Question of Silence: The Rape of German Women by Occupation Soldiers', October, 72 (1995), pp. 43–63.

[29] Alfred Maurice de Zayas, Die Anglo-Amerikaner und die Vertreibung der Deutschen (Frankfurt am Main, Ullstein, 1996), pp. 117ff.; Klaus-Dietmar Henke, 'Der Weg nach Potsdam. Die Alliierten und die Vertreibung', in Wolfgang Benz, ed., Die Vertreibung der Deutschen aus dem Osten. Ursachen, Ereignisse, Folgen (Frankfurt am Main, Fischer, 1985), pp. 49–69.

[30] Richard Matthias Müller, Normal-Null und die Zukunft der deutschen Vergangenheitsbewältigung (Schernfeld, SH-Verlag, 1994).

[31] Dan Diner, Der Krieg der Erinnerungen und die Ordnung der Welt (Berlin, Rotbuch, 1991).

[32] Antonia Grunenberg, Antifaschismus: Ein deutscher Mythos (Reinbek, Rowohlt, 1993).

[33] Sigrid Meuschel, Legitimation und Parteiherrschaft in der DDR (Frankfurt am Main, Suhrkamp, 1992), pp. 101–2.

[34] Ernst Nolte, Lehrstücke oder Tragödie? Beiträge zur Interpretation der Geschichte des 20. Jahrhunderts (Cologne, Böhlau, 1991).

[35] See arguments in Courtois et al., Das Schwarzbuch, pp. 11–50, here 29–30.

[36] Dan Diner, 'On Guilt and Other Narratives: Epistemological Observations Regarding the Holocaust', History & Memory, 9 (1997), pp. 301–20, reprinted in Dan Diner, Beyond the Conceivable: Studies on Germany, Nazism and the Holocaust (Berkeley, CA, University of California Press, 2000).

6

Comparative Evil: Degrees, Numbers and the Problem of Measure

Berel Lang

It is a universally acknowledged truth that some wrongful acts are more wrongful than others. Why is this? That is, why the universal acknowledgment, and (before that) why the 'truth' itself? These are the first questions I address, since comparisons among specific instances of wrongdoing presuppose responses to these more general issues. How, after all, could we distinguish even wrongful from rightful acts without assurance from moral history (not the history of ethical theory, but the history of ethical practice) of a means and not only the fact of moral discrimination? Ideally, such assurance would establish not only the possibility but the necessity of moral judgment through gradations of value (or, inverting the order, gradations of disvalue) – and we do indeed find this in that history. What are the specific steps in the gradation of wrongful acts, and how are the distinctions among them made? This second, in many ways more dramatic, set of issues bears on specific comparisons through the measurement of 'evil' – for example, by counting the numbers of victims or by distinguishing degrees of particular intentions. The difficulties of managing such specific comparisons are greater than those raised by the prior question of the status of those comparisons in principle – but this is due, I would argue, more to our excessive demands on the process of measurement than to the process itself. Aristotle's stipulation that we may require of a subject or a science only the degree of precision of which it is capable can, of course, be used in a self-serving way – but in this instance, that view seems a cogent response to the common objection that because moral comparisons may in the end be inconclusive or at least imprecise, the very attempt to make such comparisons is valueless if not altogether impossible. Quite the contrary, in fact: because comparison is at the very heart of moral judgment and assessment – no right without a wrong, no justice without injustice – the intrinsic vagueness of specific comparisons pales beside the case for the necessity of such comparison. (To be sure, such comparisons may always seem, and be, invidious – even when they conclude – without finding for one side over (or below) another.)

Thus, to begin: some words about my claim for the universal acknowledgment of the principle of discrimination among degrees or kinds of wrongdoing. This principle, put more concretely, holds that wrongs come in – certainly are known by – degrees of 'wrong-ness' (that is, of what makes them wrong); and that the moral differences thus found are at least in principle so clear and so significant that the principle is generally (even, I suggest, universally) recognized.

This claim of universal acknowledgment may seem exaggerated, but if it is overstated, it is not by much. The one historical counter-example of which I am aware is quasi-mythological and remains at best a solitary exception. That deviant case is the Code of Dracon, dated to 621 BC, of which few details survive but which has nonetheless become emblematic of a rare (and rarified) ideal of justice. 'Draconian' laws are now usually cited for their harshness, but a more notable feature structurally is their denial of any significant difference between lesser and greater transgressions. One punishment for all crimes was Dracon's rule – with the implication that wrongful acts provide no grounds, in themselves or their consequences, for distinguishing gradations or degrees of 'criminality'. The uniform punishment imposed, moreover, was harsh; namely, death. Hence, the association of 'draconian' laws with severity – although, strictly speaking, this reference is less tied to the punishment imposed than to its extended range. By contrast, legal systems which sanction capital punishment more typically reserve it for only certain (that is, 'capital') crimes, thus distinguishing such major offenses from lesser ones – itself a 'fine' distinction rejected on the Draconian view. 'Small offenses', Dracon is said to have observed, 'deserve death, and I can think of no more severe penalty for larger ones.'

The theoretical grounds on which Dracon drew are unknown, but there might well have been a principle – a theory of justice – underlying his harsh table of laws. For if we think of justice (at the level of laws) or the good (in terms of moral obligations) as circumscribed domains then any violation of them might be viewed as equivalent to every other one just insofar as it is a breach. To be sure, the grounds that determine prohibitions or norms are variously construed – as expressions of natural law, or dictates of the rule of state or conscience, the word of God or social convention. But so long only as the norm invoked has some such authority, all violations of it would have the common character of transgressing whatever it is that within the given community of discourse commands obedience. Since all violations are then at one as violations, it could also be argued that there is no basis – certainly no overriding basis – for introducing variations in punishment. (Determination of the specific uniform punishment is obviously a separate issue from the question of whether the punishment should be uniform.)

But, there have been few, if any subsequent advocates of this view, whether among political theorists or rulers and legislators. It might be argued that, for the sake of consistency, Kant should have been a Draconian, and certainly there is something of a kindred echo in Kant of Dracon's unflinching view of the status of the law. But Kant did not in the end take that position, arguing instead for a proportionality, or 'fit', between crime and punishment in contrast to the one-size-fits-all model – and there are, it seems, no likelier Draconian successors.[1] The distinctiveness of the Draconian Code, furthermore, pertains not only to individual rulers or thinkers: there appear to be and have been no states or societies which have not identified certain transgressions as more wrongful than others. The hierarchical ordering of moral and/or legal violations thus persists as a genuine, if rarely noted instance of a 'cultural universal', accepted and practiced without exception among otherwise very different cultures and traditions. This universal acceptance of the principle does not mean, of course, that the specific hierarchy of values or prohibitions asserted in any one society will apply generally. So, for example, the death penalty is mandated in the Hebrew Bible for violations of the Sabbath but not for serious bodily harm that stops short of murder – an order of judgment which would obviously differ elsewhere (together with the more general definition of what even counts as a 'crime'). Such inter-cultural differences, however, do not affect the claim of universality for the intra-cultural gradation of moral offenses.

The explanation of why this differential pattern holds so widely may seem self-evident. Of course, there is a difference between murder and wounding, between telling a lie and ordering a massacre – moral differences which quickly translate into legal distinctions and then into gradations of punishment. But for the most basic ethical issues there is (of course) no 'of course' – and some explanation is thus required, with the most obvious place to look for an answer being in the consequences of actions. Thus, where human life is a primary good, murder would be a more serious offense than an assault which left the victim alive (even if the assault was an unsuccessful attempt at murder). Even punishment that involves the taking of life is held – however ironically – to reflect the high value attached to life. The 38 states of the United States which have capital punishment on their books typically restrict that punishment to murder (and not even for all of its several versions or degrees). Nowhere, to the best of my knowledge, is execution indicated as a punishment for speeding or illegal parking, although it seems certain that in contrast to the non-deterrent effect of capital punishment for murder, if it were mandated for speeding or illegal parking, it would indeed be likely to reduce their incidence.

100

The underlying principle here – indeed, the basis for any system of differential punishment – is some version or other of the maxim that 'the punishment should fit the crime': a principle, in effect, of proportionality between the two (separate) acts of crime and punishment. The latter principle itself depends on two assumptions. First, that punishments differ in severity (that is, in the degree to which they indeed do punish). Second, that crimes differ in their severity (that is, in respect to whatever makes the crime a crime, in moral and/or in legal terms). Fitting the punishment to the crime thus argues for proportionality between the two, independently hierarchical sides of that relation. It asserts such proportionality, moreover, not only as warranted but as required; that is, as itself a moral condition to be met.

To be sure, the consequences of an act are not the only considerations affecting judgments of crime or punishment; intentions are also commonly recognized as a factor, at times a decisive one. In the distinction between murder and manslaughter, for instance, the consequences are identical: a death has been caused. It is the intentions (or their absence) underlying the acts that lead to differences in judgments of the various agents and punishments imposed. Philosophical views of the elements of moral judgment have been more 'purist' than legal systems in defining those elements: thus the Kantians' total exclusion of consequences as relevant to moral assessment and the consequentialists' counter-claim of the irrelevance of intentions. But beyond their other differences, all these systems distinguish between more and less serious transgressions. On that point, the most extreme intentionalists and consequentialists are at one, and hence the claim I have made for the universality of this principle.

It is in this sense, too, that I should argue that comparative assessments are intrinsic to moral judgment, certainly its constant companion. Only consider a possible moral world without gradations, or even such a world with only the Manichaean dualism of good and evil – and we find what in practice becomes an unrecognizable, and still more certainly an uninhabitable, world. However compelling dramatically or heuristically, that dualism is quite underdetermined in practice; that is, in the only too familiar moral world, where gray is much the more common color than black or white. In other words, the sub-branches of the tree of the knowledge of good and evil – the distinctions within those concepts – turn out to be as significant as the distinction itself; indeed, they arguably comprise the distinction. This holds, I should claim, not only for establishing a basis for degrees of wrongdoing but also (through the same process) for gradations of the good, although the focus of moral and certainly legal analyses has been on the former. The category of 'supererogatory' acts – heroic deeds, for example – marks a stage or degree in 'right-doing' that goes beyond any obligatory requirement but is nonetheless highly esteemed.

It seems clear, however, that these same graded distinctions, however necessary in establishing and sustaining moral judgment, pose difficulties for moral comparisons in practice – especially (although not only) where the wrongdoing at issue involves irreparable harm to human life (and that, on a scale where more than one life is involved). The very formulation of a 'mass comparison' of human lives presupposes the possibility of ascribing responsibility for large-scale acts involving the murder, intentional or adventitious, of large numbers of people, and the twentieth century offers two remarkable examples of this in the policies and acts of Nazi Germany and the Soviet Union, respectively, over the periods during which they were in power. The structural – and moral – questions begin as soon as this juxtaposition is made: Can we distinguish or compare those acts and agents in moral terms? Is numerical computation the key to such comparison – a double murder counting as twice the wrong of a single one, two million twice that of one, and so on? And would the agent's guilt – or wrongdoing – be similarly tabulated? For the utilitarian or consequentialist, such a 'felicific' calculus (in such reckoning, not at all a 'happy' choice of terms, although that itself says something about consequentialism) is not only all that a moral judge requires in order to answer such questions, but all that anyone can ever have. On the face of it, however, any such computational view of ethical judgment is too gross a standard to serve. If this is not evident from comparative examples of murder, it becomes clearer where human lives are pitted against other social goods – as the consequentialist may require that some lives ought to be sacrificed in order to increase the 'well-being' or perhaps even pleasure of a larger number of others.

Is there an alternative to this that does not take numbers alone or decisively into account? I should argue that we do not here have to concede an either/or – but that the two extreme alternatives (ethics by the numbers or ethics by pure form) themselves impel a third way. For there is here the option also of a distinction in moral degrees, in contrast to measurement by numbers – a distinction already alluded to in my reference to the contrast between manslaughter and murder and which seems to find a clear analogy in the difference, even on a much larger scale, between mass murder and genocide. If we recognize Cain (whether symbolically or literally) as responsible for the first murder on record (and so also as the inventor of the very idea), we find that even in the brief course of Biblical time an extension was made to murder in larger numbers, although still, it seems, as groups of individuals. Like individual murder, mass murder, too, might be either premeditated or ensue as a consequence of what has been called double causality: the unintended, even unforeseen consequence of another act.

Since the events of World War II, however, there has also been a second direction that might be followed – in effect, a quantum leap – in the phenomenology of murder; this, in the conceptualization of the crime of genocide as that which involves what is in effect single causality but a double murder. Central to the issue here is not whether the formulation of the concept of genocide in 1944 attested to its first occurrence at that time (by the Nazis) or whether it designated a practice that had occurred earlier but gone unnamed. But the concept does point to a distinction in kind or degree from other acts (or crimes) that fall under the heading of culpable killing – since here it is not only individuals who are murdered but the group of which they are members, with the killing of those individuals due to their membership in the group, membership which, in the clearest instances of genocide, was and would be involuntary.

The break and extension that genocide marks in the hierarchy of culpable killing requires more detailed analysis than I can provide here. But that it represents such a development (in a perverse sense, progress) seems evident. My conclusions here are thus more formal than substantive. At certain junctures of moral and/or legal judgment, the quantification of wrongdoing by numbers and not only by degrees is unavoidable – but, where that is necessary, there seems no possible formula that can serve satisfactorily as a basis for comparative judgments. On the face of it, someone responsible for a million deaths has done something larger in moral enormity than the murderer of a single person – although, also on the face of it, the claim is compelling that nothing could be more wrongful than the murder of a single person. Sentencing a serial killer to four or five 'life terms' may serve some symbolic purpose, but it hardly answers to the moral issue at stake here – and the latter difficulty is of course compounded where mass murder or genocide is at issue. The conventional formulas by which damages for 'wrongful death' are assessed in terms of economic loss do not pretend to (and do not) provide a moral estimate of the criminality or evil attached to the act or the agent – and it seems even clearer that, within the kinds of crimes committed, numbers are an inadequate basis for further moral distinctions. The difference between the deaths of a million people and of ten people is surely significant in its consequences – but there seems to me no way of defining that difference in respect to the act of murder or the agent responsible by a contrast which is at once based on those numbers and establishes a moral distinction. In this sense, it seems to me that within the kinds of crimes committed, numbers do not resolve moral comparisons or, for that matter, moral dilemmas. Even the repetition of the same crime at different times – with the implication this might carry of a failed or rejected opportunity of change or repentance – does not provide a sufficient basis for additive computation.

On the other hand, and by contrast, moral differences in terms of degrees of wrongdoing are both measurable and relevant to the judgment of morally significant acts. Here, too, the distinction between 'degrees' and 'numbers' becomes crucial. The number of victims of an act of mass murder may be larger than the number of victims of an act of genocide – as there may be more victims of an accident caused by a driver under the influence of alcohol (and so guilty of manslaughter) than of a premeditated murder which claims a single victim. But in neither case does (or, in my view, should) the difference in numbers override the differences in the moral quality of the two acts. That qualitative difference is crucial, I suggest, for the larger-scale distinction between mass murder and genocide – not because of the absence of premeditation from the former (since intention may be present there as well), but because of one aspect of intention which is necessary for the latter – directed at the group – but is by definition absent in the former. Even within genocide, moreover, gradations are indicated which override the issue of numbers or of percentages. The forcible dispersion and assimilation of members of a group is no doubt a version of genocide (sometimes called 'ethnocide') – but it, too, is distinguishable from the act of genocide involving the physical murder of the members of a group because of that membership. Thus, within genocide itself, as well as between genocide and other forms of culpable killing, distinctions by degree emerge as markers, analogous to familiar distinctions of degree within the category of individual murder.

Where does this leave – or take – us on the question of the comparability of the acts of Soviet Russia and Nazi Germany? The comparative numbers of victims, I have suggested, can never be morally irrelevant – but neither, on the account here, are they in themselves decisive unless everything else is equal, which it is almost invariably not, certainly not for measurements involving degrees and kinds. The number of Soviet victims (even apart from the years of World War II) is generally recognized as larger than the number of victims for which Nazi policies and acts were responsible – and the number of Mao's victims in his rise to and exercise of power were arguably larger than either of the others. On the other hand, if one raises the difficult question of how to characterize the acts responsible for those two sets of consequences, there seems nonetheless to be a difference, conceptually and, as that leads further, morally. Insofar as genocide represents a distinctive act (and crime), it is indisputable that Nazi Germany was responsible for genocide against the Jews and the Gypsies – with Heinrich Himmler's words at Poznan about the former still ringing in our ears: 'This people should be made to disappear from the earth.' That the Nazis failed in this attempt was due neither to their lack of will nor to deficiencies in their conceptualization of their goal. The argument has been made that the planned famine in the Ukraine initiated by the Soviets, and which then claimed between one and five million lives, was genocide, and that the dispersion of the Chechens to Khazakhstan and the oppression of the Tatars is at the very least a version of ethnocide. In both those cases, there are counter-claims, and I hesitate here to judge the substantive issue, whatever its outcome. In any event, insofar as the charge of genocide admits of degrees, there still would remain a difference in terms of such degrees between Nazi Germany and Soviet Russia as reflected in those acts. Such distinctions (and comparisons) are bound to seem invidious – indeed, offensive – as comparisons also appear invidious and offensive in the judging of differences of degree for occurrences of individual murder. Yet for the latter, too, such differences turn out indeed to be significant, and this seems to me no less cogently the case where the distinction between genocide and mass murder, with particular reference to distinctions within types or degrees of genocide, are concerned. What bearing this, or any moral assessment, has in analyzing the comparative structures of the two systems that have been mentioned, or in articulating the concept of totalitarianism more generally, is an important but separate question.

I hope it will be evident that nothing said here has been meant to provide a cover for or to excuse the effects of barbarism and brutality intrinsic to totalitarianism, part of its very definition: force mobilized and exerted in the interest of mobilizing and exerting force. Nor do I mean to rule out the possibility that at some point in moral history – perhaps even now – an entirely new system of measurement may be required. It may be, as Lyotard proposed (see Note 4), that the instruments of measurement have themselves been 'broken' by the enormity of recent events – or if not now, by some other event. But the graded distinctions of kind or degree seem the one means available – and, I suggest, also necessary – for assessing comparative moral significance on the scale of the regimes of Soviet Russia and Nazi Germany. If that basis for judgment applies anywhere, surely it applies to the two regimes in common; they are, in fact, a principal – and lasting – reason for its existence, a quite sufficient basis even if there were no other.

NOTES

1. Cited in Plutarch, 'Solon', in The Lives of the Noble Grecians and Romans, trans. John Dryden (Chicago, IL: Brittanica, 1952), p. 70.
2. Kant himself uses the expression, advocating the 'fitting of punishment to the crime'. '... [W]hatever undeserved evil you inflict upon another within the people, that you inflict upon yourself'. The Metaphysics of Morals, trans. Mary Gregor (Cambrige: Cambridge University Press, 1996), pp. 105–6.
3. For Himmler's speech at Poznan, see Peter Padfield, Himmler: Reichsfuhrer SS (New York: Henry Holt, 1990), p. 469.
4. Jean François Lyotard, The Differend: Phrases in Dispute, trans. G. Van den Abbeele (Minneapolis, MN: University of Minnesota Press, 1983), p. 56.

Part II

Frames of Comparison

7

The Institutional Frame: Totalitarianism, Extermination and the State

Sigrid Meuschel

Theories of totalitarianism have sprung from the emergence of a historical phenomenon experienced as radically new and unique. This perception was first displayed in reference to the 'total state' in Fascist Italy during the 1920s and 1930s. Later, the horrors of the Holocaust and the Gulag made the focus of analyses shift towards extreme violence and the dynamic of extermination; Hannah Arendt's work is still the outstanding example. Yet the longer the Soviet system survived Stalinism and its Nazi antipode, the less theory concentrated on mass murder. Instead, the totality of political power and social control became central. Here, Carl Friedrich's ideal-typical model exercised considerable influence. It too, however, was soon confronted with a twofold critique. On the one hand, it was charged with being static and therefore unable to explain the changes taking place in the Soviet hemisphere since the 1950s. On the other hand, as a general model primarily focusing on totalitarian institutions, it could not grasp crucial differences between Fascism, Nazism, Stalinism and post-Stalinism.

In what follows, I divide approaches to totalitarianism into two types, which I call 'totalitarianism as extermination' and 'totalitarianism as total control'.[1] Both categories come up short conceptually and historiographically when it comes to explaining the emergence of state-induced mass murder. To make up for this, I will focus on the degree to which state institutions withstand the undermining force of charismatic claims to authority.

TOTALITARIANISM AS EXTERMINATION

In general, the horror produced by the historically unprecedented violence of the Holocaust and the Gulag brought exterminism to the center of attention. This applies both to terror and to its ideological justification.

The ideological project of a 'radiant future' aimed at the total reshaping of man and society and legitimated terror. Classics of totalitarian theory, such as by Hannah Arendt[2] or Sigmund Neumann,[3] saw the violent dynamic of 'permanent revolution' as a novelty for its time. This position is still maintained today by those who regard the 'mass grave' as 'an appropriate metonymy for totalitarianism' and thereby emphasize racial-ideological or historical-philosophical legitimations of 'purposes identified as purposes of mankind', which make 'politics in the specifically modern sense liable to terror'. Not instrumental reason but, on the contrary, the 'absolute dominance of ideologically interpreted value rationality ... in short, political faith in salvation' is thus regarded as a necessary but not sufficient condition of totalitarian annihilatory politics.[4] As I argue in this chapter, the disintegration of formal-rational state institutions is another crucial precondition. Moreover, most authors see the violent excesses of Nazism and Stalinism in relation not only to a new and modern type of ideology, but also to World War I. For Neumann, François Furet[5] and many others, World War I was the watershed that marked the beginning of the age of European catastrophes. In the face of the general devaluation of life, politics could appear to be a continuity of war, including violence as a source of unbound revolutionary dynamic.

In her analyses of imperialism, pan-movements and anti-Semitism, Arendt underlines the importance of the decay of the nation-state, i.e., the decay of the institutional guarantees of the rule of law and of politics oriented toward achievable aims. Her phenomenology of the totalitarian exterminist dynamic perceives ideology and terror as the 'essence' of a 'novel form of government'. All this is well known; I will only point out the way she depicts the general context in which the totalitarian temptations arose. The starting point is what she calls 'classlessness' or loss of 'consciousness of common interest'. She refers to an anomic social constellation: intermediate institutions ('stable social bodies') are shattered. Such destruction of the social fabric induces a peculiar distance to reality and stresses a 'passionate inclination toward most abstract notions as guides for life'.[6] In situations of social anomie and alienation, totalitarian ideology offers a new meaning of life and certainty of purpose; it answers to the longing for 'consistency' and alleviates the escape from reality into fiction. With the masses subject to 'infallible leaders', the ideological horizon becomes dominated by logical deduction and the execution of 'immutable laws'. The terror makes those laws come true, excluding and snuffing out the lives of those who are 'superfluous' anyway, be it for reasons of historical or biological necessity.[7] The conjuring up of 'a "truer" reality concealed behind all perceptible things' makes totalitarian terror, for Arendt, different from any other.[8] It singles out 'objective enemies', and starts only when the regime is consolidated. 'Only after the extermination of real enemies has been completed and the hunt for "objective enemies" has begun does terror become the actual content of totalitarian regimes.' Ideology and terror set into motion a process of permanent revolution, which prevents totalitarianism from ossification and transition into an 'absolute' regime.[9]

New, for Arendt, is not the content of totalitarian ideologies – laws of history and nature. Rather, what makes ideologies totalitarian are their modes of thinking and organizational forms. In order to gain a new, exterminist quality, the ideological code has to be transferred from the written word into propaganda and mobilization for action.[10] Arendt's analysis of totalitarian organization appears up-to-date. She emphasizes characteristics, such as 'fluctuating hierarchy', 'constant addition of new layers and shifts in authority', or 'techniques of duplication', which undermine existing institutions.[11] In pointing out both the overall 'shapelessness' or 'structurelessness' of the regime and the 'intentionally vague' character of law, orders and commands, she refers to Ernst Fraenkel's Dual State, Franz Neumann's Behemoth, and to Nazi jurists such as Werner Best. Best – as Ulrich Herbert has shown in his fascinating study – made it perfectly clear that only those who were acting within the law executed 'the will of the leadership'.[12] Arendt had thus a clear understanding of the totalitarian dynamic; in her analysis the notion of 'working toward the leader' already resonates.[13]

However, there is a caveat in the concept of exterminist totalitarianism. Although there is no doubt that Stalinism, like Nazism, regarded the law as a fluid and flexible instrument at the service of revolutionary will power, and that it claimed to obey higher laws instead of petty legality, there is still some doubt about whether institutional 'structurelessness' characterized Soviet totalitarianism as it did Nazism. Also, the partial dissolution of the social fabric, which induced the fascination with Nazism, in the Soviet Union only followed from revolutionary, especially Stalinist, politics. The concept therefore still has to prove itself in historical research. It must be able to integrate the differences National Socialism and Stalinism display in regard to their ideology and dynamic and to the genesis of the Holocaust and Gulag. While there seems to be agreement that violence was immanent to Nazism from the beginning, the path to Stalinism is historiographically highly disputed. If genesis is not clarified then the concept's central criterion – extermination – is only named without being sufficiently analyzed. There is a further problem inherent in this approach: it ignores Fascism as potentially totalitarian. Therefore, I will now discuss whether total control – the fusion of subsystems for the sake of power concentration – can function as a substitute for terror.

THE LESSER EVIL

TOTALITARIANISM AS TOTAL CONTROL

This concept was meant to encompass Fascist Italy, to which the critique of totalitarianism addressed itself in the 1920s, as well as Nazism and Stalinism. Moreover, the notion of total control usually also includes – not to say that it primarily puts under scrutiny – post-Stalinist dictatorships. It identifies 'core' structures common to all forms of total domination, and by necessity relativizes physical terror. Terror now figures either as a phenomenon of 'early' totalitarianism or is not regarded as a specific characteristic at all.

In terms of sociology, Johann Arnason defines totalitarianism as the reaction to a central conflict in modernity, that which derives from the tension between the rationality of self-determination and the rationality of world domination. This 'polarized basic structure', expressed in the conflict between capitalism and democracy in Western societies, he sees as 'partially mediated and partially overlaid by a dynamic of fragmentation'.[14] In the face of fragmentation and differentiation of autonomous spheres of action, integration is also required. Totalitarianism, then, is to be understood as an answer to these modern structural problems insofar as it abolishes the institutional forms of capitalism and democracy, integrated in Western development through the nation-state, and eliminates their dynamic in order to outdo them. It aims at an order open for change but free of antagonisms, an order capable of increasing capitalism's economic and technological dynamic by means of rational planning, on the one hand, and of overcoming democracy's precarious relation between people's sovereignty and the rule of law by reconciling the will of the people with absolute state power, on the other.

Such systemic characterization of total power structures stresses, first of all, the fusion of otherwise distinct sources of power, especially concerning the economic, political and cultural spheres. An institution sui generis, the apparatus coordinates and leads the absolute power within these three spheres. The differentiation of relatively autonomous subsystems is either severely cut back on, or blocked outright. Legitimization both rejects the legal-rational mode of domination and claims cultural sovereignty over all tradition. The totalitarian core structures avoid the contradictions of capitalism and democracy, but produce 'specific dissonances and dysfunctionalities' of their own. The outcome is a 'simultaneously over-integrated and a new kind of fragmented society'. As already mentioned, this conception of totalitarianism understands terror and extreme ideology as 'special cases or peaks within the frame of a more comprehensive historical configuration'.[15]

Although this concept is theoretically attractive, it also faces historical and conceptual problems. If we leave aside for a moment that it fits

Soviet-type dictatorships better than Nazism or Fascism, there is the question of how the general theory comes to grips with the problem of system integration, which in the exterminist model is a function of terror and ideology. How to explain what Arnason calls terrorist and ideological 'peaks'? Is terror a 'rather extreme aberration' from a 'typical model of a totalitarian dictatorship',[16] so that its 'mature' and 'modern' form appears above all in the advanced technology of secret-police surveillance and the sophisticated methods of psychic manipulation?[17] Does the concept boil down to what Havel and others have called 'soft' totalitarianism, i.e. a regime which no longer conjures up the future but forces upon its subjects a 'life in inauthenticity', owing to forced accommodation to a dictatorial present? This clearly is not Arnason's argument. But, since ideological orientation toward a new civilization, whether or not it legitimizes terror against objective enemies, is part and parcel of totalitarianism and therefore is hardly to be regarded a special case or peak within an overall totalitarian setting, what else, then, can be considered as extreme ideologization? If we assume that ideological extremism relates to terror, and terror is excluded by definition from the basic constellation of the total-control type, does it then regard the fusion of subsystems as its substitute, as generating the dynamic of which any regime of a radiant future is in need of so as to prove itself? What, then, does it mean in terms of the concept if there is a totalitarian fusion of subsystems without ideology and void of dynamic? Does not such a constellation rather fit into Juan Linz's concept of post-totalitarianism?[18]

There is a similar problem with the phases of totalitarian development. In his seminal study from 1975, Juan Linz proposes a periodization which begins with the seizure of power as an intensive ideological phase, followed by a consolidation characterized by a far more instrumental relation to ideology, since institutionalization and rationalization establish greater calculability and continuity. The 'final phase of administering society' opens up 'a moderate degree of pluralism among decision makers', and eventually the possibility of a transition to non-totalitarian rule.[19] He grounds his decision not to treat terror as a central characteristic by pointing out that there is terror without totalitarianism and totalitarianism without terror. On the other hand, he identifies specific aspects of totalitarian terror that are unique in comparison with the terror of authoritarian dictatorships.[20] Totalitarian terror is distinguished by its unprecedented scope, its systemic policies, its ideological ('objective') definition of enemies, and the absence not only of an emergency situation but also of any formal-legal basis. Like Arendt, Linz assumes that totalitarian terror is not confined to the takeover but increases when power is consolidated aiming for unity, atomization and mobilization of society. There seems to be a dissonance in these two models, since in one terror plays no role at all, whereas in the other the specifics of totalitarian terror are minutely identified. This dissonance is dissolved, however, as soon as we find a substitute for terror equally capable of mobilizing society and achieving its unity. Here, Linz suggests to look at concentration of power and the fusion of subsystems.

Yet there appear to be conceptual problems with this model, too. One version of the notion of 'extreme concentration of social functions in the political system at the expense of other social systems' characterizes totalitarianism as the monopolization of the power of decision, the principly unlimited scope of decisions, and the similarly unlimited intensity of sanctions.[21] Accordingly, determinate forms of sanctions are less important than the indeterminacy of political sanctions, which includes in principle the possibility of terror but not its necessity. Thus, the emphasis lies on the total power of control over all social domains of action, not simply on the form and intensity of sanctions. But, on the other hand, the system's claim to monopolistic planning and steering cannot succeed, for the regime attempts too much. Its performance never matches its goals, and conflicts are inevitable. The focus, therefore, shifts from fusion to ideology. Ideology has the specific function of enabling the leadership both 'to decide authoritatively the socially relevant values and norms' and 'to impose on society binding schemata for interpreting reality'.[22] The leadership's steering capacity depends decisively on both; it presupposes monopolistic control of social communication, thus the political monopoly entails the economic and especially the cultural one. Briefly put, the ideological dimension is so important because totalitarian dictatorships are in fact not capable of 'surpassing' capitalism. Because there is a systematic contradiction between aims and performance, ideology has to provide interpretative schemes that integrate rulers and ruled alike, if each in their own way. What, though, will become of cultural hegemony if ideological manipulation becomes obvious and thus incapable of concealing reality? Then the interpretative monopoly threatens to fall into jeopardy – through pressure from above or from below – and the erosion of one monopoly of power threatens its other forms.

This, again, raises the question as to when the system stops being totalitarian. For Arendt the answer was comparatively easy. The dictatorship will either end in an exterminist paradox – it will be complete only when all are dead – or, it will transform itself into an 'absolutist', that is, a, at least minimally, stable and calculable regime. This happens when ideological beliefs get lost and reality returns as a substitute for fiction.[23] For Claude Lefort, the destruction of ideological certainty breaks up the totalitarian universe. As far as Stalinism is concerned, this was the unintended outcome of the XX Party Congress of 1956.[24] Stalinist terror had one function to fulfill: to force the heterogeneous classes and strata into the 'unity' of a new formation, to produce a single world in which the political no longer existed as a distinct societal sphere but rather gained a 'monstrous autonomy', produced by the 'complete penetration' of society.[25] In 1956, even the restricted criticism of Stalin's 'errors' destroyed the myth of unity and opened up the possibility of discussion and political action. From this point on, it was in principle possible to ask 'where error begins and ends', 'where politics begins and ends'; 'if Stalin's personality is no longer sacred, then the entire leadership past and future, the regime as a whole, lose their divine right to historical truth. The system becomes, like any other, an object of analysis and critique.'[26] Indeed, in the post-Stalinist Soviet system ideological certainty eroded slowly but surely, and politics adapted, somewhat at least, to the norms and demands of contemporary, real-existing society.

The most comprehensive answer to the question of the end of totalitarianism and its transition is given by Linz.[27] In his version, post-totalitarianism arises under the condition of weakened ideological and power monopoly, lost interest in mobilization, and reappeared pluralism. The 'mature' or 'frozen' state of post-totalitarianism depends on further moves from above or from below, to extend the room for a parallel society and second economy. But, if we correctly assume that the notion of transition does not apply to Fascism or National Socialism, does it not follow that Stalinism/totalitarianism and post-Stalinism/post-totalitarianism are synonymous? Why, then, not place terror and extreme ideology at the center of totalitarianism, whereas the model of total control fits the frozen state of post-totalitarianism much better?

As already mentioned, the total-control type does not refer to Nazism or Fascism. They professed to a much lesser extent the aim to rationally planned economy, society and culture. Accordingly, the de-differentiation of subsystems, which went a long way in Soviet-type societies, took the comparatively mild form of Gleichschaltung in Germany and Italy, while capitalism remained basically untouched. Perhaps we should look for another substitute for terror than the concentration of power and institutional fusion. I suggest a third approach, which focuses on the various degrees to which different types of charismatic domination destroy the formal-legal state.

TOTALITARIANISM AS CHARISMATIC DOMINATION

Emilio Gentile analyzes Fascism as 'the Italian road to totalitarianism'.[28] He regards the sacralization of politics and the cultural dimension of totalitarianism as of primary importance. In conceiving of totalitarianism as an 'experiment', moreover, he focuses on its character as a continuous movement much more than on its existence as an institutionalized regime.

Because in post-Stalinist societies neither sacralization nor dynamism was dominant, they are clearly not cases in point. But Fascism, Nazism and Stalinism certainly are to be subsumed under one heading because of their revolutionary movement character, their integralist concept of politics, and their sense of heading towards a new civilization. Similarly, violent coercion, social mobilization and the 'capillary organization' of the masses are doubtlessly part of all three cases, and that applies to the role of the one and single party, the strong emphasis laid on action, and, last but not least, the aesthetical dimension of politics and its sacralization, too. Rather than terror and ideology, or the fusion of subsystems, sacralization and mobilization – ideology as practice – are the crucial elements in this concept.

However, I am going to argue that there is a difference among Fascism, Nazism and Stalinism, namely the myth of the Fascist state. In Fascist Italy, it is the state which was sacralized and supposed to 'assume the role of a religious institution',[29] whereas in Nazism we observe the charismatization of a single person, the Führer. Stalinism differs from both cases because it was dominated by the charisma of the party of which Stalin's personal charisma was only a derivative, however indispensable. This difference among the three totalitarianisms, concerning the main subjects they sacralized, leads me to suggest the following differentiation: we can distinguish exterminist from non-exterminist totalitarianism in regard to the degree to which totalitarian movement regimes destroy the institutions of the state. This distinction is important if we assume that legal-rational state institutions (as with formal rationality in general) are the only safeguards against annihilatory barbarism on a mass scale.

As Gentile shows, the Fascization of the Italian state emerged from diverse sources. The secular-religious idea of the nation was to lay the foundation of the 'rebirth' of Italian greatness. It gained its specifically Fascist momentum when combined with the myth and modes of action of the militia party, on the one hand, and its integration into the cult of the fatherland, and finally the state, on the other. The symbols of the state were Fascized, the state itself sacralized and hailed as the 'new church', aiming at the advent of a 'new man' and a 'new civilization'. As for the party's function, it was to ensure the ecclesiastical role of the state and to make Fascism its secular religion, a religion intended to integrate state, party and Duce, and endow this religion with myths, rituals and cults. The state became 'both an institution and a collective faith',[30] an institution itself institutionalizing the political religion and its cults. To put it differently, Gentile diagnoses a process of continual sacralization, which entails the potential successively to dissolve the formal structures of the state; the more the state's 'ethical essence' serves the mobilization of the masses and the totalization of politics, the less formal procedures are to prevail. In all probability, such a dynamic of sacralization went much further than what Nazi jurists, such as Wilhelm Frick, the minister of the interior, had in mind when he suggested the incorporation of Nazism into the German state and constitutional law. However, Fascism's subservience to secular religion and political repression notwithstanding, its dynamic stopped short of destroying the Italian state – if not necessarily for endogenous reasons but rather because of war and defeat. Although we admit that all totalitarianisms remained 'incomplete',[31] there still is the question of why in the Italian case terror remained at a comparatively low level. Was it because either Fascism's ideology or its mode of organization did not support such tendencies? Since Fascism was excessively fascinated with death and the movement was extremely violent, I regard its institutionalized structure as most important.

Charismatic theories may help to clarify this institutional aspect. According to Max Weber's sociology of domination, different claims to legitimacy establish distinct social relations, attitudes and expectations, which, in turn, characterize institutions. The charismatic mode of domination is the only revolutionary one; therefore it is highly fragile and exposed to different forms of routinization. In his comparative study of Fascism and National Socialism, Maurizio Bach analyzes the impact which the seizure of power and its subsequent consolidation exerted on charismatic political agencies, such as the party or its leader, on the one hand, and on the formal-rational institutions of the state, on the other. Was the charisma incorporated into the inherited state institutions or was it rather routinized? In Italy, Bach argues, there emerged a specific compromise from the conflicts between the charismatic claims to authority and the representatives of the state executive.[32] While the party and its leader succeeded in successively establishing Mussolini's power over government, parliament and administration, the power center itself stayed dependent on the cooperation of the state executive. The latter remained intact, and at the same time it gained a political role: to support the Duce in fulfilling the legislative functions which he usurped. The dictator was tied to the bureaucracy; the latter defended its relative autonomy. This constellation limited the potential for the appropriation of power based solely on charismatic sources. While there existed party- or Duce-dominated agencies running parallel to and duplicating state institutions, they did not undermine their formal rationality. If Bach is correct, in Italy the charisma-tization of the normative state went less far than in Nazi Germany because institutional compromise lasted longer than in the German case.

In Germany, according to my tentative approach, the personal charisma of the Führer dominated the party long before the seizure of power. This type of charisma formed the social relations within the party as a classic 'emotional community' in the Weberian sense. After the

117

takeover, Hitler's charisma was not routinized but, on the contrary, it prevailed and spread along with affective anti-formalism. As is well known, there developed a highly fluid, extremely personalized constellation of authority in which mere will power was decisive. The predominance of 'decisionism' opened up occasional power chances completely apart from legal norms and formal procedures.[33] In the course of a dual process, the inherited normative state was ever more integrated into the Führer absolutism, and formal rationality eroded with the arbitrary state's continual extension of extra-bureaucratic, charismatic agencies. Apart from Nazi crown jurists such as Huber or Schmitt, or politicians such as Frick, National Socialists were not interested in preserving formal-legal norms and procedures – if we leave aside the standard administration of the German Volksgemeinschaft's (national community's) everyday life.

As Martin Broszat and Hans Mommsen have shown, the National Socialist exterminist dynamic was a consequence of the de-institutionalization of the formal-legal state and the rise and extension of the SS-state.[34] Both historians have convincingly argued against intentionalism in favor of their structuralist approach. Yet the most impressive research result – Mommsen's famous notion of 'cumulative radicalization' – seems to ask for explanations additional to and partly different from those they offer themselves. As it seems to me, they tend to reduce the radicalizing dynamic to striking political 'errors' of the Nazi leadership. Instead of selecting 'positive' objectives – so we are told – National Socialists chose the 'negative' elements of their Weltanschauung; instead of compromising with the normative state they continually dismantled it. In an alleged difference from Stalinism, Nazism did not create 'lasting political structures'. And because it did not head toward 'partification', i.e. the strengthening of the structure and role of the party, Nazism ended in self-destruction and collapse.[35]

While there is agreement concerning Mommsen's argument that Nazism's 'purely destructive nature' was the consequence of polycracy and institutional chaos, his notion of political errors needs further consideration. I would suggest – as does Ian Kershaw – a charismatic theoretical approach. Only if Hitler had not been a charismatic leader, and if his charisma had not induced an extreme personalization of politics and informality of procedure, could the Nazi party have gained the possibility of routinization, rationalization and collective decision-making. Because Mommsen ascribes such attributes to the Soviet party, he came to conclude that Stalinism was more rational (or less irrational) than Nazism. This conclusion, however, seems to be highly questionable, for the more Stalin's own charisma and his personal cult developed, the less the Soviet party lived up to its rational standards. Kershaw's theoretical design bears the potential to combine both approaches of intentionalism and structuralism in that it discerns the personal charisma of the leader as the motor both of the state's destruction and of its final consequence, exterminist politics.[36]

Before proceeding with Stalinist totalitarianism, let me briefly sum up my arguments. I suggest that we should see the state as Fascism's main subject of sacralization. Italy's totalitarian tendencies notwithstanding, the regime possibly did not last long enough to incorporate successfully the Duce's or the party's charisma into the state so as to finally abolish its formalism, which blocked development of a fully fledged terrorist dynamic. On the other hand, Nazism's main subject of sacralization was the Führer and nothing else but him. His personal charisma had developed long before the seizure of power. Accordingly, the party was organized around him and completely depended on him. After the consolidation of power, Hitler's charisma did not become routinized and not only prevented the party from gaining structural stability, but induced the rise of the SS-state and the chaotization of the institutions of the normative state as well. The subversion of formal institutions set free a dynamic leading toward exterminism.

What, then, was the Stalinist constellation? In contrast to Hitler, Stalin was – as Kershaw and many others point out – 'the man of the machine', the 'creature of the party';[37] his cult was 'superimposed upon the Marxist-Leninist ideology and the Communist Party, and both were capable of surviving it'.[38] However, Stalin was not only the man of the machine, he also went far in destroying it, that is to say in its Leninist form. During the Leninist period, the main subject of sacralization was neither the state (as in Fascism) nor the leader (as in Nazism), but the party – the party as scientific socialism incarnate. While Nazism from the beginning rested on the classical type of charisma attached to a person, Communism produced quite a different type, the 'charisma of reason'. According to Max Weber and his interpreter Stefan Breuer, this specific charismatic type is tied not to a person, but to ideas and institutions.[39] French Jacobinism serves Breuer as his first historical example, and for the Russian case he points out that Leninism claimed the right to power of the party, of an institution which drew its charismatic force from revolutionary theory – socialism as science – and from the idea of the avant-garde. The emotional community which characterizes classic charismatic relations is replaced here by an ultra-rational construction.[40]

The tightly organized party which characterized Leninism – and which post-Stalinism tried to reinstall – attempted to place itself above all other bureaucracies and to create a mono-organizational structure with immediate goal orientation. As both Rigby and Pakulski have argued, these bureaucracies were quite different from Max Weber's idea of socialism. They intended to pursue substantive instead of formal rationality.[41] The 'organization as hero', a party idea not present in Nazism, united opposites such as superordinate, impersonal (scientific and organizational) authority and personal (collective and individual) heroism. To unify these oppositions between action-oriented heroism and scientific authority, the definition of a charismatic 'correct line' and a corresponding 'combat ethos' were proferred.[42] This, however, threatened to fail once power had been seized and control over society gained. The Soviet party's charisma faced two alternatives: either routinization and formalization, or the option of continual revolution. While the NEP (New Economic Policy) incorporated the first alternative, Stalin's policy of 'socialism in one country' stood for the second. I contend that Stalin's decision involved a twofold consequence: transformation of Marxism-Leninism into what Arendt calls 'fiction', and substitution of the cult of the leader for the charisma of the party. It was this replacement of institutional by personal charisma, which subsequently worked toward the destruction of the old party and the destabilization of the new state. As a result, there remained no institutional bulwark against terror on a mass scale.

In his study of the Soviet 'state against its people', Nicolas Werth analyzes two cycles of terror.[43] The first, beginning with the October Revolution, he sees against the background of World War I and the breakdown of Russia's ancien régime. Even if Lenin's revolutionary politics induced only in part this period's violent excesses, the terror of the political police and other extra-legal agencies, which hit workers, peasants and especially Cossacks, already anticipated some features of the second, Stalinist, terror cycle. The latter involved deportations of social groups in their entirety; their possible death was taken into account. It was the Stalinist regime that institutionalized terror as a mode of domination; moreover, its extreme violence started from the constellation of relative regime consolidation. During the 1930s, terror became a permanent means of social transformation, with mass deportations, the great famine and purges. Considering that the Gulag resulted from a mixture of commands from the top and institutional chaos, Werth speaks of a dynamic of 'cumulative radicalization', thus pointing out similarities to Mommsen's Nazi paradigm.[44]

This interpretation will certainly be contested, for experts of Nazism define cumulative radicalization in a double sense: exterminism, on the one hand, and National Socialism's inexorable self-destruction, on the other. As far as the first aspect is concerned, the elimination of objective enemies, I regard Werth's interpretation as highly plausible, be it from the point of view either of charismatic theory or of Arendt's totalitarian theory. The second aspect, the self-destructive tendency of totalitarian regimes, appears questionable to me.[45] Although there is no denying that Stalin's policy of 'socialism in one country' followed from political decision and contingency rather than from an inexorable dynamic, his decision initiated a dynamic resulting from a shift of power from the charismatic party to personal charismatic rule. In order to pursue Stalin's politics of continual revolution, to liquidate 'the kulaks as a class', Marxism-Leninism had to be redefined and the old party smashed. The war against the peasantry, which Alvin Gouldner calls 'internal colonialism', rested upon the moral exclusion of large parts of society.[45] Its justification took the form of deductive logic, as Arendt would put it, and it conjured up 'theoretical nightmares'.[46] The identification of the kulaks as irreconcilable class enemies and agents of international capitalism turned class analysis into 'fiction', which in turn informed the terror. Virtually everybody could become an enemy by mere definition, if only because there were no longer any classes in the proper theoretical sense. As soon as property, social relations and common institutions were destroyed, a hitherto unknown situation of classlessness made the old party and its dogma a burden. Fictionalization and personal cult cleared away any hindrance to completely arbitrary definitions of social reality. Paradoxically, class fiction in a classless society invited terror to strike at society at large, and made the Gulag a microcosm of Soviet society. What is occasionally called Stalinist paranoia, then, resulted from a politically self-induced constellation; in the face of classes being smashed but with 'false consciousness' abounding, overall stigmatization, vigilance and terror were employed to bring about the unity and homogeneity of a 'new civilization'. 'As class concepts died', writes Lewin, 'they were replaced by the "demonization principle".' [47] Politics turned to 'exorcism'; ideological constructs such as 'former people', 'social aliens', 'enemies of the people' and all sorts of generalized suspects informed the terror from above and the collaboration from below.[48]

Back to Werth's analysis: as for its effects on party and state bureaucracies, Stalinism developed within a polymorphous system in which there coexisted and competed both 'hard' and 'soft' bureaucracies, functioning along the lines of contradictory forms of organization and their logics of power; the dualism between informal 'clan' relations, on the one hand, and hierarchy and competence, on the other, recalls the dual structure of the normative and the arbitrary state. It was the frustration with the permanent tensions between these two logics which nourished Stalin's anti-bureaucratic syndrome, so that, finally, the purges destroyed the apparatus.[49] It goes without saying that the Soviet dictatorship generated huge bureaucratic apparatuses that kept growing constantly. But, I would add to Lewin's interpretation, the purges attempted to do more than just overcome the 'bureaucratic maze', and derived from more than 'a sense of powerlessness' and 'institutional paranoia'.[50] The bureaucratic phenomenon was there to stay, but there are good reasons to assume that its character had changed. Oriented against the old political elite as well as the bureaucratic segments which had developed during the NEP period, the purges were meant to end the conflicts between telos and techné, to force all executive units under the teleological guide of the primacy of politics, and in the process to abolish the differentiation of planning and technocratic units trying to increase economic rationality and administrative calculability. Stalin's personal cult, to bring my point home, attempted to integrate the mobilized and atomized society, party and state bureaucracy into the hegemony of substantive rationality.[51] That this attempt was futile, as unity and homogeneity were never achieved, does not touch upon the argument that revolutionary regimes, and charismatic ones above all, generally require the very opposite of formal-rational institutions.[52]

Stalinism, as Werth reminds us, lacked the Nazi systematic will to extermination, and a simplistic parallel between class and race genocide cannot be drawn.[53] However, by abolishing the state, both dictatorships created the institutional precondition for cumulative radicalization. Flexible, extra-legal and extra-bureaucratic agencies institutionalized the terror against fictitious enemies; the fiction of a future civilization and a new moral sense legitimized it.

NOTES

[1] See Sigrid Meuschel, 'Theories of Totalitarianism and Modern Dictatorships: A Tentative Approach', Thesis Eleven, 61 (2000), pp. 87–98.

[2] Hannah Arendt, The Origins of Totalitarianism (London, Harvest [1951] 1968).

[3] Sigmund Neumann, Permanent Revolution: Totalitarianism in the Age of International Civil War (London, Praeger, 1965).

[4] Hermann Lübbe, 'Totalitäre Rechtgläubigkeit, Das Heil und der Terror', in H. Lübbe, ed., Heilserwartung und Terror: politische Religionen des 20. Jahrhunderts (Dusseldorf, Patmos, 1995), pp. 27, 33f.

[5] François Furet, Das Ende der Illusion. Der Kommunismus im 20. Jahrhundert (Munich, Piper, 1996).

[6] Arendt, Totalitarianism, pp. 315f., 348.

[7] Ibid., pp. 349f., 457.

[8] Ibid., p. 470f.

[9] Ibid., pp. 422ff, 389.

[10] For a similar argument on anti-Semitism see Shulamit Volkov, Antisemitismus als kultureller Code (Munich, Beck, 2000).

[11] Arendt, Totalitarianism, pp. 369, 371.

[12] Ulrich Herbert, Best: biographische Studien über Radikalismus, Weltanschauung und Vernunft; 1903–1989 (Bonn, Dietz, 1996).

[13] Similar to my interpretation, which underlines the institutional aspects of Arendt's aproach, Benhabib refers to Arendt's 'Tocquevillian' analysis, a 'political sociology of the public sphere and of intermediate associations'. See Seyla Benhabib, The Reluctant Modernism of Hannah Arendt (Thousand Oaks, CA, SAGE, 1996), p. 69. As for 'working towards the Führer', see Ian Kershaw and Moshe Lewin, eds, Stalinism and Nazism: Dictatorships in Comparison (Cambridge, Cambridge University Press, 1957) and Ian Kershaw, Hitler's Macht (Munich, dtv, 1992).

14 Johann Arnason, 'Totalitarismus und Modernisierung', in Lars Clausen, ed., Gesellschaften im Umbruch (Frankfurt am Main, Campus, 1996), p. 158.

15 Ibid., p. 161f.

16 Carl Friedrich, Michael Curtis and Benjamin Barber, eds, Totalitarianism in Perspective: Three Views (London, Pall Mall Press, 1969), p. 131.

17 Ibid., p. 144

18 Juan Linz and Alfred Stepan, Problems of Democratic Transition and Consolidation: Southern Europe, South America, and Post-Communist Europe (Baltimore, MD, and London, Johns Hopkins University Press, 1996).

19 Juan Linz, 'Totalitarian and Authoritarian Regimes', in Fred Greenstein and Nelson Polsby, eds, Handbook of Political Science, Vol. III (Reading, MA, Addison-Wesley, 1975), pp. 208, 228ff.

20 Ibid., pp. 217ff.

21 Peter Graf Kielmansegg, 'Krise der Totalitarismus-Theorie?', in Eckhard Jesse, ed., Totalitarismus im 20. Jahrhundert (Bonn, Nomos, 1996), p. 292.

22 Ibid., p. 301f.

23 Arendt, Totalitarianism, p. 389.

24 Claude Lefort, The Political Forms of Modern Society: Bureaucracy, Democracy, Totalitarianism (Cambridge, Polity Press, 1986), pp. 34ff.

25 Ibid., pp. 79, 83.

26 Ibid., p. 55.

27 Linz and Stepan, Problems of Democratic Transition and Consolidation, pp. 38ff.

28 Emilio Gentile, 'Fascism and the Road to Totalitarianism', paper presented at the 19th International Congress of Historical Sciences, Oslo, 6–13 August 2000, Special Themes No. 12, 'Forms of Totalitarianism and Dictatorship'.

29 Emilio Gentile, The Sacralization of Politics in Fascist Italy (Cambridge, MA, Harvard University Press, 1996), p. 11.

30 Ibid., p. 59.

31 Gentile, 'Fascism and the Italian Road to Totalitarianism'.

32 Maurizio Bach, Die charismatischen Führerdiktaturen (Baden-Baden, Nomos, 1990), pp. 110ff.

33 Ibid., pp. 35ff.

34 See, for example, Martin Broszat, 'Soziale Motivation und Führer-Bindung im Nationalsozialismus', Vierteljahresheft für Zeitgeschichte, 4 (1976), pp. 392–409; Hans Mommsen, 'Hitlers Stellung im nationalsozialistischen Herrschaftssystem', in idem, Der Nationalsozialismus und die deutsche Gesellschaft (Reinbek, Rowohlt, 1991), pp. 67–101.

35 See also recently recapitulating his and Broszat's arguments: Hans Mommsen, 'Cumulative Radicalisation and Progressive Self-destruction as Structural Determinants of the Nazi Dictatorship', in Ian Kershaw and Moshe Lewin, Stalinism and Nazism, pp. 75ff.

36 Kershaw, Hitlers Macht and idem, Hitler 1889–1936 (Stuttgart, Verlags-Anstalt, 1998).

37 Ian Kershaw, 'Working Towards the Führer: Reflections on the Nature of the Hitler Dictatorship', in Kershaw and Lewin, Stalinism and Nazism, p. 90.

38 Ibid., p. 94.

39 Stefan Breuer, Bürokratie und Charisma (Darmstadt, Wissenschaftliche Buchgesellschaft, 1994), pp. 62ff.

40 Ibid., pp. 90ff., 100ff.

41 Thomas Rigby, The Changing Soviet System (Aldershot, Ashgate, 1990); Jan

Pakulski, 'Bureaucracy and the Soviet System', Studies in Comparative Communism, 14:1 (1986), pp. 6ff.

42 Ken Jowitt, New World Disorder: The Leninist Extinction (Berkeley, CA, University of California Press, 1992), pp. 3, 17; the notion of the 'party as hero' is Breuer's.

43 Nicolas Werth, 'Ein Staat gegen sein Volk – Gewalt, Unterdrückung und Terror in der Sowjetunion', in Stephane Courtois, ed., Das Schwarzbuch des Kommunismus (Munich, Piper, 1998), pp. 51–295.

44 Ibid., pp. 290, 292, 294f.

45 It could well be argued that Stalinism was saved from self-destruction not from within but by World War II, whereas the dynamic started anew as soon as the war was won. Then, for sure, after Stalin's death, his successors tried to revive the party and its Leninist ideology.

46 Alvin W. Gouldner, 'Stalinism: A Study of Internal Colonialism', Political Power and Social Theory, 1 (1980), p. 238f.

47 Gouldner's definition, in ibid., p. 224.

48 Moshe Lewin, 'Bureaucracy and the Stalinist State', in Kershaw and Lewin, Stalinism and Nazism, p. 55.

49 Sheila Fitzpatrick, Everyday Stalinism (Oxford, Oxford University Press, 1999), esp. chs 5 and 8.

50 Nicolas Werth, 'Le Stalinisme au Pouvoir – Une mise en perspective historiographique', paper presented at the Nineteenth International Congress of Historical Sciences, p. 10.

51 Lewin, 'Bureaucracy', p. 67.

52 See also Walter Süß, 'Partei, Bürokratie und Arbeiterklasse auf dem Weg in den "Stalinismus"', in Gernot Erler and Walter Süß, eds, Stalinismus (Frankfurt am Main and New York, Campus, 1982), pp. 601–55.

53 Social scientists, such as Zygmunt Bauman (see his Modernity and the Holocaust [Ithaca, NY, Cornell University Press, 1989]) miss precisely this point when they declare 'modern' rational bureaucracy to be the core structure of the exterminist catastrophe. On the contrary, formal rationality serves as a bulwark against totalitarianism.

54 Nicolas Werth, 'Le Stalinisme', p. 17f.

8

Asian Communist Regimes: The Other Experience of the Extreme

Jean-Louis Margolin

Asia's Communist countries have experienced some of the most violent collective traumas in world history. If Mao Zedong and Pol Pot symbolize the extremes of Communist utopia – each of them attributing the failure of revolutionary expectations to excess in moderation – they have also triggered murderous processes of horrendous proportions.[1] And although a reliable death count is still out of reach, it can safely be stated that at least two-thirds of the victims of Communist regimes have been Asians. The phenomenon is partly connected to China's huge population (around 700 million at the beginning of the Cultural Revolution in 1966). Taking 58 million unnatural deaths as an average estimate would put the death toll over three decades, from 1946 to 1978, at 8 per cent of the total Chinese population. This figure is not much different from the one recently established for the three decades of the Lenin-Stalin period.[2] Figures are less accessible for Vietnam, Laos and North Korea, but as these countries followed closely Mao's and Stalin's paths, the end result should not have been very different. While the hard-line period in Vietnam lasted slightly more than 30 years, from 1953 to 1986, the Pyongyang regime remains even today as fierce as ever, after more than five decades. In Cambodia's case, the bloodbath reached the dimensions of a full-fledged genocide in just under four years, from April 1975 to January 1979. During these four years between 17 and 30 per cent of the population perished from mass killings, exhaustion, mistreatments or starvation – and that in one of the few Asian countries that is not known for large-scale famines.

Thus, the very size of these 'megadeath' experiences puts them in the center of any assessment of the twentieth century's bloody trail. Asian Communism has shown considerable creativity in oppressive and murderous methods. Mass re-education – extending to concentration camp inmates – family disintegration, refashioning of private life, mass expulsion from cities, systematic starvation of prisoners, elimination through detention or wholesale killing of their ancien régime civil service, total suppression of culture and traditions, and contempt for any kind of law and regular justice have reached a level there unsurpassed elsewhere. There has been no Auschwitz in the Far East (no gas chambers, no carefully planned, industrially organized genocide), but several features of Asian Communist regimes are apparently just as extreme and horrific as the Nazi Holocaust. Furthermore, the present Chinese, Vietnamese, Laotian and North Korean political elites are direct, proud (and, fortunately, more or less unfaithful) heirs to the vanished generation of mass murderers that gave birth to their regimes. They represent a unique case. In Italy, Germany, Spain, Portugal, Greece, in central/eastern Europe and Russia, in Latin America, and in several African countries, present-day rulers have convincingly distanced themselves from former dictatorships. Only the Arab world shows a somewhat comparable continuity – but even its most bloodthirsty tyrants pale in comparison to Mao Zedong or Kim Il Sung.

Hence the urgency to study Asian Communist regimes, if for no better reason than trying to understand how to help so many people still under their yoke. However, even though a number of historians and political scientists have recently increased and refined our knowledge, especially on China, they are still cut off from philosophers, sociologists, and 'mainstream' political scientists. The numerous theoretical or comparative works on political violence, genocide, totalitarianism or, simply, evil, tend to include, almost as a rule, considerations on the Holocaust and often allude to Stalin's Soviet Union. They seldom go further than a few footnotes or some short statements, not always up-to-date or accurate, when they mention Asian Communism.

There are several reasons for this reluctance to engage the problem. The first difficulty is linked to the questionable relevance of the very notion of Asian Communism. Is its existence more justified, more heuristic, than, say, 'European Fascism', a category not considered very useful by experts on Mussolini's Italy or Hitler's Germany? True, there have been significant differences, especially in the extension, intensity and chronology of political repression. The Khmer Rouge genocide remains unique, as do China's Red Guards. North Korean purges seem less far-reaching than their Chinese counterparts, but real détente periods are hard to spot in the long Kim dynasty history. Political liberalization started in China in 1978 and around the mid-1980s in the three Indochinese countries. We are still to see a ripple of it in North Korea. Last, but not least, the only 'wholly Communist wars' took place in 1977–79 between Vietnam and Cambodia, then in 1979 between China and Vietnam.

Second, the originality of Asian Communist regimes is suspect. It is hard to spot any of their features that had no Soviet precedent. 'Re-education through work' or criticism and self-criticism procedures were present under

Stalin, although their application was much more thorough and extensive under Mao. The concept of a 'Cultural Revolution' was also elaborated in the Soviet Union. The often quoted Mao's comparison of intellectuals to 'shit' closely follows some of Lenin's expressions.[3] The supposedly 'peasant' character of Chinese-style revolutions was actually limited to a military propaganda strategy in the period of revolutionary war. Neither the discourse nor the praxis of Asia's Communist regimes had any connection, however remote, with the aspirations of the peasantry. In fact, they were as savagely exploited and thoroughly enslaved as in Stalinist Russia, the development of heavy industry being until recently a constant magnet for their rulers.[4] Even in Democratic Kampuchea, cities (especially the capitals), where it had always been a privilege to be allowed to live, were much better protected from starvation and various deprivations than the peasantry. The progressive opening of Soviet archives, as well as new testimonies from China or Vietnam, lead to a constant re-evaluation of Soviet political influence and direct help to Asian Communist movements, especially during their early periods of power, extending from the training of political police cadres to industrial planning. One should not be misled by the strident pretension of Asian Communists to follow a specific, national way. Their tactics are not unlike those used in France, where the now well-documented servility of the indigenous party to Moscow's orders was hidden from the mid-1930s People's Front period under the claim of building 'socialism with French colors'. The claim to a national way has been used as a trick to win support on the basis of nationalism, anti-colonialism and anti-imperialism.[5] Yet many scholars of Asian Communism tend to take that claim for granted. Educated as 'Orientalists', having gone through the painstaking learning of an Asian language and usually fascinated with the great culture and long history of countries such as China or Cambodia, they tend to overestimate, sometimes in an excessive way, the indigenous anchorage of Communist policies and to underestimate their obvious 'Cominternian' origins. Such scholars usually know very little about other Communist experiences. In our globalized world – Communism itself is a failed attempt at an alternative globalization – comparative history still occupies a backseat.

The specifics of Asian Communism should not be overstressed. It is part and parcel of the wider, more easily definable reality: world Communism.[6] But its peculiarities are not insignificant. Indigenous cultural and societal features explain some of these. For example, one can argue that the Chinese Confucian notion of self-improvement opened the way to self-criticism and the practices of re-education. The imperial paochi'a (collective control of deviants) system was rejuvenated into criticism sessions. If that is the case, Cambodia and Laos, steeped in Indian-derived Theravada Buddhism, should not have followed the same path as Vietnam or Korea, influenced by China.[7] How about a genealogical explanation? As is well known,

Russian Communism was transplanted into China. For a series of practical reasons (the difficulty of maintaining the tenuous connection between Moscow and South-East Asia, the Chinese ethnicity of many South-East Asian Communist militants), since the early 1930s the overseeing of most regional parties was informally delegated to the Chinese Communists. As they began their ascent to power, and as the Soviet Union had to concentrate on affairs in Europe, Yan'an (the Chinese Communist capital from 1936 to 1947) became the new de facto center of Asian Communism. Many future Vietnamese and Korean leaders, as well as cadres from many other nations, spent several of their formative years there just as Mao was putting the final touch to his personal contributions to revolutionary practice – guerilla war, peasants' mobilization and control, and re-education. Solidarity was reinforced by the bitter struggle against the common enemy, Japan. Then, as soon as the Chinese Communist Party (CCP) had won over the whole of China in the early 1950s, it provided invaluable aid to its Vietnamese and Korean brothers. That aid was vital for achieving the local parties' goals and proved indispensable for their survival, particularly during the war in Korea. The anti-American war in Vietnam was just as resolutely supported. The ensuing fascination with the Chinese model led to indigenous 'Great Leaps', with invariably disastrous consequences for the peasants' well-being. Then, Beijing unearthed new filial connections with the Khmer Rouges, happy themselves to find an alternative, more distant protector against the hegemonic inclinations of the Vietnamese Communists.[8] Thousands of Chinese civil and military advisers helped Pol Pot throughout his genocide. The proximity, attraction and large aid packages from China drew almost all Asian Communist parties alongside Beijing when the big rift with Moscow opened in the early 1960s. Thus, between the 1930s and the 1970s, an alternative Communist camp grew in East Asia, gravitating around China, with its own connections and political features, and free of subordination to an overwhelming power, unlike Soviet-centered eastern Europe. Much of that camp survives to this day, proving the pertinence of the notion of Asian Communism.

SEARCHING FOR THE ROOTS OF VIOLENCE

It has often been argued that Communist violence has to be contextualized both within the indigenous murderous traditions and within the aggressiveness of Western interventions. Therefore, what look like horrendous extremities could actually be considered a sad routine, or a slightly excessive counter-violence. The concert between cultural and area studies experts and 'radical' thinkers eager to save something from Communist history appears to give some credibility to these, often far-fetched, hypotheses.

Summarizing in a few words the long history of violence in Asian societies is an almost impossible challenge. The Chinese example is the best known in Asia. A general feature in the Middle Kingdom was the alternation between long periods of relative calm (except on the bellicose north-western frontier) and shorter, often tragic, moments of foreign invasions or widespread insurrections. At least since the Tang dynasty, from the seventh to the tenth century, the momentum was towards a reduction of violence. For example, the Penal Code of 654 put family responsibility for crimes to an end, developed the notion of intentionality, and instituted the right to appeal. Under the Song dynasty, in the twelfth century, each death sentence had to be reviewed and approved by the emperor, aiming at reduction of capital punishment. As the country was, by and large, secure, it could reasonably be argued that, during most of the past two millennia, the Chinese have benefitted from one of the world's lowest rates of violent deaths. Voltaire's 'wise mandarin' is not a pure Western speculation. Of course, in times of trouble, violence perpetrated by invaders, insurgents or governmental troops could surge to impressive heights. It should be emphasized that the century preceding the Communist revolution of 1949 was exceptionally violent, the highlights being the massive Taiping revolt during 1851–64, the Warlords period of anarchy in the decade 1916–27, and the Sino-Japanese war of 1937–45. Each of these upsurges of violence claimed millions, or dozens of millions, of victims. A small part was killed fighting; many more died from famines caused by the plundering armies or by the general disorganization. Incidentally, Western aggressions, limited in time and even more in space, have not been major causes of mortality. Westerners have played no part in the most dramatic events in recent Chinese history. Even so, nothing foretold the systematic victimization of whole human groups during the globally peaceful Maoist period, or the unprecedented nationwide extension of the Great Leap famine, probably the worst of that category of events in Chinese, and possibly global, history. The late imperial period, after the 1900 Boxer insurrection, or the Kuomintang Nanking decade, 1927–37, had actually been rather settled and reasonably tolerant.

In many ways, Cambodian history has been just the opposite. Marked by numerous civil wars, often degenerating into foreign interventions, conditioned by Angkorian traditions of merciless killing, slavery and mass deportations, it became more peaceful after 1863, under the French protectorate. Prince Sihanouk succeeded in keeping the two Indochina wars at bay. In that fertile, not overpopulated country, mass famine was something almost unknown. Vietnam, too, had a rather tragic pre-modern history of wars, insurrections and fierce persecutions, lastly against the indigenous Catholic community. The French colonial period, 1858–1954, had begun with bitter fighting, especially in Tonkin during the period

1883–96. Revolts remained a frequent feature throughout. Their suppression was severe: death sentences by the hundreds, intermittent use of torture, and high level of mortality in jails (it could reach 4 per cent per year). But the judiciary remained partly independent, sentences were often reduced when the political situation calmed down, and press campaigns and policy changes in France could lead to the liberation of political prisoners (all were released by the People's Front government in 1936). Later on, many Vietnamese admitted that French prisons had often been their school in Communism, and had played no small role in their subsequent party promotion. Even more important was that prosecutions were always individualized and their scope was limited. Political detainees never numbered more than a few thousands. The embattled pro-US Republic of Vietnam, 1955–75, undertook much harsher repressive measures. Its Communist opponents have mentioned an (unconfirmed) figure of 200,000 political prisoners. Just one year after the 1975 'liberation' of Saigon, although all fighting had ceased, at least 500,000 former military personnel, civil servants, professionals and students had been sent to 're-education' camps, generally for several years. The judiciary and the civilian state authorities lost all control and access to information on the process, which was secretly decided by the party Politburo and executed by the political police. The size and nature of repression had fundamentally changed.

THE ENGINES OF VIOLENCE

Communist violence cannot thus be analyzed as the mere replica of ancestral practices. It is even less of a delayed response to colonial violence; a practice that had actually been limited after the bloodbaths of conquest. Communist violence also cannot be seen as counter-violence triggered by the tragedies of decolonization, Cold War and the civil wars. Had that been the case, more people would not have been detained (in Vietnam or Laos) or killed (in Cambodia and probably China) after the end of fighting. What was it, then, that set the fatal circle in motion?

Numerous accounts revolve around apparently rational explanations, related to the economic or social sphere. Killing and detaining scores of people would have been an unpalatable way to solve concrete problems. In the economic field, for example, it would have been a way to fight sabotage, to terrorize the lazy and recalcitrant, and concentrate national effort on investment and production regarded as vital for development. Unfortunately, economic decision under Communism has too often been characterized by irrationality. Collectivization and accelerated industrialization have severely disorganized the whole economy, and multiplied non-productive jobs as well as unprofitable or simply unusable productions.

Sending the few able managers and experts to piggeries (as in China), or using their bodies as fertilizer (as in Cambodia), can hardly be justified economically. Social pressures 'from below' to eliminate alleged 'enemies of the people' may look to Western intellectuals a modern and progressive explanation, but is not supported by the evidence. China's radical land reform in the 1940s and the 1950s was demanded by the peasantry. Its initiation and organization, however, were entirely in the hands of party agitators who manipulated – with difficulty – the villagers. Moreover, why should the process have 'cost' the life of between two and five million people? In Japan, Taiwan and South Korea, very thorough land reforms took place simultaneously and hardly anyone was killed. The real goal was political: to terrorize, to implant party cells everywhere, to establish a sort of blood pact between the party and the population.

Even the often-invoked nationalist quest for restoration of a country's past glory cannot be considered as the central motivation behind such radicalism. Undoubtedly, nationalism had been a central element of mobilization during the 'united front' or 'national front' years and the struggle for power during these periods. But if that strategy performed marvels during the 'liberation' wars – victory over France and successful resistance to the USA – it was put aside immediately after peace came back. The Red Guards were strongly xenophobic, but they did not care much about the world status of their country. To continue the Revolution was considered more important than to realize national empowerment. Hence the deliberate devastation, for ideological reasons, of the still fragile economic structures; acts that provoked the dismay of genuinely patriotic managers and intellectuals. Wars were won, but peace was lost. Significantly, the first Communist leaders to take care of their country's economic strength were the more moderate, second-generation leaders. Deng Xiaoping, through his 'Four Modernizations' plan, Vietnam's Prime Minister, Vo Van Kiet, and possibly even North Korea's Kim Jong Il all gave top priority to economic development as a shortcut towards increased political significance on the world scene.

The chronological connection between utopia and terror is quite obvious. The Great Leap Forward of 1958–61 attempted to create large 'agrocities' on the ashes of the village network; transplant 'scientific' methods in agriculture; and develop heavy industry on a massive scale, both in the urban centers and in the countryside. The peasants had to give up their land and almost all of their personal goods. They had to accept a kind of army barracks life, with collective meals (getting lighter as time went on), and exhausting, compulsory work assignations. Any hint of reservation was deemed 'right deviationism'. When famine struck, it was often treated as an act of sabotage: the party line could not be wrong. Thus – as in the Ukraine in 1932–33 – the army was sent to search the farms for 'hidden grain stocks' and, on not finding them, then tortured, arrested and killed the starving peasants. During the Great Proletarian Cultural Revolution of 1966–69, the genuine anger of students and young workers against the corruption, meanness and police methods of the state bureaucracy was instrumentalized by Mao and by the power-crazed Red Guard self-proclaimed leaders. It was employed in a campaign of terror against intellectuals, cadres of all kind and former capitalists, landlords and Kuomintang civil servants. Egalitarian aspirations degenerated into universal inquisition and victimization. The will to engender a new world produced only an unprecedented devastation of culture. Soon, the anti-authoritarian rebels opened their own jails and torture chambers, and were putting pressure on prison authorities for an even harsher treatment of their 'counter-revolutionary' detainees. As for Democratic Kampuchea, its goal was an accelerated Great Leap, with total collectivization and total mobilization of human energy. No country ever went so far in reshaping, in one bold stroke, geography (emptying of cities, massive population transfers, huge irrigation works), economy (suppression of currency and commerce), sociology (suppression of religion, education, the family and the most elementary individual freedoms), and psychology (quasi-prohibition of sexuality, criminalization of individual thinking and feelings). Language itself was deeply modified, and an Orwellian Newspeak became compulsory. Almost by necessity, there was some (mostly individual) resistance, widespread escapism of all kinds, regular failure to achieve the unrealistic goals and, soon, famine and massive mortality. All that was read by the central apparatus as proof that the 'enemies' were even more numerous and treacherous than expected, with the only answer being increased repression.

This utopianism with deadly consequences was based on three central assumptions. First, there was the slogan that 'everything is possible', a sentence closer to the Nietzschean 'triumph of the will' than to original Marxism, with Lenin's voluntarism bridging the gap. Mao, with his anarchist leanings and his growing separation from reality, bent the Bolshevik tradition into an increased reliance on ideological indoctrination and mass mobilization. The second adage was 'everything is political'. There were no natural constraints, no economic laws; nothing but the permanent 'fight between two lines' – the bourgeois against the proletarian – even inside the Communist Party. There were, therefore, no mistakes, but resurgences of bourgeois, imperialist ideas and no failures, but acts of sabotage of the class enemy. A poor harvest should therefore call for more repression. Third, 'only the future matters': the past had to be rejected (Mao compared new China to a 'blank page') and all present resources mobilized for a future of brightness and universal contentment, just a few years away. With such a splendid perspective in sight, who could seriously care if, in the process, lives were lost, eggs were broken?

But, to break the old society and terrorize hostile elements, the Communists also had to transform themselves into practical sociologists. They painstakingly nurtured latent resentments and hidden bitterness so as to make them explode violently, and to channel them against the party's enemies. In hierarchical Asian societies, there was no lack of such long-constricted societal antagonisms. Youth had to submit to the old; women to men; villagers to cities; peripheral, mountainous areas to the more prosperous central plains, seats of power and dominant culture; ethnic minorities to the majority group. All these sources of violence were tapped, with disastrously murderous effects. Fourteen-year-old students were deemed fountains of revolutionary wisdom during the Cultural Revolution. In Democratic Kampuchea, young uneducated peasant females often replaced, for the worse, the older experienced cadres, suspected (often rightly) to be simultaneously too corrupt and too moderate. Everywhere in Indochina, the most rejected ethnic groups formed a disproportionate number of the revolutionary troops. Nevertheless, the 'liberation' of the oppressed was short-lived. After having been cynically used by the party, they were brutally put back into place. Thus, more than ten million 'young educated', yesterday's revolutionary heroes, had to move in 1968–69 from cities to remote villages; in principle, for the rest of their life. Pol Pot's Jarai minority personal guard was wiped out with one stroke. And the large autonomous regions of mountainous northern Tonkin, where the Vietminh had its first sanctuaries in the late 1940s, were abolished soon after the victory in 1975. Party interests could not be confused with those of any social group or any specific community. The Communists had to protect their complete freedom of action for the glorious designs that only the initiated few could fully understand.

A STATE OF INHUMANITY

Total social control remains the most striking peculiarity of Asian Communism, more so than its mass crimes. There was no automatic connection between control and violence. Japan and Nazi Germany committed terrible crimes during World War II without exercising a similar control. In Asia, daily life was meticulously regulated, spontaneity reduced to the absolute minimum. Leaving one's workplace or residence was prohibited. Cities were cut off from the countryside. Pressure was constant: political meetings at the workplace and month-long 'seminars' kept its level high. Deviants and suspects were ostracized, their families compelled to reject them. Suicide (hundreds of thousands during the Cultural Revolution) was often the only escape route – but even for that families could be victimized.

Deinstitutionalization reached an extreme level. Practically no courts, no penal codes, very short and ever-changing constitutional texts, and almost no written law, that was the rule. The boundaries between party, state and society became blurred. This did not translate into more freedom and power for the individual, but into the imposition of unlimited duties (individual rights disappearing almost completely), and by a mostly ideological regulation. To be close to Mao's thought (unfortunately, ambiguous and changing) was the only law, the only strategy for survival. Education in the party truths, criticism and self-criticism procedures became universal, and were always open to re-education – the laogai. Unpredictability and insecurity were maximized.

The most elementary features of humanity were ferociously hunted down and eliminated. The Khmer Rouges took the passive ox as a model, and they only accepted love and friendship if directed towards the Organization. In Vietnam, revolutionary virtues were transferred from the traditional Confucian female devotion to the male family members. In China, the general labelization of the population led to a rigid caste system. Birth ('family color') determined rights and duties, even for those born after the revolution.

The consequences of such policies were especially dramatic for morality: one could not survive without lying, slandering, denouncing and (in Democratic Kampuchea) stealing.

The specific case of the Cambodian genocide resulted from the extreme weakness of a Communist group surrounded by hostile countries and fighting against time. It shows a nihilist trend to self-devouring and, ultimately, suicide – a trait probably present in every extreme experience, but nowhere else as obvious.

CONCLUSION: GETTING OUT OF TERROR

The contradictions, variations, and extreme tensions engendered by radical Communist policies in Asia fast exhausted the initial enthusiasm and support of the people. The sectarian regimes proved their fragility and, in one generation or less, they had to disappear or transform themselves, renouncing both utopia and terror. But these experiences of the past (with the exception of North Korea) have been so extreme that they help us understand, worldwide, what the essence of political terror looks like.

NOTES

[1] Here lies a seldom perceived cause of the escalation of terrorism along the history of Communism. Lenin, fascinated by the Jacobin phase of the French Revolution (1793–94), and attributing the rapid failure of the 1871 Paris Commune to its deficiency in revolutionary violence, organized a political police with almost unlimited powers, prohibited political opposition, and triggered the Red Terror, all in the very first months of the Bolshevik regime. Mao, seeing to his horror that the Soviet party leaders, although carefully selected by Stalin himself, had 'betrayed' him in 1956, crushed the Chinese intelligentsia through the 1957 Hundred Flowers movement, launched the ultra-collectivist People's Communes in 1958, and, in 1966, attempted the complete rebuilding of the Communist Party through the Cultural Revolution. Pol Pot, assuming power in April 1975, after the obvious failure of that strategy, decided to undermine the very bases of private property, through the suppression of money, to prohibit private life through dislocation of families and total control of the individual, and to eliminate fully 'old society' through the forced evacuation of cities and the physical destruction of civil servants, cadres and intellectuals. If Peru's Sendero Luminoso (Shining Path) had succeeded, it would have probably tried to redress 'Pol Pot's mistakes' through an even higher degree of terrorism. Incidentally, the fatal escalation demonstrates that historical and international consciousness does not necessarily play in favor of increased wisdom. There are 'abuses of history', just as Tzvetan Todorov demonstrates in his chapter in this book that there were 'abuses of memory'. There are also 'genealogies of evil'.

[2] The year 1946 marks the beginning of the large-scale land reform in Communist 'liberated' areas, fueled by quota-based, compulsory executions of 'landlords' in every village. In late 1978, Deng Xiaoping assumed supreme power, and soon proceeded to free most political prisoners.

[3] In general, Asia's 'Marxist-Leninist' theoretical works have been desperately poor. Whatever its one-time startling influence over a section of Western intellectuals, Mao's thought is nothing more than a 'pop', summarized version of Lenin's writings, read through Stalin's glasses. Yet the Chinese leader proves a major theoretician when compared with Ho Chi Minh or Kim Il Sung, despite the latter's thousands of published pages, translated at great cost into dozens of languages. Kim's famed Juche (self-reliance) concept has been taken in its entirety from Chinese theorization of the Great Leap Forward. Pol Pot has left very few texts, and nothing even remotely theoretical.

[4] The first year of China's Great Leap Forward, 1958, was marked by an increase of the state-owned industrial companies workforce by 85 per cent. Pol Pot's Four-Year Plan, presented in August 1976, devoted its longest chapter to heavy industry and that in one of the least industrialized countries in the world.

[5] History is crafty: in the past two decades or so, with the rapid, universal fading away of Marxist utopianism, and as so many Communists have been attracted to a nationalistic discourse, nationalism (sometimes under the extreme forms of xenophobia or racism) really became the central tenet of many Communist Parties, especially where they still are or have been in power.

[6] Despite some ambiguities, particularly in Africa (especially Mengistu's Ethiopia), the list of Communist countries has always been easy to establish. But was Mongolia, almost a Soviet colony since 1922, part of Asian Communism? Even North Korea, organized after 1945 under Soviet control much alike East Germany

or Poland, and to this day more repressive than inquisitive, is a kind of transition zone between Soviet-style and Chinese-style Communism.

[7] That apparent cultural contradiction could have been a factor in the specific Cambodian drama.

[8] The Cultural Revolution, with its extraordinary attempt at destroying the existing Communist Party, signaled the first rift between China and the other Asian Communist regimes, until then faithfully Maoist.

9

A Lesser Evil? Italian Fascism in/and the Totalitarian Equation

Ruth Ben-Ghiat

This chapter will address the moral implications and historiographical consequences of one narrative of a long history of regime comparison: that of Italian Fascism as a 'lesser evil' with respect to National Socialism. While the Italian dictatorship has not been included in the totalitarian equation as defined by the other essays in this volume, it ranks high on the scale of twentieth-century European evil – except when compared with Nazism and Communism. Whether the index is body counts or the dissolution of traditional state institutions, Italian Fascism comes up a distinct third, classifiable at most as an 'imperfect totalitarianism', to use an old slogan that still circulates.[1] My intent in investigating this comparison is not to ascertain its truth-value, but rather to explore its histories and symbolic value and the ways it influenced the evaluation of Italian Fascism among both Italians and foreigners. For although a wealth of studies testifies to an effort to assess Mussolini's regime on its own terms, this international historiography has also been shaped directly and obliquely by a sense of 'what [Italian] Fascism was not': a regime of genocide and mass murder in which 'ordinary men' implemented policies designed to produce a racialist utopia.[2]

'Only comparison allows an understanding of uniqueness', Ian Kershaw and Moshe Lewin have written.[3] This is certainly true, but it can also be argued that this particular comparison, which has found expression both in historiography and in popular perception, has hindered a full understanding of the particular policies and practices of the Italian regime. Specifically, it has until very recently fostered a witting or unwitting underestimation of Fascist violence committed both within and outside of Italy, and has perpetuated historiographical traditions and popular credos that minimize Italians' agency and their responsibility for such violence (such as the idea of the Italians as a brava gente, or a 'good people').[4] These 'blind spots', which also reflect the obstructionist practices of the Italian state archives, are the legacies of a wider repression of those parts of the historical record that might blur distinctions of morality, national character, etc., which are generated and renewed by the 'lesser evil' formulation. Each of these important issues merits a much fuller discussion than is possible here.[5] My aim in this chapter is mainly to map out the political, cultural and ideological factors that facilitated the circulation of this comparison, and to present some concrete examples of Italian policies and behaviors that have been slow to find acknowledgement in Italian discussions of Mussolini's regime and which remain too little known among scholars of Nazism and Communism. As I will detail later, death marches, mass population transfers, genocide and concentration camps with forced labor and starvation rations not only characterized Nazi Germany or Stalinist Russia but Italian Fascism as well. Comparison can illuminate the individual things compared, but it must commence from the kind of empirical knowledge that, in the case of Italian Fascism, has been difficult to gather, especially with regard to those topics that are the common currency of totalitarian regimes.[6]

With many accounts of European totalitarianism now centered around the development of and dance between Nazism and Communism, it is worth recalling that for many years after World War I it was Mussolini's rather than Hitler's regime that stood out as Communism's 'enemy twin'. The term 'totalitarian' had been coined as a slur against Fascism by Italy's liberal opposition, but by the mid-1920s Mussolini and his followers had appropriated the term as a means of advertising the distinctiveness and originality of their approach to governance.[7] For observers of various political leanings in the 1920s and early 1930s, the Fascist and Soviet states seemed to be engaged in a race to bury democratic and bourgeois Europe, and similar strategies of mass mobilization, political identity formation and persecution marked their quests for a perfect revolutionary one-party system of rule. In fact, even as the 'black shirts' denounced Communist internationalism, they devoted considerable resources to the establishment of their own networks of international influence that would lay the foundations for a 'universal Fascist' civilization. Mussolini bankrolled Fascist organizations abroad, encouraged an array of rightist movements inspired by him that stretched from Portugal to India and, once Stalin took power, stepped up his promotion of corporatism and other 'revolutionary' aspects of Fascist ideology.[8] This comment by a young Fascist, which was written six months after Hitler took power, captures the diffused sense that the Italian and Soviet regimes were the main competitors for control of the ideological and political spaces left open by the crisis of the bourgeois order:

> The decline of nineteenth-century civilization has left only two roads to follow: ours and theirs. And we can be sure that in time these two

roads will meet. But will we end up on their path, or they on ours? The serious person must ask himself: will it be Rome or Moscow?[9]

This early chapter of the history of totalitarianism, in which Italy and Russia were the primary referents of organized terror and state projects of human refashioning, came to an end with the start of the German National Socialist government in 1933. Although Mussolini initially welcomed the Nazi takeover as evidence of Fascism's forward impetus within Europe, the speed with which the foreign press anointed the National Socialists as the standard-bearers of rightist totalitarianism proved unsettling. Less than one year after Hitler took power, the head of Mussolini's Press Office warned the Duce that the Germans might usurp Italian Fascism's leadership position and claim to originality 'by presenting the characteristics of Mussolinian thought and action under the Nazi name'.[10]

The complex relationship between the Italian Fascists and the National Socialists over the next decade is beyond the scope of this chapter.[11] A few points do bear on the Italian contribution to the construction of the 'lesser evil' thesis in this period. The first regards the consistency of Italian perceptions of Germans as heartless materialists from the Weimar Republic through the Nazi years, and the equal consistency with which Italians saw themselves as possessed of a greater common sense and humanity. Italian anxieties about this aspect of the German national character found expression in the 1920s in complaints about the triumph of die Sachlichkeit über alles, and in the early 1930s in denunciations of the Nazis' 'fanatic' racist credos that privileged biology over family and community.[12] Such depictions of Germany as a land of extremists, and of Italy as 'a school for liberty, harmony, and wisdom about life', continued after the declaration of the Axis alliance and the promulgation of Italy's own anti-Semitic legislation.[13] If anything, the Italians increased their rhetoric about Fascism as a regime that nurtured spirituality and personhood. Far from being an example of the imitation of Germany, the adoption of racial ideology gave Italians another opportunity to articulate their differences from the Nazis. They did so by eschewing the Germans' biological racism in favor of a peculiarly Italian brand of 'spiritual racism', a distinction that was recognized by Church officials as well.[14]

Such images and self-images did not stop Fascist policymakers and intellectuals from charting a joint course of history with the Nazis, and the years 1936 through 1943 saw a flood of Italian–German collaborations in fields as disparate as biology and art restoration, as well as the creation of new labor markets for Italians within the territories of the Reich.[15] This symphony of aims and ideals continued for some Italians through the period of the Salo Republic, which was seen as a chance to realize the revolutionary promise of Fascism on an international scale.[16] For the majority of the populace, though, and for the men and women who would serve as public arbiters and custodians of Italian national memory in the postwar period, the wartime experiences of invasion, occupation and deportation by Germans proved the most salient indicators of the correctness of what the historian Filippo Focardi has analyzed as the 'bad German–good Italian' trope.[17] Indeed, by the end of the war, the Italian press and Italian purge bodies used the terms 'collaborator' and 'resister' to refer to the positions Italians took during the two-and-a-half-year span of the Salo Republic, rather than to their actions during the preceding 21 years of Mussolini's rule. Such distinctions, which originally reflected a culture and jurisprudence of transition, have become accepted in the scholarship on Italian Fascism. As Claudio Pavone has noted, this has comported a 'normalization' of the Italian dictatorship and a concomitant black boxing of genuine evil as proper to the exceptional and foreign-tinged 'Nazi Fascism' of Salo.[18]

The symptoms and effects of such exculpatory legal and ideological operations were wide-ranging in the immediate postwar period, and I will mention just a few of the most relevant consequences here. First, the desires of many leftists, liberals and even progressive Christian Democrats to de-Fascistize Italy through widespread purges and sanctions remained unfulfilled, at least in part. The need of the new political parties to gain grass-roots followings, a shared feeling of victimization at the hands of the Germans and the Allies, and a sort of collective complicity among intellectuals and civil servants who had been entangled for two decades with the Fascist state all conspired to ensure a large degree of institutional continuity between the regime and the new republic.[19]

Second, Italy did not cooperate with requests by Greece, Yugoslavia, Libya and other countries to extradite the more than 1,600 Italian civilians and military men accused of attempted genocide and other war crimes, in part to avoid public debates that would further tarnish the image of Italians during the drafting of the 1947 Peace Treaty. As recent research by Focardi and Lutz Klinkhammer has revealed, in 1946 the Christian Democrat government privately pursued a policy of stalling and dissemblance to avoid compliance with such requests. Official public discourses emphasized the relative quality of Italian guilt with respect to Germany and the victim-ization of Italians in Nazi concentration camps and during the German occupation of Italy.[20]

Third, this public silence also extended to Italy's complicity in Holocaust operations, encouraging narratives that minimized Italian agency in Jewish persecution and reduced even the prewar Italian racial laws to an imitation of German policy.[21] In the aftermath of so many Nazi atrocities committed on Italian soil, the consistent referencing of Germany as the symbol of evil was inevitable and a result of historical fact. Yet the consistent externalization of Fascist aggression on to the Germans, coupled with an equally consistent emphasis on the 'greater good' of Italians, discouraged any sustained moral debate about Italian totalitarianism and the place of violence in the ideologies and practices of Mussolini's regime. Within a few years of the defeat of Italian Fascism, official and popular narratives had merged to create what Focardi has called 'a reassuring and self-absolving self-portrait' that has depended on an ongoing comparison with the German dictatorship for its renewal and reaffirmation.[22]

Naturally, Italian policymakers and intellectuals did not operate in a vacuum. Cold War politics were a contributing and sometimes determinant factor in the shaping of the policies and assumptions described above. The popularity of the Italian Communist Party – the largest such party in western Europe – and Italy's geopolitical importance as a bridge between Europe and the Mediterranean were foremost in the minds of the Allied officials who were in charge of the wartime occupation and, later, the postwar reconstruction of the country. The goal of avoiding social revolution and ensuring goodwill toward the democratic liberators took precedence over large-scale punishment of Fascist wrongdoing. Comparing the Italian populace to a 'good boy who was led astray by a band of criminals', both American and British authorities eschewed notions of collective guilt and concentrated on Italians' greater redeemability (as compared with the Germans) for democratic life.[23] For the same ideological and geopolitical reasons, the Allies turned a blind eye to Italian obstructionism with regard to extradition of their accused war criminals, who were active in Italy's occupied territories and in the colonies.[24]

Among Italians, the very polarized climate of the late 1940s led Communists and Christian Democrats to accuse one another of being 'totalitarian' and emphasize their own repugnance at the discredited Italian regime. The Christian Democrats' leaders pointed to the Communists' links with Stalin and advanced arguments for the equivalency of Fascism and Communism, while Communist head Palmiro Togliatti stressed the continuities in membership and spirit (religious and otherwise) between Fascism and the Christian Democrats.[25] For different reasons, both parties used the conduct of Nazi soldiers as a foil for their own constructions of the 'good Italian'. For the Communists, who needed to highlight the contribution of Resistance partisans to the war at a time of American-backed political crackdowns against the Italian left, this involved the repression of information about excessive partisan violence and the diffusion of a view of the Fascist period that minimized popular support for Mussolini's regime.[26] For the ruling Christian Democrats, on the other hand, damage control was crucial to rehabilitate Italy and gain a better bargaining position with the Allies. This mandated doing everything possible to prevent Italian war atrocities from coming to international attention, downplaying the past association of Italians and Germans, and diffusing a counter-narrative that emphasized the anti-Fascist feelings of Italians and the humanity many individual Italian soldiers and officials had shown toward foreign Jews and others during the war. By 1948, an image of the Italian soldier had emerged in national films and public discourse that turned totalitarian propaganda on its head, presenting an individual who was 'intimately averse to war and reluctant to commit acts of violence and oppression'.[27]

In presenting themselves as a 'less evil' than the Germans before and after 1945, Italians could find support in the opinions of a host of foreign commentators whose works removed Mussolini's regime from the totalitarian equation. Among the most prominent and widely read of these analysts were a number of German émigrés, for whom, as Abbott Gleason has written, 'Italy was something secondary or tertiary in their attempts to analyze what had happened in Europe.'[28] In fact, Italian Fascism figures only marginally in the explorations of totalitarianism published by Franz Neumann, Hannah Arendt, Erich Fromm, Paul Tillich and others. Typical is this statement by Tillich in his essay on the conflicts between religion and the totalitarian state, a subject of great relevance for Italy. Writing in 1934, when the Nazis had been in power just over a year and the Italian Fascists for 12 years, he asserts that 'the development of totalitarianism has progressed farthest in Germany, where the totalitarian state was conceived and to a great extent realized'.[29] Such attitudes reflected these émigrés' obviously superior interest in and knowledge of the German case. But they also attest to a tendency to see the Italian dictatorship as an aside or footnote to a history of totalitarianism that was plotted from the very start around mutual reactions and rivalries between Nazism and Communism. They also convey perceptions of cultural differences between northern and southern Europe. Arendt, for one, groups Italy together with Spain and Portugal as nations in which the presence of 'Latin-European' values mitigated the spread of the kind of extremist and anti-humanist mentalities that had prevailed in Germany and in Russia.[30] Such beliefs also inform the observations and recollections of Germans who emigrated to or passed through Fascist Italy. Among these was the Jewish philosopher Karl Löwith, a student of Martin Heidegger, who took up residence in Rome after he was expelled from the German university system in 1934. 'The Italians are humane even in a black shirt', Lowith confided in his diary in 1936 as he lauded their relative indifference to racial matters. He changed his mind a few years later, when new anti-Semitic legislation forced him and all other foreign Jews in Italy to choose between expulsion and internment in an Italian concentration camp.[31]

Arendt, the most famous of totalitarianism's émigré analysts, wrote as a philosopher attempting to chart a genealogy of state-sponsored terror, and as a German Jew who struggled to understand the psychological and historical roots of the racist credos that had proved so appealing to her compatriots. Writing in the aftermath of the Holocaust, she contended that the absence of state anti-Semitism and the relatively mild way that the Italian Fascists dealt with their internal opposition justified the classification of Mussolini's regime as a 'non-totalitarian, or, at the most, semi-totalitarian' state. Indeed, until the onset of the racial laws, Italy was 'just an ordinary nationalist dictatorship [that] developed logically from a multi-party democracy'.[32] Interestingly, Arendt reproduces scornful German views of the Italian regime's 'shortcomings' to bolster her argument. Claiming that the Nazis possessed an 'unfailing instinct' for recognizing the differences between totalitarian and non-totalitarian regimes, Arendt fills footnotes with quotes from Heinrich Himmler, Josef Goebbels and others attesting to Italian Fascism's 'superficiality' and the accordingly truer affinities between Nazism and Communism. Stalin, not Mussolini, was Hitler's true partner in the awful totalitarian enterprise, Arendt concludes.[33]

Steven Aschheim's astute observation that the degree of civilization attributed to a culture often structures the reception of the violent acts carried out by that culture is relevant here.[34] The sense of betrayal these German émigré commentators manifest at the barbarization of their countrymen and women was proportionate to their view of the superior cultivation that marked their native land. Likewise, Mussolini's regime, as they depicted it, seemed to reflect essential 'Italian' qualities, both positive (a greater humanity) and negative (cowardice, untrustworthiness, attention to form over substance). In this, they follow a tradition of foreign-authored travel and historical narratives on Italy which argue that the Italian temperament, which seems so conducive to the expression of artistic genius, lacks the regimentation, cruelty and drive necessary for martial valor.[35] This legacy of perceptions accompanied observers who dismissed the possibility of 'ordinary Italians' becoming perpetrators in the service of the state. It is in this sense too, that we might read Arendt's judgment that Fascist Italy was an 'ordinary' dictatorship that committed 'ordinary' crimes, which lay within the boundaries of Western tradition, rather than a totalitarian state that fostered a culture of evil of a type and on a scale without precedent.

Such perceptions of Italian mentality and culture also inform many English-language commentaries on dictatorship published in the decades following World War II. This large body of work has been well analyzed and does not bear reiteration here.[36] I will discuss only the British historian A.J.P. Taylor, who did not explicitly treat totalitarianism in his writings but was nonetheless arguably the most influential non-German purveyor of the 'lesser evil' thesis. His controversial 1964 work The Origins of the Second World War aimed to refute the attribution of all war guilt to

Germany by challenging intentionalist views that Nazi expansionism was
the product of a well-designed Faustian plan. Hitler, in this view, was less
infallible engineer than shrewd opportunist; yet Taylor credits him with
ideological consistency and an iron will to achieve a profound transformation of Germany and the Germans. This was more than could be said
of Mussolini and Italian Fascism, for whom Taylor reserved some of his
harshest criticism:

> Fascism never possessed the ruthless drive, let alone the material
> strength of National Socialism. Morally it was just as corrupting –
> or perhaps more so for its very dishonesty. Everything about Fascism
> was a fraud. The social peril from which it saved Italy was a fraud;
> the revolution by which it seized power was a fraud; the ability and
> policy of Mussolini were fraudulent. Fascist rule was corrupt, incom-
> petent, empty; Mussolini himself a vain, blundering boaster without
> ideals or aims.[37]

Such prose reflects several traditions of commentary on Italian Fascism:
Nazi and, more broadly, German condescension toward Italian 'weakness'
and 'superficiality'; a particularly British contempt for Italian histrionics and
infantile behavior; and a broader Anglo-American tradition of caricaturing
Mussolini as a 'sawdust Caesar', petulant infant or irresponsible buffoon
that found expression in popular histories and journalism and in cartoons
in the interwar and wartime press. These stereotypes and attitudes persisted
into the postwar period, so that in his 1956 study of Italian Fascism the
Italian-American scholar Dante Germino felt obliged to emphasize that
the Italian regime was 'neither comic opera nor a South American palace
revolution', but a totalitarian state that oppressed millions for 20 years.[38]

If Taylor's The Origins of the Second World War renewed such views
of Italian Fascism among historians and the educated reader, his contem-
poraneously made documentary film Mussolini brought them to the larger
public and the schools. The hour-long movie, which Taylor wrote and
narrated, hews closely to the text of The Origins of the Second World War
in its presentation of the Duce and his regime. Indeed, the film's purported
protagonist, Mussolini, is seen mainly in relation to Hitler, and Taylor uses
the force-and-muscle German regime as a foil for his denunciations of
Italian Fascism's cult of appearances. The movie's central image and trope
is Mussolini as an actor performing from his balcony; the 'black shirts'
are ineffectual posturers who more closely resemble characters from opera
buffa than the perpetrators of terror; and Fascism is reduced to a spectacle.
Reality enters into this charade only with the appearance of Hitler in
Mussolini's life. Taylor's depictions of the Führer as a positive anchor for
Mussolini – at one point he calls him the Duce's 'only friend' – lends the

movie a strange air of Germanophilia. Throughout much of the narration, Taylor's voice fairly drips with scorn for the Fascists, especially when he refers to their military aspirations. When the Italians adopt the goosestep, they parade before Hitler but 'did it badly'; when Mussolini visits Germany and addresses a Nazi rally in German, his atrocious accent ensured that 'no one could understand him'. The Duce gets credit for originating Fascism, but totalitarianism as practiced by the Italians was 'all a sham': Hitler is the one who got it right.

The way that cultural stereotypes as well as historical fact have contributed to the dictum of Italian Fascism as a 'lesser evil' comes through clearly in Taylor's selection of the visual materials and in his editing choices. The centerpiece of the film consists of a long segment that shows Mussolini orating from his balcony at different periods of the regime. By providing no English translations of the Duce's words, Taylor places the emphasis on Mussolini's body language, which reads to Anglo-American and northern European viewers as a catalogue of exaggerated Italian gesticulation. Detached from their verbal referents, behaviors meant to be menacing come off as faintly ridiculous: the effect of this 'hyper-Italianness' is to disarm the aggression announced in the verbal text. Two segments within this gallery of oratorical performances stand out as particularly indicative of Taylor's caricaturial intentions. In the first, as Mussolini protests against foreign perceptions of Italy as flowery and picturesque, he goes into gestural overdrive, moving his hands and mouth in ways that make him an emblem of that which he denounces; in the second, which dates from just after the Nazis' 1934 murder of the Austrian chancellor Englebert Dollfuss, the Duce puffs up with nationalistic pride while he denounces the Germans as a people who barely knew how to read and write 'when Rome had Caesar and Augustus'. With no translation of the Italian dialogue, the attack on the Nazis is lost on the intended English-language audience. Attention is directed to the sights of the Duce's jutting chin, swollen chest and self-congratulatory strutting about the balcony. Even today, when shown this footage, many non-Italian viewers smirk rather than become indignant, including when, as in the case of a speech proclaiming victory in Ethiopia, they hear what they know is an announcement of the success of mass murder through gassing.[39] By rendering Italian Fascism as something essentially risible, Taylor not only confirms it as 'less evil' than Nazism, but removes it from the purview of moral judgment altogether.

Such international perceptions of Italian Fascism, coupled with an Italian tendency to repress a national history of repression, have led to a severe underestimation of Fascist violence, which in turn has influenced theorizations about Italy's place as a totalitarian state. Indeed, if Stalinist Russia and Nazi Germany are 'the two great slaughterhouses of the twentieth-century', as Michael Geyer has termed them, Italian Fascism is the neighborhood butcher: its domestic and foreign campaigns of repression evoke neither images of Gulags operating at Stakanovist rhythms nor the 'order of terror' imposed by German killing machines.[40] Consider the doxa about how the Italian regime dealt with its internal dissenters. Neither the municipal prisons where Antonio Gramsci languished, nor the confinement colonies in southern Italian villages, where Cesare Pavese and Carlo Levi briefly lived, nor certainly islands such as Ponza, where many anti-Fascist political leaders were interned, carry the resonance of the German Lager and the Soviet Gulag. Indeed, such comparisons, like the more complex one of the conduct of Italian, German and Russian troops in wartime, would seem merely to confirm the incommensurability of Italian Fascism with these other dictatorships, not just because of the smaller scale of Italian violence and the much smaller numbers of deaths it caused, but because of some qualitative difference in the nature, contexts and impulses of that violence that prevents its perpetrators from being classified as dehumanized executioners, either willing or reluctant ones.

As Kershaw and Lewin have observed, however, comparison presupposes a fairly even historiographical base, and scholarship on Nazism is by far more advanced in its scope and depth than that on any other totalitarian or authoritarian regime. In his introduction to a groundbreaking book on Italian concentration camps published in 2001, Enzo Collotti, a distinguished historian of Mussolini's regime and its relations with the Nazis, lamented the resistance Italian historians have shown to doing research that would clarify the specific characteristics of Italian totalitarianism. For all that has been written on the Duce and the dictatorship, Collotti observes, there are still no detailed studies on 'the concrete institutions through which Fascism oppressed and repressed national minorities, racial minorities [and] political adversaries …'.[41] The use of secret police and informers and the workings of racial and other persecutory bureaucracies – subjects that have been in the purview of researchers of Nazi Germany and Soviet Russia for years – are only now coming to scholarly and public attention in Italy. Italian concentration camps in the Balkans and in the colonies, which constitute Fascism's contributions to the map of European totalitarianism's 'extreme situations' also remain little known, in part due to the active denials, obfuscations and manipulations that have marked official Italian responses since World War II to revelations about the national past that might disturb the 'good Italian/bad German' trope.[42]

The issue of historiographical silences on aspects of Italian Fascism, which risks muddying the moral primacy that is assumed by the trope of the 'lesser evil', has two dimensions which correspond to two inter-related vectors of memory. The first can be termed 'institutional' or 'statist' and comes to center on the archive, an entity which has the power to promote

146

certain understandings of national collective memory over others by the decisions it makes in compiling and regulating access to documentary collections. The many lacunae within the historical record on Italian Fascism and its wars are in part a direct product of persistent practices of obstructionism that range from the removal by archivists of sensitive single documents from public domain files to the inaccessibility of entire civilian and military documentary collections. This situation is the fruit of protectionist impulses – a desire to keep information 'in house', thus forestalling the writing of histories that challenge official or convenient views of the past – and chronic (one might also say strategic) under-funding, which has prevented many collections from ever being catalogued.[43] To cite just one example, we still are not in a position to obtain a full picture of Italian actions and policies during World War II: the Italian Navy and Air Force archives are open for the years 1940 to 1943 only to Italian Navy and Air Force historians; materials on Italian colonialism were for decades open only to members of a state-appointed historical commission and still are not fully available; and research on Italian war crimes has been hindered by the continuing closure to researchers of virtually every relevant document collection. As Jacques Derrida has written, the archive is a place of both protection and concealment, in that to archive something is to classify and control it, keeping it safe but also under a sort of 'house arrest'.[44] This dual function is certainly evident within Italian state institutions, which have contributed not a little to a collective rimozione (the term in Italian means, tellingly, both 'repression' and 'removal') of parts of the historical record that might facilitate a comparison between German and Italian totalitarianisms.

These 'black holes' in the document and historiographical base correspond in interesting ways to gaps in Italian popular memory, as several fine oral history projects reveal.[45] Italian atrocities committed in their Balkan and colonial territories, the more than 50 concentration camps throughout Italy that held Jews and foreigners during World War II, the forced labor of Italian Jews in the cities and countryside – none of these events has much resonance at the level of individual recollection, even among those who witnessed or executed such policies and/or had quotidian engagements with those who were affected by them. Such local patterns of (non)recollection, which often remain unchallenged due to the continued inaccessibility of many communal and provincial archives, flow into national narratives that perpetuate the idea that the Nazis 'were the only ones responsible for massacres, deportations, and violent behaviors'. They sustain what the historian Ernesto Galli della Loggia has termed the 'singular schizophrenia' of Italian public opinion, 'which remembers German atrocities on Italian soil and represses Italian atrocities against other peoples with equal tenacity'.[46]

The case of Italian Fascism, I contend, offers an opportunity to think about the connections between agency, violence, and public and private memory in ways that might not emerge as clearly from critical conversations that include only what Italians term il caso limite, limite here meaning an extreme case that is perforce also a limited one. While Italian Fascism offers plenty of food for reflection on human evil, Mussolini's regime remains less 'fascinating' (in the sense evoked by Susan Sontag) than Hitler's Nazism and Stalin's Communism. Enveloped in a faint halo of imitation and ineffectuality, Fascism offers neither the spectacle of radical evil realized on an international scale (Nazism) nor that of epic suffering, paranoia and persecution at home (Stalinism). Even though we know that the Italians committed genocide in Libya and certainly engaged in what we now call 'ethnic cleansing' in the Balkans, Italian Fascist crimes in the service of the Axis lack magnitude and 'critical mass' when compared with those of the Nazis. Yet this post-Holocaust reasoning merely brings us back to notions of the Germans as standard-bearers of evil that are embodied in the 'lesser evil' trope.

If we are to understand the phenomenon of totalitarianism, we must guard against the temptation of assigning gradations of evil to regimes according to the body counts they produced and look instead at larger transnational questions relating to the collective desensitization to violence among European populations from 1914 to 1945. One need only think of the international range of collusion in and execution of violence during this period: after all, Nazi violence was not the work of Germans alone, but of individuals of many other nationalities who collaborated and cooperated with them or committed racial crimes on their own. The actions of the Italian Fascists, from the well-publicized squadrist violence and political assassinations to the equally well-publicized mass use of gas in Ethiopia, were essential to a process of desensitization that occurred through second- as well as first-hand exposure to violent acts.[47] Seeing the history of totalitarianism as a chain of mutual influences with regard to strategies of rule and persecution also makes it harder to sustain Cold War and neo-conservative ideological operations (which had their most recent reiteration in the Historikerstreit debates) that configure Nazism and Communism as a diabolical dyad – with one existing to provoke and/or justify evil in the other. As the historian Mariuccia Salvati has observed, 'telling the history of totalitarianism means reflecting on the political and moral dimensions of the history of totalitarianism'.[48] The fortunes the 'lesser evil' trope has had as a means of summarizing the putative differences between Italian Fascism and Nazism shows the necessity of a critical revisitation of comparative judgments about such regimes. It stands as a case study of the way that collective memory and historiography can converge in national contexts to sustain formulations that allow the moral and political legacies of totalitarianism to remain too little explored.

ITALIAN FASCISM IN/AND THE TOTALITARIAN EQUATION
NOTES

[1] For the articulations of this concept within Italy alone, see Emilio Gentile, 'Fascism in Italian Historiography', Journal of Contemporary History, 21 (1986), esp. pp. 200–3. The question of an Italian variant of totalitarianism is addressed explicitly in Renzo De Felice, Il Fascismo. Un totalitarianismo all'italiano? (Turin, 1981); and in Emilio Gentile, La via italiana al totalitarianismo. Il partito e lo Stato nel regime Fascista (Rome, 1995). The most comprehensive collection of historiographical views on Italian Fascism is Renzo De Felice, Il Fascismo. Le interpretazioni dei contemporanei e degli storici (Rome-Bari,1998).

[2] Here I am punning the title of an article by Gilbert Allardyce, 'What Fascism is not: Thought on the Deflation of a Concept', American Historical Review, 84 (1979). For a sense of the range of this international bibliography regarding Italian Fascism alone see Renzo De Felice, Bibliografia orientativa del Fascismo italiano (Rome, 1991).

[3] Ian Kershaw and Moshe Lewin, Stalinism and Nazism: Dictatorships in Comparison (Cambridge, 1997), p. 1.

[4] On this see David Bidussa, Il mito del bravo italiano (Milan, 1993).

[5] An important contribution to the critical historiography of Italian Fascism, which begins by questioning such perceptions, is Richard Bosworth, The Italian Dictatorship: Problems and Perspectives in the Interpretation of Mussolini and Fascism (London, 1998). Fundamental work on the construction and postwar utilization of the Italian–German comparison has been done by Filippo Focardi, 'L'ombra del passato. I tedeschi e il nazismo del giudizio italiano dal 1945 a oggi', Novecento (July–December 2000), pp. 67–81; Focardi, '"Bravo italiano" e "cattivo tedesco": riflessioni sulla genesi di due immagini incrociate', Storia e memoria, 1 (1996), pp. 55–83.

[6] Among the few studies that explicitly compare the two regimes are Alexander De Grand, Fascist Italy and Nazi Germany (New York, Routledge, 1995); Carl Levy, 'Fascism, National Socialism, and Conservatives in Europe, 1914–1945: Issues for Comparativists', Contemporary European History, 8, 1 (1999), pp. 97–126. See also MacGregor Knox, Common Destiny (Cambridge, 2000); and Richard Bessel, ed., Fascist Italy and Nazi Germany. Comparisons and Contrasts (Cambridge, 1996).

[7] On anti-Fascist and Fascist uses of the term 'totalitarian' in 1920s Italy, see Jens Petersen, 'Die Entstehung des Totalitarismusbegriffs in Italien', in Manfred Funke, ed., Totalitarismus (Dusseldorf, 1978), pp. 105–28; Abbott Gleason, Totalitarianism: The Inner History of the Cold War (Oxford, 1995), pp. 14–20.

[8] I have written about these initiatives more fully in Fascist Modernities: Italy, 1922–45 (Berkeley, CA, 2001), but see also Michael Ledeen, L'internazionale Fascista (Bari, 1973).

[9] Giulio Santangelo, 'La Russia: Questione di civilita', L'Occidente (July–September 1933). On public attitudes towards the Soviets, see Pier Giorgio Zunino, L'ideologia del Fascismo (Bologna, 1985), pp. 332–44; Luciano Zani, 'L'immagine dell'URSS nell'Italia degli anni trenta', Storia contemporanea (December 1990), pp. 1197–224; and Rosaria Quartararo, 'Roma e Mosca: l'immagine dell'Urss nella stampa Fascista (1925–1939)', Storia contemporanea, 27 (1996), pp. 447–72.

[10] Gaetano Polverelli to Mussolini, 1933 letter in Archivio Centrale dello Stato, Rome, Ministero della Cultura Popolare, b.155, f.10.

[11] General overviews of the Nazi–Fascist relationship and Italian–German relations are Ruth Ben-Ghiat, 'Italian Fascists and National Socialists: The Dynamics of a

Difficult Relationship', in Richard Etlin, ed., Art, Culture and the Media under the Nazis (Chicago, IL, 2002); Jens Petersen, 'Italia e Germania: percezioni, stereotipi, pregiudizi, immagini d'inimicizia', Storia contemporanea, 6 (1992), pp. 1087–124.

[12] First quotation from Gino Chiesa, 'Notiziario', L'Architettura (November–December 1927); second quotation from Partito Nazionale Fascista, Il cittadino soldato (Rome, 1935), p. 24. For relations between the two regimes in the early 1930s and the question of racism, see H. James Burgwyn, Italian Foreign Policy in the Interwar Period, 1918–1940 (Westport, CT, 1997), pp. 70–100; Jens Petersen, Hitler–Mussolini. Die Entstehung der Asche Berlin–Rome 1933–1936 (Tubingen, 1973), and Meir Michaelis, Mussolini and the Jews: German–Italian Relations and the Jewish Question in Italy, 1922–45 (Oxford, 1978).

[13] Enrico Rocca, 'Dove va la nuova Germania letteraria?', Italia letteraria (9 October 1930).

[14] On the differences between German and Italian ideas of race, see Aaron Gillette, The Defense of the Race: Racial Theories in Fascist Italy (New York, 2002); Michaelis, Mussolini and the Jews; on the Vatican's acceptance of these differences, see Ben-Ghiat, Fascist Modernity, pp. 152–3.

[15] See Mino Argentieri, L'Asso cinematografo Roma–Berlino (Naples, 1986); and Jens Petersen, 'Vorspiel zu "Stahlpakt" und Kriegsallianz: Das deutsch italianische-Kulturabkommen von 23. November 1938', Vierteljahreshefte für Zeitgeschichte, 36 (1989), pp. 41–77; Ben-Ghiat, 'Italian Fascists and National Socialists', and Bruno Mantelli, Cesare Bermani and Sergio Bologna, Proletarier der 'Asche': Sozialgeschichte der italienischen Fremdarbeit in NS-Deutschland 1937 bis 1943 (Berlin, 1997).

[16] On the Salo republic see Lutz Klinkhammer, L'Occupazione tedesca in Italia, 1943–45 (Turin, 1993).

[17] See the excellent studies by Filippo Focardi: 'La memoria della guerra e il mito del "bravo italiano". Origine a affermazione di un autoritratto collettivo', Italia contemporanea (September–December 2000), pp. 393–9, and '"Bravo italiano" e "cattivo tedesco".'

[18] Pavone, 'Fascismo e dittature', p. 68.

[19] On the purges, see the fine studies of Hans Woller, Die Abrechnung mit dem Fascismus in Italien 1943 bis 1948 (Munich, 1996), and Roy Domenico, Italian Fascists on Trial 1943–1948 (Chapel Hill, NC, 1991). On the continuity of the state, see Claudio Pavone, Lalle origini della Repubblica. Scritti su Fascismo, antiFascismo, e la continuita dello stato (Turin, 1995), pp. 70–159.

[20] Such was the fear of exposing Italian war crimes that the government decided not to bring charges against Germans for their massacres in Italy and against Italians on the island of Cephalonia. See the findings about this double obfuscation in Lutz Klinkhammer and Filippo Focardi, 'La questione dei "criminali di guerra" italiani e una Commissione di inchiesta dimenticata', Contemporanea (July 2001), pp. 497–528; Focardi, 'La questione dei criminali di Guerra in Italia dopo la fine della seconda Guerra mondiale', Quellen und Forschungen aus italienischen Archiven und Bibliotheken, 80 (2000), pp. 543–624.

[21] This historiographical operation is discussed in Bidussa, Il mito del bravo italiano. Only in the mid-1990s did a critical mass of works about Italian racism begin to appear. See on this Alberto Burgio, 'Una ipotesi di lavoro per la storia del razzismo italiano', in Burgio and Luciano Casali, eds, Studi sul razzismo italiano (Bologna, 1996), pp. 19–28.

[22] Focardi, 'La memoria della guerra e il mito del "bravo italiano"', p. 393.

[23] Quote from Gregory Dale Black, The United States and Italy (Lawrence, KS, 1974), p. 13; Ron Robin, The Barbed-Wire College (Princeton, NJ, 1995), pp. 6–8, makes a similar point regarding the different attitudes Americans held toward German and Italian prisoners of war in the USA.

[24] Focardi and Klinkammer, 'La questione dei "criminali di guerra italiani"'.

[25] Palmiro Togliatti, 'Totalitarianismo?', Rinascita (November–December 1946); see Gleason, Totalitarianism, pp. 143–6, on the Italian Communists' and Christian Democrats' uses of such rhetoric.

[26] On the histories and silences about partisan violence, see Luca Alessandrini, 'The Option of Violence – Partisan Activity in the Bologna Area, 1945–48', in Jonathan Dunning, ed., After the War: Violence, Justice, Continuity, and Renewal in Italian Society (London, 1997), pp. 59–74; and Paolo Pezzino, Anatomia di un massacro (Bologna, 1997).

[27] Quotation is from Focardi, 'La memoria della guerra', p. 393. This image was carried forth in films such as Carlo Borghesio's Come persi la guerra (1946).

[28] Gleason, Totalitarianism, p. 32.

[29] Paul Tillich, 'The Totalitarian State and the Claims of the Church', Social Research (November 1934), p. 433; also Wilhelm Reich, The Mass Psychology of Fascism (New York, 1946); Erich Fromm, Escape from Freedom (New York, 1941), esp. p. 232. Franz Neumann is the exception here, since he engages in sometimes detailed excurses on Italian history. Yet his references to Italian Fascism are designed to illuminate the radical difference and newness of National Socialism with respect to existing governments and political philosophies. See his Behemoth: The Structure and Practice of National Socialism, 1933–1944 (New York, 1944), pp. 75–7, 462–3. Gleason, Totalitarianism, pp. 33–8, and Bosworth, The Italian Dictatorship, pp. 210–12, offer more detailed discussions of German émigré views of Italian Fascism.

[30] Hannah Arendt, The Origins of Totalitarianism (New York, 1973), p. 258.

[31] See for example Karl Löwith, My Life in Germany Before and After 1933 (Chicago, IL, 1994), pp. 86–8; also the memories of George Mosse, Nazism: A Historical and Comparative Analysis of National Socialism (New Brunswick, NJ, 1978), pp. 104–5.

[32] Arendt, The Origins of Totalitarianism, p. 257.

[33] Arendt, Origins of Totalitarianism, p. 308. For a critique of Arendt's views on Italy and a discussion of their reception within Italy, see Meir Michaelis, 'Anmerkungen zun italienischen Totalitarismusbegriff: Zur Kritik des Thesen Hannah Arendts und Renzo de Felices', Quellen und Forschungen aus italienischen Archiven und Bibliotheken, 62 (1982), pp. 270–302.

[34] See Steven Ascheim, Culture and Catastrophe: German and Jewish Confrontations with National Socialism and Other Crises (New York, 1996), pp. 9–10, and his In Times of Crisis: Essays on European Culture, Germans and Jews (Madison, WI, 2001), pp. 54–6.

[35] On English perceptions of Italy and Italians through the modern era, see Maura O'Connor, The Romance of Italy and the English Political Imagination (New York, 1998). The ways such views intersected with national notions of Italianness are investigated in Giuliano Bollati, L'Italiano. Il carattere nazionale come storia e come invenzione (Turin, 1984).

[36] See, for example, Gleason, Totalitarianism, passim, and Bosworth, The Italian Dictatorship.

[37] A.J.P. Taylor, The Origins of the Second World War (New York, 1961), p. 59.

[38] Dante Germino, The Italian Fascist Party in Power (Minneapolis, MN, 1959),

p. 56. See Bosworth, The Italian Dictatorship, pp. 69–70 on the tradition of British superiority; George Seldes, Sawdust Caesar: The Untold Story of Mussolini and Fascism (London and New York, 1935), for an example of popular historical/ journalistic writing; and Niccolò Zapponi, Il Fascismo nella caricature (Bari, 1981), for cartoon depictions of Mussolini and Fascism in the international press. Luisa Passerini, Mussolini immaginario, 1919–1939 (Rome, 1990), tracks the Duce's image up to World War II.

[39] My observation here is based on ten years of showing the film in university lectures, public talks, and at conferences such as the one that gave rise to the present volume.

[40] For Geyer's definition see Michael Geyer, quoted in Moshe Lewin and Ian Kershaw, 'Introduction', in Lewin and Kershaw, Nazism and Stalinism, p. 8.

[41] Enzo Collotti, 'Introduzione', in Costantino Di Sante, ed., I campi di concentramento in Italia (Milan, 2001), pp. 9–10.

[42] On the current state of historiography on the Italians' Balkan war, see Brunello Mantelli, 'Die Italiener auf dem Balkan, 1941–43', in C. Dipper et al., eds, Europaische Sozialgeschichte. Festschrift fur Wolfgang Schieder zum 65. Geburtstag (Berlin, 2000), pp. 57–74; but see also the essays in Di Sante, ed., I campi di concentramento in Italia, and James Walston, 'History and Memory of the Italian Concentration Camps', Historical Journal, 40, 1 (1997), pp. 169–83. These, and other historiographical silences, have meant that the Italian case is often excluded from comparative examinations of police states, so that Sheila Fitzpatrick and Robert Gellately's otherwise valuable edited volume on informing and denunciation contained essays on Stalinism, Nazism, and the French Revolution but none on Fascism. See Accusatory Practices (Chicago, IL, 1997). The first books on informers and denunciation appeared only in 1999–2001: see Mimmo Franzinelli, I tentacoli dell'Ovra: agenti, collaboratori e vittime della polizia politica Fascista (Turin, 1999), and his Delatori, spie e confidenti anomini: l'arme segreti del regime Fascista (Milan, 2001). These denials and obfuscations by Italian government institutions include the creation of a phantom commission for the investigation of Italian war criminals whose purpose was to stall their extradition; the jailing of the filmmakers Guido Aristarco and Renzo Renzi on charges of treason in the early 1950s for having made a film on the Italian occupation of Greece; official denials that gas was used during the conquest and rule of the Italian colony of Ethiopia, which were reversed only in 1995; and an Allied refusal, which continues to this day, to comply with international weapons treaties by revealing the locations of stockpiles of chemical weapons from the Ethiopian war. An overview of these official manipulations is given in Rory Carroll, 'Italy's Bloody Secret', Guardian (25 June 2001).

[43] An informative rather than critical publication edited by Carlo Spagnolo, Segreti personali e segreti di Stato. Privacy, archive e ricerca storica (Florence, 2001), compares current Italian and other European archival norms and regulations. The scandal that ensued in 1999 when 'new' archival documents brought to light the leftist writer Ignazio Silone's double life as a Fascist spy was one of several recent historical 'cases' that revealed the practices of Italian archival officials (acting on their own or on orders from higher state authorities) of removing sensitive material from public domain files. In this case a Central State Archives functionary had removed the compromising documents from the files and kept them from public access for over ten years; surprisingly, debates focused less on the ethics and politics of his actions than his decision to make the documents public at that time.

[44] See Jacques Derrida, Archive Fever: A Freudian Impression, trans. Eric Prenowitz (Chicago, IL, 1996), p. 2; see also Sonia Combes, Archives interdites: Les peurs françaises face a l'histoire contemporaine (Paris, 1994).

[45] The phrase 'black holes' is taken from Carlo Spartaco Capogreco, 'Internamento e deportazione dei civili jugoslavi', in Di Sante, ed., I campi di concentamento in Italia, p. 135

[46] See the oral histories conducted by Costantino Di Sante, 'I campi di concentramento in Abruzzo', in I campi di concentramento, p. 205, and Angelo Bendotti, '"Ho fatto la Grecia, l'Albania, la Jugoslavia ..." Il disagio della memoria', in Bruno Micheletti, ed., Italia in guerra (Brescia, 1992), pp. 964–79. Quotation is from Ernesto Galli della Loggia, 'Criminali di guerra nostrani', Corriere della Sera, 'Sette' Magazine, 28 June 2001.

[47] On this issue see Omer Bartov, Murder in Our Midst: The Holocaust, Industrial Killing, and Representation (New York, 1996), esp p 40

[48] Mariuccia Salvati, 'Hannah Arendt e la storia del Novecento', in Flores, ed., Nazismo, Fascismo, Communismo, p. 241.

10

On the Moral Blindness of Communism

Steven Lukes

Among the questions which The Black Book of Communism poses is one as old as Communism itself. It is a question that has been addressed from the beginning by its enemies and by its friends and, from within, by an unending succession of heretics and renegades, each reacting, as the saying goes, to his or her own Kronstadt. (These are, of course, not mutually exclusive categories; as is shown by the perennial figure of the ex-Communist anti-Communist). All have asked the same question. What was the source of the disaster? Just where did it all go wrong?

They have offered different kinds of answer, which range from the maximally generic to the narrowly specific. The generic answers mostly come from Communism's enemies – reactionaries, conservatives, various kinds of liberals, and all those who came to be called Cold War thinkers. In countless different versions they claimed that the root of the catastrophe was (to cite only a few examples): the very legacy of the Enlightenment, including the idea of progress; 'rationalism in politics'; utopianism; the Promethean myth; political messianism (Talmon); the belief that the course of history was scientifically knowable and its future predictable (Popper's idiosyncratically named 'historicism'); the 'fatal conceit' that economic and social life could be brought under collective, rational control (Hayek); a scientistic, ersatz religion based on the philosophical illusion of 'the idea of perfect unity' to which genuine religion is an antidote (Kolakowski); or 'monism' (Berlin), 'the belief that some single formula can in principle be found whereby all the diverse ends of men can be harmoniously realized'.[1]

Different thinkers in the Western tradition were variously seen as sowers of the seeds of eventual destruction: Plato and the Neo-Platonists, Rousseau, Hegel of course, and even the allegedly naively well-intentioned thinkers of the Enlightenment. On all such accounts, Marxism-Leninism-Stalinism was viewed as the faithful historical implementation of one or another intellectual error responsible, in Berlin's words, 'for the slaughter of individuals on the altars of the great historical ideals – justice or progress or the happiness of future generations, or the sacred mission of emancipation of a nation or race or class, or even liberty itself, which demands the sacrifice of individuals for the freedom of society'.[2] According to this family of answers to the initial question, in short, some attractive and plausible way of thinking has led to 'absurdities in theory and barbarous consequences in practice'[3] – to the barbarity and mass-slaughter of twentieth-century totalitarianism in its Communist variant.

Communism's disillusioned friends offered other diagnoses. From the Bolshevik Revolution onwards the disease was not seen as congenital but as contracted at a later stage – for the Mensheviks, Kautsky and Rosa Luxemburg with Leninism, for Trotsky and his various followers with Stalinism. The canker was now not the idea but its implementation: in the wrong place at the wrong time, or in the wrong way – through a minority dictatorship conducting a civil war against the majority (Kautsky), proclaiming socialism by decree and eliminating freedom of thought (Luxemburg), through a terroristic oligarchy, substituting the Party for the people, its leaders for the Party, and the Supreme Leader for the leaders (Trotsky). Indeed, Trotsky and the Trotskyites were always notably forthright about Stalinism's crimes and falsifications, however illusory their unshakable belief that the Revolution had been 'betrayed' and remained 'unfinished'.

As for the heretics and renegades, mostly in the West, their answers were many and various, colored in each case by personal experience, sometimes rendered the more vivid in powerful confessional writing characterizing the 'god that failed', though after 1956, and definitely after 1968, the supply of 'true believers' and thus of apostasy ran dry. From such writings one can learn much about the distinctive appeal of the combination of Marxist belief and Communist commitment, above all under conditions of real danger where anti-Fascism rightly seemed to have an overwhelming priority. It was a winning combination that simultaneously offered explanation, justification and practical instructions: an elaborate but readily intelligible cognitive map of the entire social universe and indeed of the whole span of human history that presupposed a universalistic picture of human liberation and entailed a clear-cut imperative of collective action, a package bound together by a doctrine of the indissoluble unity of theory and practice. No attempt to answer the question at hand can neglect to consider the powerful motivational force of such a comprehensive system, above all in a context of social and economic crisis and, for a significant time, impending military defeat, which it explained and from which it promised a release. There were many diverse reasons for the loss of faith, but chief among them was an ever-more pervasive awareness of the mounting disasters of 'actually existing socialism'.

In addition to this there are substantial bodies of different kinds of literature addressing these disasters and reflecting on their causes. Prominent intellectuals, from Bertrand Russell and Tomas Masaryk to Sidney Hook and Raymond Aron, faced them from the beginning (Russell's The Theory and Practice of Bolshevism dates from 1921 and Masaryk's The Making of a State from 1927). After World War II there were abundant writings on 'totalitarianism', beginning with Hannah Arendt's classic work. There were numerous academic studies by political scientists and historians of the Soviet system (Merle Fainsod, Brzezzinsi, Huntington, Leonard Shapiro, Adam Ulam and many others) and of other Communist systems, some of the more critical, indeed, being Marxist or Marxian in inspiration (Barrington Moore, Marcuse), not to mention specific studies of the disasters themselves, such as Robert Conquest's The Great Terror. And then, of course, there was an ever-increasing flow of compelling writings of all kinds from within the disaster area (Pasternak, Mandelstam, Solzhenitsyn, of course, and countless others from Russia and elsewhere) circulating as samizdat within and readily translated abroad.

Given all of this, how can Stephane Courtois write, in his Introduction, that 'scholars have neglected the crimes committed by the Communists', that the 'revelations' concerning these 'cause barely a stir', and of a 'silence born of cowardliness or indifference' which is 'the most tenacious in western societies [sic!] whenever the phenomenon of Communism came under the microscope'? And does he really believe that 'Communism is again re-asserting itself – in Eastern Europe and Russia'?[4] Doubtless John Torpey is right to attribute such eccentric judgements to the 'persistent provincialism of the French intellectual scene'.[5] The old story of Communism's long-lasting hold over French intellectuals is not uninteresting and perhaps deserving of repeated study but it is, after all, a local problem and one that is strictly irrelevant to the question with which I began and with which The Black Book's chief editor is concerned. Yet the rhetorical strategy of The Black Book, and more particularly of that editor, is that of a wake-up call, to break the supposed silence and 'cause a stir' (in this it succeeded) by amassing all the currently available evidence of Communism's crimes within two covers. Comparison with the atrocities of Nazism makes obvious sense in the light of that rhetorical purpose. To juxtapose mega-death counts, to write that 'the genocide of a "class" may well be tantamount to the genocide of a "race"'[6] and suggest that the starvation of a Ukrainian kulak child is 'equal to' the starvation of a Jewish child in the Warsaw ghetto, and to point to the 'animalization' of the adversary common to both Nazis and Communists is a good way to challenge, or perhaps pillory, any surviving leftists who are still able to believe that there are 'no enemies on the left' at a time when 'the Holocaust' has come to dominate, even obsess, the collective memory of the twentieth century. But are there really any such leftists left?

And were they ever, inside and outside France, so uniformly cowardly and indifferent towards, and willingly ignorant about, Communist crimes? Martin Malia, author of the Foreword to the US edition of the Black Book, endorses this suggestion, arguing that in the twentieth century 'morality is not primarily a matter of eternal verities or transcendental imperatives', but is 'above all a matter of political allegiances. That is, it is a matter of left versus right ...'.[7] In other words, Malia is here suggesting that the left, committed to 'the priority of compassionate egalitarianism', is inherently blind to the consequences of the Communist project. Indeed, he claims, 'we will always encounter a double standard as long as there exists a left and a right'. But this is a polemically driven travesty, disappointing in a historian who (rightly) commends this book for its reliance on the available evidence. It is denunciatory ideological talk, echoing the very practice of branding a group seen as an enemy that Courtois identifies as a distinguishing Communist trait. Pro-Sovietism and fellow-traveling were indubitably part of the story of the twentieth-century left in most places but so, in most places, were principled opposition to and struggle against Communism in all its forms, from Kautsky (explicitly quoted to this effect by Courtois) onwards. Malia here diverges from his French colleague by effectively defining the left as the political tendency immune to the book's message.

But Courtois's rhetorical strategy does not, in any case, assist his explanatory aim. Indeed, it probably obstructs it. Courtois concludes his Introduction by asking what he describes as 'the essential question, "Why?"' Why did Lenin, Trotsky, Stalin, and others believe it was necessary to exterminate all those whom they had branded as 'enemies?' What made them imagine they could violate one of the basic tenets of civilization, 'Thou shalt not kill'?[8] It is not at all clear how the task of answering this question is furthered by Nazi–Communist comparisons. It is, of course, a general truth that anything can be compared with anything else; any particular comparison is to be justified by its likely explanatory pay-off. There are, undoubtedly, many illuminating parallels to be explored in studying, for example, the organization of prison camps or the effects of propaganda and, in general, the dynamics of terror. But Courtois's 'Why' is a question about the specificity of Communism, each national variant of which, he plausibly writes, 'has been linked by an umbilical cord to the Soviet womb' – or (making the point even more clearly) 'by a sort of genetic code of Communism' to 'the pattern elaborated in Moscow in November 1917'.[9] So we do not want to know what was common to the two cases which subverted or precluded 'respect for the rules of a representative democracy and, above all, respect for life and human dignity'.[10] Rather we want to know what it was about Communism that had these momentous consequences.

Actually, the question 'Why?' – the ambitiously promissory title of Courtois's concluding chapter to The Black Book – is, in this domain, a question that is, to put it mildly, far from simple. At its least simple it could be interpreted as an expression of incomprehension at the depth and scale of human cruelty – an incomprehension that derives mostly from our general assumption, from which it is hard to escape, that humans are mostly, at some level and to some degree, humane, that they possess a range of human traits, including sympathy, pity and compassion, which must, we suppose, render such things impossible. It was, perhaps, in this sense that Primo Levi addressed the question 'Why?' to a camp guard at Auschwitz and received the chilling answer 'Hier ist kein warum' ('Here there is no why').[11] And it is in response to this sense of 'Why?' that Christopher Browning concludes his remarkable book Ordinary Men: Reserve Police Battalion 101 and the Final Solution in Poland, after hazarding several individually and jointly plausible explanations of what facilitated ordinary men's repeated participation and complicity in extreme atrocities, with the telling observation that one comes away from the story 'with great unease'.[12] For what none of these explanations can approach is an answer to the question: how could such things be possible?

But let us take Courtois's 'Why?' in the simplest sense that he himself specifies: why did the Communist leaders believe it necessary to exterminate all those whom they had branded as 'enemies'? He goes on to amplify and extend his understanding of this 'fundamental question':

> Why did modern Communism, when it appeared in 1917, almost immediately turn into a system of bloody dictatorship and into a criminal regime? Was it really the case that its aims could be attained only through such extreme violence? How can one explain how these crimes came to be thought of as part of normal procedure and remained such for so many decades?[13]

How far does he, together with his fellow contributors, take us in answering this set of questions? The answer must, I fear, be: not far at all. Thus we are reminded of the tradition of revolutionary violence stemming from the Terror during the French Revolution, of the Russian culture of violence from above and below, and of the violence of World War I and its postwar impact; of the Leninist innovatory conception of the revolutionary party and illusory hope of imminent world revolution; of the Bolsheviks' appeal to a 'scientific' warrant for their faith, their manipulation of language and their rejection of representative democracy in favor of a systemic war mentality; of the next stage of systematic and contagious terror under Stalin, with the executioners becoming victims, first criminalizing, then excluding, and then exterminating the enemy (though in Asia there was a distinctive belief in 're-education'); and of the de-humanizing, sometimes 'animalizing', rhetoric employed. It would, of course, be absurd to expect originality here. There is no particular reason to suppose that the composite explanandum of The Black Book, gathering together inventories of Communism's crimes across the globe, is likely to generate some hitherto unsuspected explanans. But it might perhaps have generated some fresh or at least structured synthesis of the familiar factors heretofore listed, yielding, for instance, some insights into the iterative logic of revolution and counter-revolution, as, for example, in Arno Mayer's recent book, The Furies: Violence and Terror in French and Russian Revolutions.[14]

Instead, what we get is an encyclopedia of terror, as indicated by crimes against civilians. Focusing explicitly on these, The Black Book provides a comprehensive and, it would seem, reliable catalogue, given presently available sources, of their extent, nature and incidence. We learn, in short, 'how many', 'how', 'when' and 'where'. It is a devastating record of human disaster, all the more effective and affecting when it is dryly factual and statistical, avoiding, in Primo Levi's phrase, 'the lamenting tones of the victim' and 'the irate voice of someone who seeks revenge'.[15] In this significant respect the bulk of the book contrasts favorably with the moralizing tones of its Introduction and Conclusion and, in particular, its Foreword, in which Malia deplores a 'fact-for-fact's-sake approach' and informs us that moral judgment is 'inseparable from any real understanding of the past – indeed, inseparable from being human'.[16]

But the 'Why?' will not go away. Let us recall Courtois's first formulation of its import: why did the Communist leaders 'believe it necessary to exterminate all those whom they had branded as "enemies"'? Clearly, any attempt at answering this must point in several directions: to a study of their beliefs, their origins, content and structure, their inculcation and transmission within the Communist movements and parties, through texts, but also party schools, symbolism and ritual, and, generally, an examination of Communist political culture; but also to a study of the constraints and opportunities they faced, in revolutionary, post-revolutionary and non-revolutionary situations. To what extent, we would need to know, were their beliefs about what was necessary, given their goals, justified? Were there alternative paths of Communist development that were never taken? How did their beliefs interact with their constraints and opportunities? Such historical (including counterfactual-historical) questions remain alive and open; and, although The Black Book makes no progress in answering them, its sheer accumulation of factual material should be indispensable to future attempts to do so.

There is, however, a less ambitious version of the 'Why?' on which something even now can, perhaps, usefully be said. Courtois asks why the Communist leaders believed it 'necessary to exterminate all those whom they had branded as enemies'. But suppose we replace 'necessary' here with 'possible'. Are there features of their system of beliefs that can account for their lack of moral restraint? This seems an appropriate question to ask in the context of this book. Did the Communist leaders have beliefs that allowed them to take human rights seriously?

Both Malia and Courtois refer to Marx's picture of the Communist future as latent in the womb of the capitalist present, a picture tellingly expressed in the metaphor of the revolutionary as midwife. It was a disastrous picture, absolving both the theorists and the practitioners of revolution from both moral deliberation and institutional planning, since, as Thomas Nagel has well put it, 'midwives do not have to design the babies they deliver'[17] (they do not normally use violence either, but here, it seems, the metaphor was subject to interpretation).

The metaphor is revealing but it does not reveal what was so powerfully attractive and inspiring about Marx's vision as transmitted to his successors. This is best captured by another metaphor, that of 'emancipation'. Like the midwife metaphor, it dispenses the revolutionary from moral judgment (since there is no need to ask whether slavery is to be condemned or criticized). But it also suggests, through a series of extreme contrasts, a compelling vision of the future of mankind, the End, not of History, but of Pre-History. For what Marxism, and subsequently Communism in all its variants, promised was liberation, not only from the wage slavery of capitalism, but from those very conditions of human life that render rights in general, and human rights in particular, necessary. Briefly (and without entering into various academic controversies about how to analyze rights), we may say that human beings need rights to protect their central and basic interests in the face of threatening existential conditions that are to be found in all hitherto existing societies. Two of these were identified by David Hume as what rendered justice necessary: selfishness and scarcity or, as Hume put it, the 'confin'd generosity of man, along with the scanty provision nature has made for his wants'.[18] Both of these need some elaboration and justification but, basically, the idea in each case is clear. Being selfish, or at least not perfect altruists, individuals and groups pursue their partial and particular interests, which sometimes get in the way of others who need protection from such invasions. As for scarcity, not all good things can be had by all and, indeed, some are inherently scarce (such as time and positional goods), and so principles are needed to specify who is entitled to what. Two further existential conditions can be added to these: the plurality of values and imperfect rationality. Here too, elaboration and specification are needed but the central idea is, once more, in each case clear. Plural values mean that human ends and conceptions of what is valuable in life are irreducibly diverse and often incompatible, and so people need protection to be able to pursue their own course: the idea that

160

conflicting values can be rendered harmonious is an illusion and any attempt to do so can result only in tyranny. And humans are imperfectly rational because their capacity to absorb and control information and to predict and control their environment, natural and social, has significant limits (though there are of course different views about where these lie); so social and individual lives need protection against illusory and misguided attempts to control them on the basis of knowledge that is inherently unattainable. Let us call these four conditions 'conditions of morality' (for they are at least conditions for that part of morality occupied by ideas of human rights).

The promise of Marxism was precisely to free humankind from these conditions of morality: from scarcity (through unlimited development of the forces of production, especially once released from the fetters of capitalist relations of production); from the selfishness or partiality of conflicting individuals and groups (which Marx explained as deriving from class interests and class conflict); from non-convergent and incompatible values (tied to religious or cultural differences that would wither away, since these too were linked to class); and from the anarchy and opacity of a world not subject to collective human control (as opposed to a future transparent world of 'associated producers' in full control of their natural and social environment). Emancipation, in short, was to be emancipation from the conditions that rendered human beings' interests precarious and in need of the guarantees that constitute rights and human rights in particular. Communism was the promise of a world beyond justice and rights, in which individuals would flourish, free from alienation and exploitation, in a unified society of abundance, free of religious and cultural particularity and conflict and in full, transparent control of their economic and political life.

These, I believe, are parametric features of the structure of Marxist thinking, fully present and articulated in the classic texts of Marx and Engels and reproduced throughout the canon. They were constitutive of the tradition, which was, of course, highly bibliocentric, and so were taught in Party schools everywhere that Communist culture was transmitted. Taken together they tend to subvert all talk of morality and concern with equal human dignity or with human rights. (And throughout their writings Marx and Engels were scornful of such talk, as indeed were virtually all the mainstream Marxist thinkers after them.[19]) For if you really believed that history offers a route to a world in which scarcity, selfishness, particularistic narrowness and subjection to an economic system beyond political control would wither away, why would you flinch from whatever you thought necessary to bring it about? In this respect, one could say, Marxism offered the emancipatory vision of a world in which the principles that protect human beings from one another would no longer be needed. How could it then be justifiable to respect and act on those principles if doing so would block and even delay the advent of such a world? As Bertolt Brecht asked, 'If at last you could change the world, what / Could make you too good to do so?'[20] If emancipation required what Nicholas Werth calls 'an implacable class war pushed to its extreme',[21] why would you not fight it?

We should probably assume (though we can never know for sure) that at least sometimes Communist leaders believed themselves to be facing just this choice. Assuming this would make non-cynical sense of two passages quoted by Courtois. The first is from Isaac Sternberg, a left Socialist Revolutionary allied with the Bolsheviks:

> Old-fashioned violence is merely a protection against slavery, while the new violence is the painful path towards emancipation ... That is what should be decisive in our choice. We should take violence into our own hands to be sure that we bring about the end of violence.[22]

The second passage is from Gorky describing Lenin:

> ... he told me once as he was stroking some children, 'Their lives will be better than ours: they will be spared many of the things we have been forced to live through. Their lives will be less cruel.' He stared off into the distance, and added dreamily, 'Mind you, I don't envy them. Our generation will have carried out a task of tremendous historical importance. The cruelty of our lives, imposed by circumstance, will be understood and pardoned. Everything will be understood, everything.'[23]

And Brecht voiced the same sentiment thus:

> You who will emerge from the flood
> In which we have gone under
> Remember
> When you speak of our failings
> The dark time too
> Which you have escaped.[24]

But what of Communism's 'ordinary men'? How did the belief structure I have identified influence them? I conclude these observations by quoting at some length the precious testimony of Lev Kopelev, on whom Rubin, the staunchly Communist linguist in Solzhenitsyn's The First Circle, was modeled:

162

With the rest of my generation I firmly believed that the ends justified the means. Our great goal was the universal triumph of Communism, and for the sake of that goal everything was permissible – to lie, to steal, to destroy hundreds of thousands and even millions of people, all those who were hindering our work or could hinder it, everyone who stood in the way. And to hesitate or doubt about all this was to give in to 'intellectual squeamishness' and 'stupid liberalism', the attributes of people who 'could not see the forest for the trees'.

That was how I had reasoned, and everyone like me, even when I did have my doubts, when I believed what Trotsky and Bukharin were saying, when I saw what 'total collectivization' meant – how they 'kulakized' and 'dekulakized', how mercilessly they stripped the peasants in the winter of 1932–3. I took part in this myself, scouring the countryside, searching for hidden grain, testing the earth with an iron rod for loose spots that might lead to buried grain. With the others, I emptied out the old folks' storage chests, stopping my ears to the children's crying and the women's wails. For I was convinced that I was accomplishing the great and necessary transformation of the countryside; that in the days to come the people who lived there would be better off for it; that their distress and suffering were a result of their own ignorance or the machinations of the class enemy; that those who sent me – and I myself – knew better than the peasants how they should live, what they should sow and when they should plough.

In the terrible spring of 1933 I saw people dying from hunger. I saw women and children with distended bellies, turning blue, still breathing but with vacant, lifeless eyes. And corpses – corpses in ragged sheepskin coats and cheap felt boots; corpses in peasant huts, in the melting snow of the old Vologda, under the bridges of Kharkov ... I saw all this and did not go out of my mind or commit suicide. Nor did I curse those who had sent me to take away the peasants' grain in the winter, and in the spring to persuade the barely walking, skeleton-thin or sickly-swollen people to go into the fields in order to 'fulfill the Bolshevik sowing plan in shock-worker style'.

Nor did I lose my faith. As before, I believed because I wanted to believe. Thus from time immemorial men had believed when possessed by a desire to serve powers and values above and beyond humanity: gods, emperors, states; ideals of virtue, freedom, nation, race, class, party ...

Any single-minded attempt to realize these ideals exacts its toll of human sacrifice. In the name of the noblest visions promising eternal happiness to their descendants, such men bring merciless ruin on their contemporaries. Bestowing paradise on the dead, they maim and destroy the living. They become unprincipled liars and unrelenting executioners, all the while seeing themselves as virtuous and honourable militants – convinced that if they are forced into villainy, it is for the sake of future good, and that if they have to lie, it is in the name of eternal truths.

Und willst du nicht mein Bruder sein
So schlag ich dir dein Schadel ein.
(and if you won't be my brother
I'll crack your skull open),

they sing in a Landsknecht song.

That was how we thought and acted – we, the fanatical disciples of the all-saving ideals of Communism. When we saw the base and cruel acts that were committed in the name of our exalted notions of good, and we ourselves took part in those actions, what we feared most was to lose our heads, fall into doubt or heresy and forfeit our unbounded faith.

I was appalled by what I saw in the 1930s and was overcome by depression. But I would still my doubts the way I had learned to: 'we made a mistake', 'we went too far', 'we did not take into consideration', 'the logic of the class struggle', 'objective historical need', 'using barbaric means to combat barbarism ...'

Good and evil, humanity and inhumanity – these seemed empty abstractions. I did not trouble myself with why 'humanity' should be abstract but 'historical necessity' and 'class consciousness' should be concrete. The concepts of conscience, honour, humaneness we dismissed as idealistic prejudices, 'intellectual' or 'bourgeois' and, hence, perverse.[25]

So, how to answer the question with which I began? Obviously, there is no one answer. But if we interpret the question to be asking whether there were specific beliefs central to the culture of Communism everywhere that made its crimes against humanity possible, then the answer has to be affirmative. The defect in question, causing moral blindness on a heroic scale, was congenital.

NOTES

[1] Isaiah Berlin, Four Essays on Liberty (London: Oxford University Press, 1969), p. 169.
[2] Ibid., p. 167.
[3] Ibid., p. lvi.
[4] Stephane Courtois et al., The Black Book of Communism: Crimes, Terror, Repression (Cambridge, MA: Harvard University Press, 1999), pp. 17, 26, 28.

5   John Torpey, Typescript, p. 3.
6   Courtois et al., The Black Book, p. 9.
7   Ibid., pp. xvi, xvii, xx.
8   Ibid., p. 31.
9   Ibid., pp. 28, 754.
10 Ibid., p. 30.
11 Primo Levi, If This is a Man and The Truce (London: Abacus edition, Sphere Books, 1987), p. 35.
12 Christopher Browning, Ordinary Men, Reserve Battalion 101 and the Final Solution in Poland (New York: HarperCollins, 1992), p. 188.
13 Courtois et al., The Black Book, p. 727.
14 Arno Mayer, The Furies: Violence and Terror in French and Russian Revolutions (Princeton, NJ: Princeton University Press, 2000).
15 Levi, If This is a Man and The Truce, p. 382.
16 Courtois et al., The Black Book, p. xvi.
17 Thomas Nagel, 'Getting Personal', review of G.A. Cohen, If You're an Egalitarian, How Come You're so Rich? (Cambridge, MA: Harvard University Press, 2000), Times Literary Supplement, 23 June 2000, p. 6. Cohen's book discusses the 'midwife' metaphor.
18 David Hume, A Treatise of Human Nature (Oxford: Clarendon Press, 1888; reprinted 1951), p. 495.
19 For numerous examples, see Steven Lukes, Marxism and Morality (Oxford and New York: Oxford University Press, 1985), in which the foregoing argument is spelt out at greater length. See also 'Can a Marxist believe in Human Rights?', in Steven Lakes, Moral Conflict and Politics (Oxford: Clarendon Press, 1991).
20 Bertolt Brecht, The Measures Taken and Other Lehrstucke (London: Eyre Methuen, 1977), p. 25.
21 Courtois et al., The Black Book, p. 75.
22 Ibid., p. 744.
23 Ibid., p. 756.
24 Bertolt Brecht, 'To Those Born Later', in Bertolt Brecht, Poems 1913–1956 (London: Methuen, 1956), p. 319.
25 Lev Kopelev, No Jail for Thought (Harmondsworth: Penguin edition, 1979), pp. 32–4.

Part III

Legacies

11

Totalitarian Attempts, Anti-Totalitarian Networks: Thoughts on the Taboo of Comparison

Ulrike Ackermann

'In the 1950s and the early 1960s', wrote Milan Kundera in his novel Incomprehension,

> the immigrant who had left his Communist country for good found little compassion in Paris. Back then the French believed that Fascism had been by far the greatest evil ... It was only by the end of the 1960s and in the course of the 1970s that the French began to think of Communism as another evil. Still, it was considered the lesser evil, so to say, Evil Number Two. About that time, in 1969, Irina [the protagonist in the novel] and her husband immigrated to Paris from Prague. It did not take them long to understand that in comparison to Evil Number One the catastrophe that had befallen their country was not bloody enough to impress their new friends.[1]

In this short paragraph, Kundera, a great writer and an émigré himself, captured in a nutshell the problem of the differing assessments of the crimes of Nazism, Fascism and Communism. One needs only to recall that it was in the mid-1950s when Jean-Paul Sartre confronted Albert Camus on the issue of the existence and implications of the Soviet Gulag camp system. 'Like you, I find these camps unacceptable', wrote Sartre. 'But I find just as unacceptable the use to which the bourgeois press is putting them.'[2]

Sartre's injunction strikes me as paradigmatic of the mental attitude that informed a good deal of the intellectual debates in France and Germany from the end of World War II to the present: the concept of anti-anti-Communism. This attitude is responsible for engendering the taboo to the comparison of Nazism, Fascism and Communism. It impeded the development of theoretical approaches to totalitarianism. A unified tack on the problem appeared suspicious, for it would question the magnitude of Nazi crimes and the exceptionality of Auschwitz. What ensued, in the definition of the French historian Alain Besançon, was 'a hypermnesia of Nazism and amnesia of Communism'.[3] It seems to me that a comparative analysis of the French and German debates on totalitarianism in recent decades would allow us to track down the resistance to compare and theorize to liberal-leftist intellectual quarters.

The twentieth century came to a close with a war in which the West justified its military intervention in foreign affairs with the defense of democracy and human rights. Not surprisingly, the intellectual debates over the war in former Yugoslavia (Kosovo) climaxed in a confrontation about the definition of the old and new forms of totalitarian rule. The debates gave rise to references to Hitler and Stalin, to Munich 1938, to the Civil War in Spain, and issued forth in a dispute that, in a sense, had already taken place back in the 1950s. Tragically, the debates gained a new legitimacy after the events of 11 September 2001. The terrorist attacks in New York and Washington opened a war on the open society, on democracy and freedom. It will not be inappropriate to qualify these attacks as a totalitarian challenge that caught the West by surprise and left it speechless. Only gradually, as the numbness went away, the debates over the meaning of war and peace, over the ways this outburst of totalitarianism should be confronted began in earnest.

Against this background, it makes sense to revisit the intellectual debates in the early 1950s. Back then, intellectuals from Europe and the USA came together in a struggle for democracy and human rights, a struggle that, if necessary, was to be waged with armed force. A forum to publicize their concerns was devised, a Congress for Cultural Freedom. They worked out a network, which, in time, contributed to the fall of Communism in 1989. Their activities were quite effective, so effective in fact as to pose the question of why they have been neglected in the discussions on the reaction to totalitarianism. Was it because these intellectuals were both anti-Fascists and anti-Communists? Was it because they were financed by the US government? Or was it because while campaigning for a united Europe long before 1989, they at the same time worked to undermine the traditional ideological status quo? These questions are worth asking, given the impressive presence of the Congress. It met for the first time in West Berlin on 26 June 1950, with a spectacular opening at Titania Palace, and was active until well into the 1970s. In all aspects, it was an extraordinary enterprise of committed intellectuals. It reflected both the exuberance and the apprehension of the intellectual establishment of postwar Europe. Fascism and Nazism had been overcome, but Stalin had re-drawn the political map of Europe and was expanding his influence through the so-called 'people's democracies' in eastern Europe. The Stalinist terror within the Soviet Union belied the image of a great champion for peace that the great power had built for itself through the victory over Nazism.

Berlin, then divided between an Eastern and a Western sector, was a condensed version of the new order brokered at Yalta. The blockade of the city in 1948 gave the world a foretaste of the forthcoming Cold War. It was not by accident that Berlin was chosen to host the Congress for Cultural Freedom. The organizers were the author Arthur Koestler and the American journalist Melvin Lasky, who belonged to the independent New York leftists. The call for the Congress was well received in the city, where the feeling of being a 'frontier town' had set in and there was wide approval for the formation of the West German state. The mayor, Ernst Reuter, opened the Congress. The atmosphere became tense right from the beginning. As speakers were addressing the more than 1,800 delegates from all over the world, news came in that North Korean troops had just invaded South Korean territory. The Cold War had suddenly heated up. More than 15,000 Berliners gathered at the Sommergarten during the concluding ceremony to listen to the farewell addresses. Among the speakers were Eugen Kogon, the chairman of the German section of the Movement for Europe, David Rousset, Ignazio Silone, Carlo Schmidt and Irving Brown. All the speakers called for a free and united Europe. Kogon closed the Congress with the dramatic slogan, 'Friends, freedom is on the offensive!'

This anti-Fascist and anti-Communist intellectual forum provoked angry outbursts in both Moscow and East Berlin. US financial support for the Congress was described as 'the Wall Street specter's attempt to turn the tables on us'. Pravda, the newspaper of the Communist Party of the Soviet Union, labeled the Congress 'a gathering of war-mongers'. The accusations were quite unrestrained, for they were aimed at deserters of the Communist cause, those 'renegades' who had turned their pens against their ideal. For decades, the Soviet regime had sponsored and orchestrated peace and writers' 'congresses' under Communist auspices. Now the free artists, writers and scholars were fighting back with a Congress of their own. Little wonder Moscow was outraged. The intellectuals who kept the Congress going had all experienced the totalitarian regimes of the twentieth century, Nazism, Fascism and Communism, first-hand. In their literary, scholarly and public activity they drew a clear line between these experiences as a whole and their subsequent lives. Their cooperation in the Congress was informed by their anti-Communist and anti-Fascist principles. The anti-totalitarian consensus united them for the common goal. Before the Congress's first session closed in 1950, it assessed the conditions in the Soviet Union and east-central Europe and sent out a 'Message for the intellectuals in the East'. 'It is clear', asserted the message, that the greatest contemporary conflict is not a conflict between the West and the East. It is the conflict between tyrants and the people who yearn for their freedom. Hereby we all ensure all those people who stand for their freedom and fight against oppression of our moral solidarity and material support. We express our passionate hope that they all will be free soon and will be able to partake of our common intellectual heritage.

As a result of the founding Congress in Berlin, during the 1950s–1970s there formed a network of American and European intellectuals, whose activity has remained practically unnoticed. Among them were Raymond Aron, Albert Camus, Alexander Weißberg-Cibulsky, George Orwell, Daniel Bell, Manès Sperber, Czeslaw Milosz, Leszek Kolakowski, François Fejtö, David Rousset, François Furet, Eugen Kogon and Margarete Buber-Neumann, to name but a few. The French writer and journalist David Rousset, a former Trotskyite, joined the French Resistance, fell in the hands of Gestapo and was tortured and sent to Buchenwald. He published his sufferings in L'Univers concentrationnaire,[4] which received the Renaudot literary award. He then led a campaign, supported by former concentration-camp inmates, for the abolition of all camps world-wide. On 12 November 1949, Figaro Littéraire published Rousset's 'Appeal to the Inmates of the Nazi Camps: Help the Inmates in Soviet Camps!' as its title-page headline. The publication led to acrimonious rebukes from Communists in France and abroad and sharp attacks from leftist Parisian intellectuals. The precursor of this exemplary attempt to put Nazism and Communism on the same plane of comparison was the so-called 'Kravchenko trial', which took place in Paris in 1949. Kravchenko, a Russian immigrant, had been a high-ranking Soviet official who defected to the West and later published a book about the Stalinist dictatorship, I Chose Freedom.[5] The book sparked an ideological controversy about the existence of civil rights in the Soviet Union. The trial was triggered by the challenge to the authenticity of the facts Kravchenko revealed. At the trial, Margarete Buber-Neumann appeared as a witness for Kravchenko. She had been among the active supporters of Rousset's appeal to help the Soviet camp inmates. On 25 February 1950, Figaro Littéraire published her article, 'An Inquiry into the Soviet Concentration Camps: Who is Worse, Satan or Beelzebub?', wherein she recounted her double sufferings, as both an inmate in a Nazi camp and a prisoner in a Soviet camp. Her political autobiography, A Prisoner of Stalin and Hitler, which appeared in 1948, was a sensation.[6] She had spent two years in Siberia and then, in 1940, after the Stalin–Hitler Pact, was delivered into the hands of the Gestapo, who sent her to the female camp in Ravensbrück for another five years.

The very title of Buber-Neumann's book and her experiences ran against the conventional wisdom underlying the political division which emerged during World War II and held after the war. The leftists found it provocative. To them Nazi crimes were beyond any comparison. Their position was to keep them that way by accusing those who spoke of Stalin's crimes of anti-Communism – thus diminishing the value of the evidence – or of outright fabrication of the facts about the Soviet camps. The right-wing ideologues sought, claimed the leftists, to relativize Nazi crimes with reference to Stalin's reign of terror. A model exponent of this position in the 1950s was Jean-Paul Sartre, whose open letter to Camus has already been mentioned.

The cooperative effort of German and French intellectuals to counter such attitudes, exemplified by the fellow camp inmates Buber-Neumann and Rousset, was taken up in Berlin as well. The Executive Committee of the Congress for Cultural Freedom opened branches in Paris and Rome. The Secretariat of the International Executive Committee was based in Paris, on Boulevard Haussmann. Its task was to organize conferences and found new periodicals – besides Monat, which Melvin Lasky had been publishing regularly since 1948. In 1951, François Bondy began publication of a French version of Monat, the magazine Preuves. The close cooperation between the two editors-in-chief, Lasky and Bondy, marked an innovative German–French dimension of the intellectual debate about the future of Europe. Moreover, Bondy was instrumental in the effort to bring together Eastern and Western intellectuals in defiance of the Iron Curtain long before 1989. He involved in the activity of the Congress two prominent Polish émigré writers, Czeslaw Milosz and Konstanty Jelenski, who published a Polish magazine in Paris, Kultura. It was the Executive Committee of the Congress which extended a very special and symbolically significant welcome to Czeslaw Milosz at his arrival in Paris in the spring of 1951. Milosz had worked for the Communist government in Warsaw as cultural representative in Paris and Washington, but in 1951 he broke with the regime and went into exile to Paris. At the ceremony, Denis de Rougement and Ignazio Silone greeted him with welcome speeches. The Committee organized a press conference for the 'defector' Milosz. Two years later he published his masterpiece, The Captive Mind (the German edition being published with a preface by Karl Jaspers). Milosz clearly separated himself from the intellectual fascination with Communism. His analysis counts, along with Raymond Aron's The Opium of the Intellectuals, as one of the most impressive intellectual responses to totalitarianism.[7]

For east European émigrés Paris was a safe haven, a headquarters of their struggle against the Communist regimes in their respective countries. Hungarian émigrés were the first group to arrive, after the revolution of 1956. In the aftermath of the Prague Spring of 1968 there came Czech and Slovak intellectuals, led by Milan Kundera and Antonin Liehm. The latter founded Lettre International in 1984. In 1981, when the military took over in Poland, a wave of Polish dissidents took to Paris, among them intellectuals such as Adam Michnik, Bronislaw Geremek and Andrzej Wajda. Finally, Romanian and Russian artists and writers, as well as intellectuals from Serbia, Bosnia, Croatia and Kosovo, found refuge in Paris in the 1980s and 1990s. Their presence called for a re-assessment of the concept of totalitarianism, past and present. The East–West interaction that grew out of this migration of intellectuals was in part influenced by the redefinition of totalitarianism as a mental category (after Jean-François Revel), and clearly demonstrated the intellectuals' attitude toward any and all totalitarian systems and ideologies.

French intellectuals' reflections on the ideological straitjacket and totalitarian structures of their Communist Party found its way into many of the biographies published in the period – for example, on the break with the Communist Party, the examination of their own political evolution and structure, and the specifically French culture of political discussion and theoretical analysis that characterize the debate to this day. Experiences within the Stalinist French Communist Party and the reactions to which these gave rise sharpened French intellectuals' analytical approach to totalitarian structures in the countries of 'real socialism'. This evolution can be explained, to a substantial degree, by the presence of east European émigrés in Paris. These émigrés helped the French to step back and see the larger picture, and were instrumental in the transformation of the intellectuals' fascination with left totalitarianism in the 1950s into a strong anti-totalitarian tradition, which – unlike the situation in Germany – informs the intellectual landscape in Paris.

Between 1953 and 1955, the network of publications that sprang from the activities of the Congress for Cultural Freedom spread wider. In 1953, along with the already established Monat and Preuves, the first issue of Encounter appeared in London. Tempo presente and Cuadernos followed, in Italy and Spain, respectively. The Austrian journal Das Forum, under Friedrich Torberg as editor-in-chief, joined the network at the same time. In 1957, the Comité des écrivains et des éditeurs pour une entr'aide intellectuelle européenne was founded to coordinate the Congress's activities in support of Hungarian intellectuals, who had been persecuted and repressed since the revolution of 1956. The Comité organized symposia, made books published in the West available to intellectuals in Communist countries, and helped with publication of books and journals. These activities were not carried out within the existing institutional frameworks of international cultural cooperation, which involved governmental representatives. Rather, those who launched them relied on individuals and independent organizations and movements in eastern

Europe. The top priority – this is how Ignazio Silone formulated it – was the free circulation of people and ideas. This unofficial and partly underground support was strengthened by the Foundation pour une entr'aide intellectuelle européenne, established in Geneva in 1966. The foundation subsequently moved to Paris and, sponsored by the Ford Foundation and the Soros Foundation, took over from the Congress for Cultural Freedom. Its activity was not limited to facilitating the exchange of literature between East and West. Its representatives would travel to Hungary, Czechoslovakia, Poland and Romania, financially supporting intellectuals who had come under duress for political reasons and gathering information about the political and intellectual climate in these countries.

In April 1966, a scandal broke out which, in the long run, brought the Congress to an end. In a series of articles, The New York Times alleged that the Congress had been financed to a significant extent by the CIA.[8] These allegations caused a wave of indignation. To the European public, the Congress appeared to be a puppet of 'American anti-Communism and imperialism', an 'instrument of the Cold War'. The scandal and the sharply negative attitude to the war in Vietnam gave rise to a Renaissance of Marxism and anti-American sentiments. The shift in the political and ideological climate at the end of the 1960s and the beginning of the 1970s forced Monat to close down in 1971. In spite of all efforts, mostly by the then editor-in-chief, Klaus Harpprecht, the journal could not be saved. Subsequent attempts to reopen it, most notably by Michael Naumann in 1978, also failed. The political atmosphere in West Germany during the 1970s was not conducive to such publications. The order of the day was Entspannungspolitik – diffusion of the tensions with the East. The political rapprochement with Communist east central Europe was believed to be the true road for securing global stability and peace. Unlike in Paris, in Germany Communist dissidents were met with some skepticism and distrust. They were regarded as trouble-makers and were either outlawed or ignored. Against this background, institutions like the Congress and the Geneva Foundation, dedicated to anti-totalitarian pursuits, were seen as dangerous agents intervening in the internal affairs of neighboring Communist countries.

In Paris, in the meantime, the intellectual and political climate was much more receptive. The publication, in 1974, of Alexander Solzhenitsyn's Gulag Archipelago had prepared the intellectual soil in France. When civil rights movements, such as Solidarnosc in Poland or Charta 77 in Czechoslovakia, began in earnest in eastern Europe, French intellectuals mustered their unconditional support. Antonin Liehm, the founder and publisher of Lettre International, and the political scientists Jacques Rupnil and Pierre Hassner played a decisive role in this endeavor. Vaclav Havel, Istvan Eörsi, Tadeusz Mazowiecki, Adam Michnik and Bronislaw Geremek

– who after 1989 became ministers and presidents of their respective countries or turned their samizdat publications into national newspapers for the fledgling east European democracies – had close ties with the Paris Foundation. So did Parisian intellectuals, such as the historian François Furet and the sociologist Edgar Morin, both former leftists who had separated themselves from the Communist Party back in the 1950s. Their cooperation before 1989, which was without doubt a significant factor in the toppling of the Communist regimes and the fall of the Berlin Wall, was, of necessity, to a great extent clandestine. The price was the public's ignorance of their activities. It is surprising, however, that the lack of attention to and acknowledgement of what was accomplished – and theirs were impressive breakthroughs – continues even today, long after the fall of Communism and the victory of democracy. It is as if the main actors of the pre-1989 pan-European intellectual achievement had faded away from the public memory of a united Europe.

The open challenge to the totalitarian establishment initiated by the Congress in 1950 and the struggle of the intellectuals for democracy and for a united Europe was a remarkably far-sighted policy. People engaged in passionate debates about how to burst asunder the existing ideological and political establishment. In Germany, however, this anti-totalitarian impulse is, even after the end of the order of Yalta, still a taboo and meets with great resistance. In this sense, one finds it hard to accept the year 1989 as a watershed. Liberal-leftist quarters are dominated, pretty much as in the past, by the conviction that 1945 is the only historical change that matters. Challenging the singular importance of this date would mean to the liberal-leftists that the significance of the implications of Auschwitz is undermined. The unconditional support for the post-World War II arrangements, that is, the division of Europe and Germany proper as a punishment for the crimes of the Nazis, was closely linked to the taboo of comparing Nazism, Fascism and Communism.

It is worth noting in this connection the evolution of French and German intellectual attitudes to totalitarianism in the past century. Although unfolding as if in lockstep, the German and French traditions appear as mirror images of each other. Thus, in the 1950s, French intellectuals were positively fascinated with the Communist establishment. By contrast, in Germany, the political climate was characterized by an anti-totalitarian consensus. As a reaction to it, an anti-anti-Communist sentiment developed, reaching beyond the left-wing parties and extending to independent intellectuals of liberal-left convictions. Then, in May 1968 in France, a new stage began, which in the long run spelled the end of Marxism. The protests of the students in Paris were directed partly against the Communist Party, and marked the beginning of the disenchantment with Marxism which reached its climax in the 1970s. In Germany, the same period of student unrest witnessed a revival of Marxism, which stimulated the development of old and new analyses of Fascism. The publication of Gulag Archipelago in 1974 caused a shockwave in France. An anti-totalitarian front emerged in the public debates of the decade and brought together intellectuals of different political generations. In Germany, by contrast, the trend was to stay aloof from theorizing on totalitarianism. Discussions of the issue were banned from universities and public political debates. Unlike in France, Solzhenitsyn's stunning revelations about the Gulag, the Soviet system of penal colonies and labor camps, got a cool reception in Germany. Anti-totalitarian theories that considered Nazism, Fascism and Communism as political phenomena of the same kind, and which were an essential part of the French intellectuals' contribution to the political culture of the country, remained a taboo in Germany long after 1989.

That was the case not only during the German Historikerstreit (historians' quarrel) of 1986. The same attitude was evident in the 1997/98 discussion of the Black Book of Communism,[9] prepared by French historians. Just a year before, a great debate, sparked by François Furet's The End of an Illusion, had seized French public opinion over the seductive powers of Communism. In Germany, however, this debate hardly caused a ripple. German intellectuals were highly suspicious of the French push for revision of long-standing paradigms. Germany remained true to its own, tested tradition of anti-Fascism and anti-anti-Communism. While in the 1970s and 1980s Parisian intellectuals took to the streets in support of the civil movements in eastern Europe, in Germany demonstrations were for peace or against the planned Starbahn West. East European dissidents' calls for freedom and democracy sounded too 'bourgeois' to find a warm reception in Germany. The anti-capitalist attitude counted as a crucial component of the self-identification of the leftist and liberal-leftist quarters in West Germany. Bourgeois democracy did not appeal to them. While the democratic movements on the other side of the Iron Curtain finally broke through to Europe in a drive to partake of its freedom and prosperity, visions of 'socialism with a human face' still filled many a West German head. An honest debate about the blindness to the developments in totalitarian eastern Europe, about the bias toward, sometimes even the fascination with, Communism, and the tendency to underestimate its crimes has still to take place. While in France this debate has been going on for decades and has caused shifts in the entire French intellectual landscape, the German mentality is still closed to that aspect. Not before 1993, for example, was Jürgen Habermas able to acknowledge publicly that he had held back from a fundamental discussion of Stalinism. He had to accept the remonstrance of the Polish historian Adam Michnik that a critique of Stalinism had no systematic value in his theory. Fear of joining the wrong side had silenced him. Habermas did not want, according to his own confession, to fall into an anti-Communist position. Renegades from the old mentality, in other words, are still not looked at very positively. An anti-totalitarian attitude on our side of the Rhine still means the safe old anti-Fascism – and not much beyond that.

It was against this mentality that the former Buchenwald inmate Jorge Semprun spoke in 1994, when he described death, following Celan, as the 'Master from Germany'.

> The death that devastated Europe in the wake of Hitler's victorious march was, yes, it was the Master from Germany. But we all know that the death that hides deep into the totalitarian beast disguises itself in other robes as well, takes the cheap ornamental finery of other nations. I know personally the Master from Spain, and have fought it. The Jews whom the thoroughly French Vichy government hunted down and deported knew death as the Master from France. And Warlam Schalamov tells us, in his shocking Tales from Kolyma, about the Master from the Soviet Union. Death is the Master from Humankind.

These diametrically opposed attitudes to the concept of totalitarianism in France and Germany were reflected in the position their respective public opinions adopted in reference to the war in former Yugoslavia. The French organized impressive public rallies. More than 300 committees for support of Bosnia and against ethnic cleansing were set up. The intellectuals who gathered in the Vukovar Committee, active in Paris from 1991, advanced the Bosnian cause by referring to political traditions which transcended day-to-day Western political practices. When the military took over in Poland on 13 December 1981, French intellectuals led by Michel Foucault organized a demonstration that same night. There was a clear consensus in Paris that defending democracy in Poland against the military was intimately linked to promoting democracy at home. Unlike their German colleagues, French intellectuals very early on criticized the official position of the French government, and that of the West as a whole, on the issue of the Serbian–Bosnian conflict. From the beginning of the war, the French press was flooded with articles. Among the most outspoken critics were Pascal Bruckner, Claude Lefort, Cornelius Castoriadis, François Furet, Bernard Kouchner, Edgar Morin, Marcel Gauchet, Jacques Julliard, François Fejtö, André Glucksmann, Bernard Henri Lévy and Alain Finkielkraut. The Vukovar Committee united anew French intellectuals from different leftist and liberal-leftist denominations in an anti-totalitarian consensus that went back decades.

In Germany, the situation was quite different. In left-liberal quarters, Tito's government had been seen as the essential guarantor of stability and peace in the region. The priorities evoked in the slogan 'peace and stability' informed the German reaction to the war in Bosnia just as it had determined the German position to developments in Poland a decade earlier. A decade later, the same attitude was still to be seen in the reaction to the break-up of the Soviet Union. The civil movement in Poland was believed to be too Catholic and fundamentalist, something like a 'fifth column' of the Papacy. Ten years later, similar explanations were offered with reference to the Bosnian conflict. The Bosnians, it was stated, were the representatives of Islamic fundamentalism, now becoming active in the heart of Europe. Some did not shrink from asserting that a new evil apparent in the customs of blood vengeance was taking over where previously Tito's rule had supposedly kept law and order. Needless to say, on both sides of the war zone much was done that did not conform to reason. Military confrontation spilled over into vendettas, Islamic fundamentalists fought in the Bosnian army, and the war gave vent to ethnic, religious and other deep-seated, centuries-old hostilities. But rationalizing the war entirely by such criteria indicates the presence of a deeply rooted traditional mentality prone to employing ethno-historical explanations even while criticizing their effects. This mentality detached social structures and old and new political regimes from their immediate historical contexts and thus excluded them from the domain of the political analyst. Until NATO bombed Serbia in 1999 this political attitude of the German intellectuals conformed to the long-standing policy of the West: 'No intervention in the internal affairs of a sovereign state', and held them back from assessing developments that occurred, so to speak, before their very doors.

The most conspicuous differences between French and German attitudes transpired in the debate over the Western intervention in the war in Kosovo and the German contribution. The reference point for both sides was Auschwitz. One of the dimensions of the discussion was whether the Bosnian genocide could be compared to the Nazi mass murder of European Jews and whether Western aloofness in the Bosnian case could be likened to the Western handling of Munich 1938 and the Spanish Civil War. It is telling that although both sides agreed on the unique character of Auschwitz, the conclusions they drew from that were diametrically opposite. Since 1995, German intellectuals had taken it as a decisive argument against intervention, on the strength of the maxim that there should be no war, 'never again!' For the French that was exactly why the West had to intervene. But as the war went on, attitudes changed. In 1999, the German foreign minister Joschka Fischer, formerly the most outspoken opponent of military intervention, justified the participation of Bundeswehr troops in the NATO-led mission in Kosovo by comparing the situation there to the atrocities of Nazism.

All in all, the debates about the Black Book of Communism during 1997–98, the controversy over the war in former Yugoslavia, and the current debates about military action against terrorism in the wake of the terrorist attacks of 11 September 2001 give an added impetus to the debates about totalitarianism.

The history of the Congress for Cultural Freedom is the history of the passionate attempts of European intellectuals to understand and fight totalitarianism. It is also an impressive example of French–German cooperation in the face of totalitarianism. The attack on 11 September clearly demonstrated that it is too early to bury the totalitarian threat. The appreciation and remembrance of the European anti-totalitarian tradition could facilitate the further development of the European political establishment as a political system that holds democracy and human rights as its most precious possession. It would provide a fresh opportunity to assess the condition of democracy in Europe and its long-delayed expansion eastwards. The active remembrance of past anti-totalitarian efforts would allow us to grasp the paradoxical relation of German and French perceptions of totalitarianism, to overcome national myths and taboos, and to enforce productive revision of long-standing mentalities and attitudes. Until 1989, the Iron Curtain conditioned our perception of totalitarianism. Now it is finally the time to build a common memory. Among other things, that would allow us to confront the 'hypermnesia' that characterized our perceptions of totalitarianism during the past century.

In 1989, it seemed that democracy and freedom had finally won in Europe. A decade later, it appears that the European position on human rights, lawful governance and protection of minorities, will need to be defended again and again. Democracy is an extension of the uncertain – so claimed Jean-François Revel. The events of 11 September 2001 have brutally reminded us how vulnerable an open society is and how easy it is to attack democracy. This is enough of a reason for French and German intellectuals to continue, in a productive manner, their old and new debates before the united European public.

NOTES

1 Milan Kundera, Ignorance (New York: HarperCollins, 2002).
2 Jean Paul Sartre, 'Réponse à Camus?', in Situations, IV (1995).
3 Alain Besançon, in Commentaire, Bd. 20, Nr. 80, Winter (1997).
4 David Rousset, L'univers concentrationnaire (Paris, 1946).
5 Victor Kravchenko, I Chose Freedom (New York: Charles Scribner's Sons, 1946).
6 Margarete Buber-Neumann, A Prisoner of Stalin and Hitler (London: Henry Holt, 1988).

[7] Raymond Aron, The Opium of the Intellectuals (New York: Transaction, 2001). Czeslaw Milosz, The Captive Mind (New York: Vintage Books, 2001).
[8] New York Times, April 1967.
[9] Stephane Courtois et al., The Black Book of Communism (Cambridge, MA: Harvard University Press, 1998).

12

If Hitler Invaded Hell: Distinguishing between Nazism and Communism during World War II, the Cold War and since the Fall of European Communism

Jeffrey Herf

In a discussion of the moral comparison between Nazism and Communism, it is appropriate, indeed essential, to discuss World War II. During the war, this comparison and the question of lesser and greater evil was not only, as the editors of this volume put it, a chapter in 'the history of the mentality of the intelligentsia in the twentieth century'; it was an urgently practical issue, whose resolution had a direct impact on the outcome of the war. Second, it seems to me that the intellectual debates of the 1990s recall those of the postwar decade. The organizers of the conference on which this book is based spoke of a 'growing consensus that neither the condemnation of Communism should imply a rehabilitation of Nazism, nor should a condemnation of Nazism be taken as implying a rehabilitation of Communism'. To the extent to which such a consensus has grown, it amounts to a reconstruction of an even-handed defense of liberal democracy against its antagonists. During the early Cold War such a stance was known alternatively as 'the vital center', in the United States, and 'militant democracy' or 'the anti-totalitarian consensus', in West Germany. The renewed exploration of these themes in recent years has taken place against the crystallization of the Holocaust and the Soviet Gulag into far sharper focus than was the case in the postwar decade. Recollection of those wartime and postwar views should help us in clarifying the old and new elements in more recent reflections.

Practical consideration of the question of the lesser evil should begin with an examination of Winston Churchill in the summer of 1940. As the correspondence between Churchill and President Franklin Roosevelt makes clear, there was an alternative to continuing to fight on alone against Nazi Germany: namely, to accept Hitler's offer of a negotiated settlement that would leave Nazi Germany in control of the continent, freed from a threat from the West and able to hurl all its armed might against the Soviet Union. Desperate to convince Roosevelt that Britain would fight on if the United States sent military assistance, on 18 May 1940 Churchill assured his long-time friend that 'in no conceivable circumstances will we consent to surrender'. However, 'if members of the present administration were finished', that is, if the current Churchill government fell, pressures might grow in the British political establishment to make a deal with Hitler. Following the evacuation from Dunkirk at the end of May 1940 and the entry of the German army into Paris on 14 June 1940, Churchill wrote an even more dire letter to Roosevelt:

> Although the present government and I personally would never fail to send the fleet across the Atlantic if resistance was beaten down here, a point may be reached in the struggle where the present ministers no longer have control of affairs and when very easy terms could be obtained for the British island by their becoming a vassal of the Hitler empire. A pro-German government would certainly be called into being [in Britain] to make peace and might present to a shattered or starving nation an almost irresistible case for entire submission to the Nazi will. The fate of the British fleet as I have already mentioned to you would be decisive on the future of the United States because if it were joined to the fleets of Japan, France, and Italy, and the great resources of German industry, overwhelming sea power would be in Hitler's hands. He might, of course, use it with merciful moderation. On the other hand, he might not. This revolution in sea power might happen very quickly and certainly long before the United States would be able to prepare against it.[1]

Churchill appealed to Roosevelt's understanding of US national interests and the threat that Hitler's Germany would pose should Britain cease its resistance. Churchill's determination to keep fighting rested on the moral conviction that Nazi Germany was by far the greatest threat to Europe and to humanity, and on the political hope that the United States would continue to aid Britain in practical terms by staying in the fight. Churchill thereby made it impossible for Hitler to turn Nazi Germany's undivided resources to waging war on what the Nazis called 'Jewish Bolshevism' in Moscow. In contemporary terms, this meant that he saw Stalin's Soviet Union as the lesser evil.

Churchill further elaborated on this point in a letter he wrote on 25 June 1940 to Joseph Stalin. It occurred to Churchill that Hitler, if frustrated in the West, might attack the Soviet Union to deprive Britain of hope, bring about a fall of the Churchill government and arrange a negotiated settlement, leaving Nazi Germany dominant on the continent.

The new British Ambassador in Moscow, Stafford Cripps, was directed to deliver it personally to the Soviet dictator. This, too, rejected the idea of the moral equivalence of Nazi Germany and the Soviet Union. Churchill noted the 'widely differing systems of political thought' of Britain and Russia, but believed that 'these facts need not prevent the relations between our two countries in the international sphere from being harmonious and mutually beneficial'. Despite past mutual suspicions and the Soviet Union's current 'close relation with Germany' (as a consequence of the Hitler–Stalin non-aggression pact of August 1939) and thus that 'Germany became your friend almost at the same moment as she became our enemy', a 'new factor has arisen which I venture to think makes it desirable that both our countries should re-establish our previous contact'. That new factor was 'how the States and peoples of Europe are going to react to the prospect of Germany establishing hegemony over the continent'.

Churchill assured Stalin that Britain's policy was 'concentrated on two objects – one, to save herself from German domination, which the Nazi government wishes to impose, and the other, to free the rest of Europe from the domination which Germany is now in process of imposing on it'. The Soviet Union 'alone' could judge whether 'Germany's present bid for the hegemony of Europe threatens the interests of the Soviet Union, and if so how best these interests can be safeguarded'. Yet Churchill wanted Stalin to know of Britain's determination to continue resistance and 'readiness to discuss fully with the Soviet government any of the vast problems created by Germany's present attempt to pursue in Europe a methodical process of successive stages of conquest and absorption'.[2] During the debates over appeasement, Churchill was exceptional among British Conservatives because he was willing to entertain the policy of an alliance with the Soviet Union to deter Nazi Germany. Now, as Prime Minister, he offered Stalin a similar opening. Stalin did not respond. Britain, with American aid but not direct involvement, fought on alone, denying Hitler victory in the West and destroying his initial strategy to win a European war quickly.[3]

Equally telling for our purposes is Churchill's response to the German invasion of the Soviet Union on 22 June 1941. In the weeks and days before the invasion, British intelligence was finding increasing evidence of its imminence and sent warnings to the Kremlin. Sir John Colville, Churchill's private secretary, recorded the dinner conversation of 21 June as follows. 'During dinner Mr Churchill said that a German attack on Russia was now certain, and he thought that Hitler was counting on enlisting capitalist and Right Wing sympathies in this country and the USA. Hitler was, however, wrong and we should go all out to help Russia ...'. Colville asked if this was not strange coming from Churchill, an arch anti-Communist. Churchill replied: 'Not at all. I have only one purpose, the destruction of Hitler, and my life is much simplified thereby. If Hitler invaded Hell, I would make at least a favorable reference to the Devil in the House of Commons.'[4]

Churchill, upon hearing the news of the invasion, 'had not the slightest doubt where our duty and our policy lay', and immediately offered to ally with the Soviet Union against Nazi Germany. His 1,200-word broadcast on the BBC on the evening of 22 June 1941 is as important a political statement about the comparison of Nazism and Communism as I can think of in twentieth-century European history. For Churchill, one of these two evils was clearly and unequivocally worse than the other:

> The Nazi regime is indistinguishable from the worst features of Communism. It is devoid of all theme and principle except appetite and racial domination. It excels all forms of human wickedness in the efficiency of its cruelty and ferocious aggression. No one has been a more consistent opponent of Communism than I have for the last twenty-five years. I will unsay no word that I have spoken about it. But all this fades away before the spectacle which is now unfolding. The past, with its crimes, its follies, and its tragedies, flashes away.[5]

Churchill then spoke of the 'hideous onslaught of the Nazi war machine' on Russia and behind it 'that small group of villainous men who plan, organize, and launch this cataract of horrors upon mankind'. Faced with the invasion of the Soviet Union, the British government had

> ... but one aim and one single, irrevocable purpose. We are resolved to destroy Hitler and every vestige of the Nazi regime. From this nothing will turn us – nothing. We will never parley, we will never negotiate with Hitler or any of his gang. We shall fight him by land, we shall fight him by sea, we shall fight him in the air, until, with God's help, we have rid the earth of his shadow and liberated its peoples from his yoke. Any man or state who fights on against Nazidom will have our aid. Any man or state who marches with Hitler is our foe ... That is our policy and that is our declaration. It follows, therefore, that we shall give whatever help we can to Russia and the Russian people. We shall appeal to all our friends and allies in every part of the world to take the same course and pursue it, as we shall faithfully and steadfastly to the end ...
>
> It is not for me to speak of the action of the United States, but this I will say: if Hitler imagines that his attack on Soviet Russia will cause the slightest divergence of aims or slackening of effort in the great democracies who are resolved upon his doom, he is woefully mistaken. On the contrary, we are fortified and encouraged in our

efforts to rescue mankind from his tyranny. We shall be strengthened and not weakened in determination and in resources.

The invasion of Russia was 'no more than a prelude to an attempted invasion of the British Isles'. Churchill noted that Hitler hoped that 'the process of destroying his enemies one by one by which he [Hitler] has so long thrived and prospered' would continue until he dominated the Western hemisphere. 'The Russian danger is, therefore, our danger, and the danger of the United States, just as the cause of any Russian fighting for his hearth and home is the cause of free men and free peoples in every quarter of the globe. Let us learn the lessons already taught by such cruel experience. Let us redouble our exertions, and strike with united strength while life and power remain.'[6]

Their Finest Hour and The Grand Alliance, the first containing Churchill's correspondence with FDR in the summer of 1940, and the second his statements regarding the alliance with the Soviet Union, were published in 1949 and 1950, respectively. They comprised the second and third volumes of Churchill's six-volume The Second World War, one of the most widely read histories of World War II. Within three and four years of his 'Iron Curtain' speech in Fulton, Missouri, in 1946, which was one of the earliest and most influential of the early challenges to the Soviet Union after the war, Churchill reminded a broad reading public that he, in the crucial weeks and months when the world hung in the balance, had found no difficulty whatsoever in making a clear distinction between Nazi Germany and the Soviet Union. His decisions were not agonizing ones. In the summer of 1940 he did not wonder if Britain could live with a Nazi-dominated Europe, nor did he ever debate the pros and cons of whether to leave Nazi Germany and the Soviet Union to fight it out to the death. Hitler had invaded the hell Stalin had created and Churchill did indeed rise publicly to say many favorable words, if not about Stalin, then certainly about Russia and the need to form a Grand Alliance against Nazi Germany. His reference to the cause of 'free peoples' in connection with Stalin's Russia was an instance of rhetorical excess, which, of course, he did not repeat after 1945 or in the Iron Curtain speech.

Churchill's statements cast some doubt on the juxtaposition that became conventional wisdom in many postwar debates: namely, between a presumably exclusively leftist anti-Fascism and a presumably exclusively conservative anti-totalitarian consensus. In fact, during the war, there existed a broad consensus of opinion in the West from center-right to the Communists that Nazi Germany was by far the greater threat to humanity. (It was a view that prevailed in full knowledge, on the most part, that the Communists had turned their backs on the liberal democracies between 1939 to 1941 and had thus eased Hitler's decision to launch World War

186

II.) It found expression in the work of a number of prominent critics of Communism during the Cold War. George Orwell, Albert Camus, Arthur Koestler, Hannah Arendt, Raymond Aron, Vasilly Grossman and, among the German opposition and resistance, Kurt Schumacher, Willy Brandt, Ernst Reuter — all had impeccable anti-Fascist credentials and yet all, during the Cold War, were active opponents of the Communists. To be sure, the popular front mentality of 'no enemies on the left' placed a taboo for many on sharp criticism of Communism. Yet for opponents of the Communists such as these figures, diminishing the inhumanity of Nazism by comparison to the crimes of the Stalin era was simply a non-issue, because the evil of Nazism in the immediate aftermath of the war seemed to them so self-evident. As François Furet reminded us in The Passing of an Illusion, there were many in Europe drawn to Communism who were unable or unwilling to keep such a complex view in mind and who excused, ignored or denied Communism's crimes because of the role the Soviet Union had played in defeating Nazi Germany.[7]

Kurt Schumacher emerged from Nazi concentration camps to become the leader of postwar West German Social Democracy. In his early speeches of the postwar years, in which he called his fellow Germans to account for the crimes of the Nazi past, he also denounced the policies of the Soviet and German Communists, called them a threat to freedom and democracy in Germany, and even went so far as to compare the repression in the Soviet zone in 1946 with the Nazi repression of 1933. In so doing, Schumacher and other leaders of Social Democracy made strong efforts to distinguish their opposition to Communism from the racist and anti-Semitic attack on 'Jewish Bolshevism' of the Nazi era. American intellectual historians, following in the footsteps of George Mosse and Fritz Stern, have focused on the anti-Western political culture of Nazism.[8] Yet, as becomes apparent when we read Joseph Goebbels's public speeches and radio broadcasts, journal articles and commentaries for the period of the Third Reich, with the important exception of 1939–41 during the Hitler–Stalin Non-aggression Pact, Nazi propaganda presented Nazi Germany and Hitler as defenders of Western civilization against the threat posed by Jewish Bolshevism. Indeed, a major reason why Goebbels and Hitler detested Churchill and Roosevelt so profoundly was their view that, as puppets of Western Jewish plutocracy, they had betrayed the West by weakening its resistance to the Soviet Union through their otherwise incomprehensible decision to form the 'Grand Alliance' with the Soviet Union.[9]

Goebbels elaborated on this theme in 'The Prisoner of the Kremlin', an address of 24 August 1942.[10] Not only, he wrote, had Churchill changed his colors 'like a chameleon' from that of a life-long anti-Communist to Stalin's ally, but he had become 'the Kremlin's prisoner'. On 22 June 1941, the anti-Bolshevik became a friend of the Soviets. With his visit to Moscow, he became their tool. In the course of the war he has emancipated himself from the House of Commons but now carries the yoke of Bolshevism which becomes heavier from day to day. He has to dance to the Soviets' tune.'[11] Indeed, the Western coalition with the Soviet Union served for Hitler and Goebbels to confirm the existence of an international Jewish conspiracy bonding Western 'plutocracy' with 'Jewish Bolshevism' in Moscow. In other words, and in terms relevant for this volume, Hitler and Goebbels denounced Churchill and Roosevelt because, when asked to choose which was the greater evil, Nazi Germany or Stalin's Soviet Union, they both showed no hesitation whatsoever in making, in their view, the wrong choice.

For the Nazi leaders, the roots of this profound error lay in the power of 'Jewish plutocrats' working behind the scenes in London and Washington. Goebbels and his ministry repeatedly proclaimed that had it not been for them, 'the West' would have been able to unify and destroy the Bolshevik menace. Indeed, in the spring of 1945, Goebbels articulated a version of a second stab-in-the-back legend to explain why Nazi Germany was losing the war. On 28 February 1945, as Allied armies were closing the ring around the Third Reich, Goebbels spoke to the nation over the radio to bolster morale and to offer an explanation of how things had come to this grim state.[12]

> We are not ashamed of our setbacks in this gigantic struggle. They were possible only because the European West and the plutocratically led USA gave the Soviet military backing on the flanks [Flankendeckung] and tied our hands with which we still today seek to strike Bolshevism to the ground ... It will be the eternal shame and disgrace of this century that in the moment of its greatest threat from the East, Europe was shamefully left in the lurch and abandoned by the Western countries. Indeed, these nations sunk so low that they even encouraged the storm from inner Asia and at the same time tried to break apart the last protective dam on which it could have been broken. In any case, we expected nothing else.[13]

Like the proverbial rats leaving a sinking ship, Göring and even Himmler put out feelers to the Western Allies to sign a separate peace treaty and join forces against the Red menace. They found no takers. No one in a position of responsibility was interested in anything short of destruction of the Nazi regime and in holding the alliance with the Soviet Union together at least until the end of the war, and, it was hoped, well beyond that. In his own self-serving and distorted manner, Goebbels understood how important recognition that the Soviet Union was the lesser evil had been to the Allied victory and German defeat in World War II.

Churchill was an exceptional but not totally unique example. Some of the classic works of the postwar era express the same complexity born of anti-Nazism and anti-Communism. George Orwell, who broadcast for the BBC during the war, published 1984 soon after. Despite the book's prominence during the Cold War, it was as much about Hitler and Goebbels as about the Soviet Union in the Stalin era. Similarly, Hannah Arendt's Origins of Totalitarianism, a classic of the Cold War's anti-totalitarian consensus, had more about the mass murder of European Jewry than about Stalin's camps. Albert Camus's The Rebel, a break with French Communism and Jacobinism, is filled with trenchant insights into the intellectual origins of Fascism and Nazism. Vasilly Grossman, whose novel Life and Fate was repressed by the Soviet government and remained unpublished in his lifetime, combined vast reportage and documentation of the genocide of the Jews of eastern Europe and the Soviet Union with a subsequent denunciation of the Stalin dictatorship. Similarly, the anti-Communism of the intellectuals in and around the Congress of Cultural Freedom – Raymond Aron, Daniel Bell and Arthur Koestler, among others – had nothing to do with minimizing, relativizing or in any way making light of the crimes of the Nazi regime. To the generation who lived through the war, any policy option other than that adopted by Churchill on 22 June 1941, and later by Roosevelt, seemed beyond the range of respectable discussion.

This was certainly the case for one key group of political opponents of the Communists, the West German Social Democrats of the late 1940s and early 1950s, in particular the chairman of the SPD, Kurt Schumacher, the mayor of West Berlin during the Berlin Airlift, Ernst Reuter, and the party's young, rising star, Willy Brandt.

Schumacher was not outdone by anyone in West German politics in the vigor of his criticism of the German Communists. He was also the first national political figure to call for restitution payments to Jewish survivors of the Holocaust and the one who gave prominence to the Jewish catastrophe in his public speeches from 1945 to 1952. Ernst Reuter attained international renown as the defiant mayor of blockaded West Berlin in 1948, who insisted that the citizens of West Berlin were not willing to succumb without a fight to the imposition of yet another totalitarian dictatorship in Germany. Reuter was also one of the German politicians most sympathetic to Jewish survivors, most critical of the climate of forgetting and avoidance of the postwar years, and most willing to speak – albeit not often – of the mass murder of German and European Jewry.

Willy Brandt, who spent the war years as a politically active leftist journalist in Scandinavia, was another of the Social Democrats who led the political fight against Soviet and East German Communist policies in Berlin in the early years of the Cold War. Given that Brandt did more than any other Western political figure to displace the hard anti-Communism of the Cold War with a new political culture of Östpolitik in the 1970s, it is important to recall that he, no less than Schumacher and Reuter, was comfortable warning of the 'totalitarian threat from the East' in the first postwar decades.[14] In the 1960s, the neo-Marxist attack on the political culture of the Cold War included the assertion that the category of totalitarianism served as, and thus presumably had its origins in, an effort to obscure the differences between Nazi Germany and the Soviet Union by placing them under the identical, pejorative rubric. In that light it is interesting to note an aspect of the appeal of the theory of totalitarianism for Brandt, which has not received as much attention. There is in Brandt's archives a (presumably unpublished) 1952 essay, entitled 'Anti-Bolshevik Race Theory?' ('Antibolschewistische Rassentheorie?'), a review of a book by Franz Conradi, Vom Romischen bis zum Slavischen Imperialismus.[15] The essay was trenchant in its observation of the emergent mood in West German politics and suggestive of Brandt's subsequent views and policies. It is also revealing as to why Brandt found the theory of totalitarianism a welcome concept to describe previous forms of opposition to Communism in Germany. Many politicians in the West and in West Germany as well, he began, were indulging in ever more 'unsupportable and damaging generalizations', such as that Soviet Russia was expansionist and imperialist due to the force of Russian nationalism. Some even referred to the 'Slavic soul'. Such starting points could, however, 'end in a kind of anti-Bolshevik race theory'.[16] Russian history, in this view, was 'an unbroken chain of brutality, murder and humiliation'. For Brandt, this was a caricature, one which reminded him of an English characterization of German history as defined by a similar and grim continuity. 'Apparently', countered Brandt, 'one author knew as little about the autonomy and patterns of totalitarianism [Eigengesetzlichkeit des Totalitarismus – emphasis in the original] as the other.' The development of 'Soviet totalitarianism' had to be derived from social and economic conditions of the Soviet Union as well as from knowledge of 'totalitarian forms of domination'. Reference to 'the Slavic soul' only caused 'confusion'.[17] 'In Berlin, we tried to keep cool heads in the hot climate of the blockade and to avoid referring to "the Russians" when it was the Soviet regime that we had in mind.' In the western part of Germany, there was still too much inclination to accept 'politically fateful and objectively unjustified collective accusations', an inclination which Brandt found in Conradi's 'anti-Bolshevik race theory'. In the postwar West German context, Brandt saw the effort to apply the theory of totalitarianism to the Soviet Union as well as to Nazi Germany as an antidote to racist forms of opposition to Communism. It was part of the development of 'the anti-totalitarian consensus' that was left-of-center, democratic and reformist. Neither in motive nor in consequence, in this context and for Brandt and the Social Democrats in these early years, was the effort to apply the theory of totalitarianism to the Soviet Union part of an effort to relativize or minimize the horrors of the Nazi regime. This is not to deny, as many authors have noted, that the anti-Communist mobilization in the Cold War went hand in hand with a forgetting and avoidance of the crimes of the Nazi era. However, for Brandt and others, even-handedness and sharp rejection of both evils were possible.

The fact remained that in post-Nazi Germany, all opposition to and even criticism of Communism and the Communists took place in the shadow of the Nazi war on the Eastern Front and the racist and anti-Semitic crusade it represented. During the postwar occupation, the Western allies, for all of the well-known failures of de-Nazification, succeeded in their effort to prevent Nazism from becoming a major force in West German politics. Clearly, if a Cold War were to break out with the Soviet Union, it would not be fought in the Federal Republic with Goebbels's slogans of the renewed war against Jewish Bolshevism. Nevertheless, any massive mobilization against the Soviet Union and the Communists after Hitler and Goebbels would take place in a society in which millions had learned and relearned their anti-Communism from the Nazis. In the Nazi era, Hitler, and especially Goebbels, had presented Nazism as the bulwark and defender of Europe and Western civilization against the threat from the East. This was a grotesque falsehood – yet the challenge remained for politicians in West Germany to distinguish their defense of the West from that proclaimed by the Nazis.

The key political figure in such an effort was Chancellor Konrad Adenauer. We need here briefly to recall the following. First, though he placed his anti-Communism on a foundation of Christian natural right, Adenauer did not acknowledge the specific historical burdens of anti-Communism created by the link between anti-Semitism and racism, on the one hand, and the Nazi war in eastern Europe and the Soviet Union, on the other. Nor did he mention the Christian roots of modern anti-Semitism. Second, he denounced both Nazism and Communism as products of the secularization of the modern world and the celebration of false gods. The phrase 'godless' or 'atheistic' Communism was a common one in conservative West German opposition to Communism. Both devalued the individual. Both celebrated the state. Both viewed individuals as instruments for the working out of a grand and dangerous historical teleology. Third, Adenauer did not, nor as far as I know did any West German Chancellor, assert that the Soviet Union was a more evil or more awful form of government than Nazi Germany had been. On the other hand, despite some early speeches making clear his rejection of Nazism, Adenauer devoted vastly more time and effort to denouncing Communism than he did to denouncing the crimes of the German dictatorship. Indeed, as is now well known, he did his best to integrate former and hopefully disillusioned or cynical adherents of Nazism into his electoral base and to prevent the emergence of a separate hard right to the right of Christian Democracy. In this effort, silence about the Nazi past and a focus on the sins of Communism was a matter of personal conviction and political calculation.[18] Fourth, in his policy as well as his actions, Adenauer recognized that the Soviet Union, as oppressive as it was, was a power that would respond rationally to traditional balance-of-power politics. No matter how fierce his discourse about atheistic Communism was, he clearly understood that, in contrast to the Nazi regime, the Soviet government was one that Germany could coexist with. Indeed, his arguments concerning eventual German unification rested on the assumption that this would come about as a result of a change in Soviet policy, not as a result of war.

Yet the conservative mode of viewing the past was manifest in obscuring the distinctions between Nazism and its victims. The West German national day of mourning, established in 1952, recalled in a most abstract manner the victims of war and dictatorship and made no effort to distinguish between German perpetrators and their victims. Adenauer fostered this climate with his early and repeated references to 'the honor' of German soldiers merely doing their duty in Hitler's armies. In this atmosphere of avoidance and abstraction, Theodor Heuss, the Bundespräsident, initiated what became the distinctive West German, then German, form of memory of the Holocaust. In so doing, most famously in his speech at the memorial ceremonies in Bergen-Belsen in 1952, Heuss explicitly rejected efforts to avoid German confrontations with the Nazi past by pointing to the misdeeds of others. Genuine patriotism and honor, in his view, entailed a sharp and unvarnished look at the truth of the Nazi past. Richard von Weizsäcker's famous address of 8 May 1985 was the most important and clearest continuation of this distinctive Heussian tradition. Heuss and Weizsäcker recognized that, especially in West Germany, efforts to obscure the distinctive features of the Holocaust were key elements of nationalist revivals.

The historian of postwar Germany, Frank Stern, among others argued that Heuss's public memory of the Holocaust served cynical purposes – helping to burnish the moral reputation of a fundamentally whitewashed Bundesrepublik.[19] Yet, from the time of Nahum Goldmann's speech at the memorial ceremonies in Bergen-Belsen in November 1952 to the Weizsäcker speech of 8 May 1985 the memory of the Holocaust in West German political culture, implicitly and at times explicitly, also evoked the memory of the Eastern Front and the German attack on the Soviet Union. Indeed, in his ill-fated address on the anniversary of the pogrom of 9 November 1938, then Bundestagspräsident Phillip Jenninger angered his conservative colleagues by explicitly connecting the attack on the Jews in 1938 to the racist assumptions of the German attack on the Soviet Union – the first time, to my knowledge, that a member of the CDU (Christian Democratic Party) had acknowledged the racist legacies of Nazi anti-Communism. In all of these examples, memory of the Holocaust did not fit at all well into the political culture of Cold War anti-Communism.

As we now know, based on historical work on the postwar decades in East Germany, the Communists in the postwar period failed sufficiently to distinguish their own brand of opposition to the West from that of the Nazi past. In the anti-cosmopolitan purges, first in Moscow, then in Budapest, Prague and East Berlin, attacks on Communists, most of them Jews, drew on shockingly familiar tales of a powerful international Jewish conspiracy. Now, however, this conspiracy was supposedly aimed at destroying Communism.[20] Research in the recently opened Communist archives has confirmed, again, the presence of anti-Semitism in the Communist governments in the postwar purges. As one of the historians who wrote about these shameful episodes, I have no problem in asserting that, as morally deplorable as the anti-cosmopolitan purges followed by avoidance of Holocaust memory and active hostility to the state of Israel were, these policies, which in my view do deserve the adjective 'evil', were a lesser evil to those the Nazis pursued during the Holocaust. Making such distinctions is a matter of writing history, not writing excuses and apologetics.

The tortured history of anti-Communism in West Germany came to the fore again during the period after the 1960s. Following the New Left of the 1960s, along with Brandt's Östpolitik, one key feature of West German, as well as American, political culture was the erosion of the liberal and social democratic criticism of Communism.[21] While West German liberals and leftist intellectuals understandably focused their energies on dissecting the Nazi past, sharp and unambiguous criticism of Communism fell under suspicion. The practical consequence of this development was made apparent during the battle over the Euromissiles, in which frightening rhetoric from Washington helped to obscure the deeper reality in West Germany. The erosion of the older liberal and social democratic criticism of Communism and the Soviet Union had gone so far that it led to reluctance to face obvious facts about the Soviet Union's military build-up. During the Euromissile dispute, Germany's current foreign minister, Joschka Fischer, made a striking comparison between the policies that led to Auschwitz and those, not of the Soviet Union, but of Western and US deterrence. In one of the most heated exchanges in postwar German parliamentary history, Heiner Geissler, the General Secretary of the Christian Democratic Union, denounced Fischer's comparison and evoked the memory of Winston Churchill's rejection of appeasement of the Nazi regime in Munich. The bipolarity of the political culture was striking. The left remembered Auschwitz and associated it with Western nuclear deterrence. Conservatives and a small remnant of the postwar Social Democratic 'anti-totalitarian consensus' supporting Helmut Schmidt recalled Munich and associated it with the policies of the Greens and west European pacifists. In 1983, Nazism's shadows remained long enough to cast suspicion on any consequential West German leftist opposition to Soviet policy.

In the late 1990s, in response to Serbian ethnic cleansing in Kosovo, German liberals and former New Leftists – Cohn Bendit, Peter Schneider and, of the generation in power, Foreign Minister Fischer, Chancellor Gerhard Schröder and Defense Minister Rudolf Scharping – rediscovered the verities of the Churchillian critique of appeasement in their response to ethnic cleansing in the Balkans. Whereas in 1983 the memory of Auschwitz inspired Fischer's rejection of Western containment policy directed at the Soviet Union, the same memory now inspired a determination to embrace the tools of power politics to stop Serbia's ethnic cleansing. This was certainly a dramatic change, one that recalled the moral complexity of Churchill and the mentalities of the Second World War.

Churchill's moral and political complexity found expression in his ability to remain a sharp critic of the Soviet Union and Communism, while having no doubt ever as to the priority of defeating Nazi Germany. For the generation of politicians and intellectuals who lived through World War II and then fought the political fight in the Cold War, the obviousness of the evil character of the Nazi regime was taken for granted. Recognizing the lesser but potent evil of Communism and the Soviet Union, which too many leftist anti-Fascists were loath to admit given the saving role of the Red Army in the defeat of Nazism, was the more challenging intellectual and moral task. In the post-Cold War climate, we should at last be able to appreciate fully both the uncomfortable complexity of the anti-Hitler coalition in World War II and the political and moral legacy of the generation that fought first against Nazism, and then fought the good political fight with the Communists during the Cold War.[22]

NOTES

[1] Winston Churchill, The Second World War, Vol. II: Their Finest Hour (Boston, MA: Houghton Mifflin, 1949), pp. 134–5.

[2] Ibid., pp. 49–50.

[3] On the importance of preventing an early Nazi victory see Gerhard Weinberg, A World at Arms: A Global History of World War II (New York: Cambridge University Press, 1994).

[4] Churchill, Second World War, Vol. III: The Grand Alliance (Boston, MA: Houghton Mifflin, 1950), p. 370.

5 Ibid., p. 371.
6 Ibid., pp. 372–3.
7 François Furet, The Passing of an Illusion: The Communist Idea in the Twentieth Century, trans. Deborah Furet (Chicago, IL, Chicago University Press, 1999).
8 See George Mosse, The Crisis of German Ideology (New York: Grosset & Dunlap, 1964); Fritz Stern, The Politics of Cultural Despair (Berkeley, CA: University of California Press, [1965] 1974).
9 I am elaborating on these issues in a work in progress, 'The "Jewish War": Goebbels and Nazi Anti-Semitism in World War II'.
10 Joseph Goebbels, 'Der Gefangene des Kreml', 24 August 1942, in Joseph Goebbels, Das Eherne Herz, pp. 443–50.
11 Ibid., p. 448.
12 Joseph Goebbels, 'Nr. 30, 28.2.45 – Rundfunkansprache', in Helmut Heiber, ed., Goebbels Reden, Vol. II (Dusseldorf: Droste Verlag, 1972), pp. 429–46.
13 Ibid., p. 433. The German reads as follows: 'Es wird die ewige Schande unseres Jahrhunderts bleiben, dass Europa in seiner durch die Bedrohung aus dem Osten hervorgerufenen schlimmsten Gefahr von seinen westlichen Ländern schmälich im Stich gelassen wurde, – ja, dass diese sich sogar so weit erniedrigten, dass sie den Sturm aus Innerasien noch antrieben und zugleich die letzten Schutzdämme niederzulegen versuchten, an denen er gebrochen werden konnte … Wir haben allerdings nichts anderes erwartet. Das internationale Judentum hat es duch eine jahrelange systematische Zersetzungsarbeit fertiggebracht, die Öffentlichkeit in diesen Ländern so zu vergiften, dass sie zu eigenem Denken – von eigenen Entschluessen ganz zu schweigen – gar nicht mehr fähig ist.'
14 Willy Brandt, 'Fünf Jahre Danach', Der Berliner Stadtblatt (7 May 1950), p. 1.
15 Willy Brandt, 'Antibolschewistische Rassentheorie?', Willy Brandt Archiv, Archiv der sozialen Demokratie, 65 (15.3–30.3, 1952).
16 Ibid., p. 1.
17 Ibid., p. 2.
18 Jeffrey Herf, Divided Memory: The Nazi Past in the Two Germanys (Cambridge: MA, Harvard University Press, 1997).
19 Frank Stern, Im Anfang War Auschwitz (Gerlingen: Bleicher-Verlag, 1991).
20 Herf, Divided Memory, Ch. 6, 'Purging "Cosmopolitanism": The Jewish Question in East Germany, 1949–1956'; see also Joshua Rubenstein and Vladimir P. Naumov, eds, Stalin's Secret Pogrom: The Postwar Inquisition of the Jewish Anti-Fascist Committee (New Haven, CT, Yale University Press, 2001).
21 I explored this trend in War by Other Means: Soviet Power, West German Resistance and the Battle of the Euromissiles (New York: The Free Press, 1991).
22 After the terrorist attacks of 11 September 2001 we have a renewed sense of the importance of the category of 'evil' in contemporary history. In lieu of a postscript, I note the following essay: Jeffrey Herf, 'What is Old and What is New in the Terrorism of Islamic Fundamentalism', Partisan Review (Winter, 2002).

13

The Memory of Crime and the Formation of Identity

Gabriel Motzkin

After several years of neglect, one issue that has recently resurfaced is the retrospective question of whether Hitler or Stalin was 'worse'. This chapter will not address that question.

The focus of this chapter is the question of the different treatment of Nazism and Communism since World War II. The answer to that question may appear blindingly obvious: Nazism and Communism were differently received because they were different, because they advocated such different things. Another facile and true answer is that Nazism and Communism were differently received because it was dazzlingly evident that the Communists had won and the Nazis had lost. But such explanations fail when they are applied to the question of why the Nazis have become much more central in our cultural self-understanding than the Communists. Admittedly, the perception that the West feels itself more affected by Nazism than by Communism may also be temporary, but it nonetheless requires an explanation. It is not true that losers always have more historical influence than winners.

This differing valuation is reflected in the places allotted in cultural memory to the victims of Nazism and those of Communism. We all know who the victims of Nazism were. First of all, the Jews. Then the Gypsies, who have been somewhat neglected. Finally, the homosexuals, who are a fuzzier group, perhaps because they are not an ethnic or national group, and so do not possess a publicly organized identity and memory. But the victims of Nazism also include other Europeans, who did not fall into any of these categories, and who are not so well remembered. Finally, many Germans must also be counted among the victims of Nazism but they, too, are not remembered as members of a collective of victims.

Who were the victims of Communism? The answer provided by cultural memory is vague. The Communists claimed that their primary enemy was the bourgeoisie. Should we, then, infer that Communism's primary victims in countries under Communist control belonged to the bourgeoisie? Certainly, many of Communism's victims were members of the bourgeoisie, but it does not seem quite right to claim that the bourgeois victims of Communism were its first or primary victims. At the very least, many bourgeois survived as individuals even if they did not survive as bourgeois. Then, perhaps, the aristocracy should be figured in. They, too, were despoiled and liquidated; those who survived were even less recognizable than the former bourgeois. But the aristocracy did not function as a conceptual object of Communism's persecutions. In a vague sense, the aristocrats were unintended victims – the Communists claimed that the bourgeoisie had already disposed of the aristocracy. In other words, bourgeois and aristocrats were either indirect victims of the Communist ideology or they had to be conceptually transformed in such a way that they could serve as proper victims. Declaring the intended group a class enemy of the people effected that conceptual transformation.

The conclusion, then, must be that any social class that was perceived as being less identified with Communism than some other class was a victim of Communism. But that does not sound quite right either. Moreover, it does not identify specifically the victims of Communism, defining, as it does, Communism's victims as anyone who was not a Communist. Such an approach weakens the idea of 'victim'. It also does not allow for degrees of victimization. Most Russians did not belong to the Party, but that does not make them victims of Communism in the narrow (Nazi-defined) sense of being intended for extermination. One could claim that Communism not only victimized the 'other' classes, it also victimized the working class (even in its deportation and killing policies). That, however, would only contribute to the confusion, diminishing our capacity for realizing the true horrors of Communism. So then one can focus on a specific group, such as the kulaks. It is indeed difficult to distinguish between the Communist treatment of the kulaks and the Nazi extermination of the Jews. Yet there is one cardinal distinction: Communist theory did not focus on the kulaks in the same way Nazi doctrine made out the Jews to be the prime movers of the evils besetting the world. That does not make Communism better; it only makes it less fantastic. One might argue that the Communist policy of extermination could be turned against anyone, whereas some part of society would always be exempt from Nazi persecution. That may be debatable, but it is certainly true that the lack of specific connection between Communism's theoretical enemy and its current victims made it more difficult to remember these victims later. In other words, the perpetrators' attitudes to their victims, not only their deeds, helped define the availability of those victims to cultural memory. There is another reason why the Jews are more present in memory than the kulaks: the kulaks did not survive as a group with its own institutional memory. The salience of the Jews in cultural memory therefore derives from two factors: the possibility of institutionalizing Jewish memory in the postwar period; and the place of the Jews in Nazi ideology. In other words, there was no reason for a successful Communism to remember the kulaks, but the Nazis, had they been successful, would have remembered the Jews forever. Their plan to construct a museum to house the relics and stuffed corpses of an exterminated people is proof enough of that attitude.[1]

The kulaks could not have been remembered in the same way as the Jews because they lacked cultural institutions. Social classes, such as the kulaks or the bourgeoisie, do not establish group memory because they do not possess institutions that cultivate and preserve memory. Such institutions are almost always either national or religious. Therefore the memory of atrocities practiced against national or religious groups will always be more salient than the memory of atrocities perpetrated against social groups. That is as true of perpetrator memory, the memory of the killers, as it is of victim memory. Recent debates in Germany have shown that the memory of the Holocaust is quite alive there; one reason for that is the organized nature of German national memory. The Germans 'remember' the Holocaust because their institutions are making an effort to 'remember' it.

The memory of the atrocities perpetrated by Communism is certainly a less central factor in the formation of current Russian national identity. The Russians have a difficult time deciding whether they should remember Communist rule as perpetrators or as victims. This problem exists for the Germans as well; but the Germans have no doubt about the significance of the Holocaust for their national memory (although there are some Germans who question the fixation on the Holocaust in German national memory).[2] By contrast, those like Reinhart Koselleck, who have criticized Germans for adopting (falsely) victim memory, do not do so because they wish to forget the Holocaust, but rather because they believe that the structures of perpetrator memory must be different from the structures of victim memory.[3] Be that as it may, organized German identification with the victims is something quite different from the organized victim memory that exists in Israel or in Jewish communities around the world. Organized German memory will always have to confront the possibility of oscillating between perpetrator memory and victim memory, whereas organized Jewish memory will by definition never be able to consider seriously the possibility of taking the stance of perpetrator memory. Hence a determinant in the question of memory is the possibility of choice of memory, i.e. the question of whether or not historical collective memory can be consciously selected. The answer to this question differs from group to group.

One should keep in mind that the normal human condition is forgetting: organized cultural memory requires an enormous effort. It is because cultural memory is an intentional activity that its conscious motives can be queried and analyzed. By contrast, the well-known reaction of Holocaust survivors who wanted to forget what happened to them and did not like talking about it is the normal human reaction. What one should really investigate are the motives behind the effort to record Holocaust survivors' memory. What was abnormal on the personal level was their opening up themselves and their pasts as a result of enormous cultural pressure. The reason for the drive to forget is quite clear. If something bad has happened to you, it is in your interest to minimize its importance. The opposite reaction is useful only when there is an advantage in dwelling on the past. Even then, both perpetrators and victims often display great reluctance when asked to recount their experiences, unlike their successors and children, for whom these memories are second-order events; for the descendants of the victims can detach specific lessons and morals from the multifaceted flow of their parents' experience. Although successive generations produce and perpetuate these memories, they do so in order to consume memories. Those for whom memories are part of their own experience have no interest in adopting the position of a 'memory consumer'.

States and national institutions are not distinguishably different from religions in their construction of memory. That is why it is so easy to analyze their organization of memory in the same terms as those applied to religious institutions, in spite of the differences in belief. That also implies that the categories for analyzing religious experience are applicable to organized memory. Thus, it is meaningful to speak of the sacralization, secularization and desecration of memory. The sacralization of memory refers to the process by which a cultural memory is turned into a sacred experience for a given society. The secularization of memory is a more ambiguous process. It is sometimes difficult to distinguish it from banalization of memory, the process by which a previously holy memory is turned into a common experience. Finally, desecration of memory, like the desecration of a religious object, refers to the challenge to a previously sacred memory, the process by which a memory is violated or consciously destroyed (analogously to the destruction of a sacred religious object). The desecration of memory can sometimes imply that those who violate it remain aware of its religious power. The memory of the Holocaust has been sacralized, it has been secularized and banalized, and it has also been desecrated. If, in the nineteenth century, the emancipation of the Jews was associated with the process of secularization in many European states, in the post-World War II period the universalization of the Holocaust has had the capacity to endow the Jews in Gentile perception with a numinous and auratic quality, one placing the Jews in the context of sacralization and desecration. That quality derives in part from older associations, in part from the Holocaust. By contrast, nothing in the wake of Communism has been perceived in such quasi-religious categories. The dialectical association of the perception of the Jews with the Holocaust means that this quasi-religious experience is partly a response to the Nazi demonization of the Jews. It helps keep the memory of the Holocaust alive.

The qualification of a memory as quasi-religious is not static: it heightens the contrast between this kind of memory and other collective memories. The sense that there is a contrast fosters the impulse to reduce the difference. Then, quasi-religious memory is either secularized to look like other memories, in which case there will be no difference between the memory of the sacred event and other events, or, on the contrary, other memories are assimilated to the sacred memory. In the latter case, all memory comes to resemble Holocaust memory. Finally, the contrast between the two kinds of collective memory can lead to a transfer of value between them, so that Holocaust memory, for example, becomes just another collective memory, while at the same time cultural memory itself will henceforth be inextricably associated with trauma. No capacity for interpreting memory will continue to exist except in terms of the traumatic origin, as, for example, in the case of multiple personality disorder. This can have a rebound effect, so that memory itself, not only its origin, will be understood as a traumatic situation. One can term this a secular experience of catharsis analogous to the religious experience of grace. If, however, the religious experience of grace was understood as the anticipation of the fulfillment of God's promise to man after death, the catharsis being a harbinger of the future, the secular experience of memory indicates that its quasi-religious cathartic moment is henceforward past-oriented, with no possibility of transcendence, except through deciphering the enigma of that past. Unless the trauma is understood, there will be no possibility of escaping it. The only way of overcoming the Holocaust would be through returning to it. In such terms, Holocaust obsession and Holocaust fatigue are both signs of the burden of the discipline of the past.

The real competition for memory in the postwar period was not between Stalin and Hitler, but rather between Auschwitz and Hiroshima.[4] The Japanese, however, having waged war, were never able to establish themselves as convincing victims in the eyes of others. Thus the predominant memory of Hiroshima in the West was not a case of victim memory, but rather one of perpetrator memory. The battle over this memory was fought in moral categories. Both camps, those who endorsed the bombing of Hiroshima, and those who condemned it, viewed Hiroshima as a value-laden event, the one side with positive and the other with negative value. Despite all efforts, however, Hiroshima never attained the sacred value assigned to Auschwitz. That failure was, perhaps, the result of a fundamentally ambivalent attitude toward the use of nuclear power in the postwar period. Hiroshima could have been transvalued like Auschwitz if nuclear power, analogously to genocide, had been banned and criminalized in the postwar period. Hiroshima could then have become the quasi-religious focus of the postwar period's past-orientation. But the possibility of the use of nuclear power was a present danger in the postwar period; since all felt themselves to be vulnerable, no focus on the Japanese as victims occurred. They had, after all, been the wartime enemy. In the postwar period, Auschwitz could be sacralized in the West because the chance of its recurrence seemed remote.

Sacralization also requires that the memory of the sacred event be fixed in time and place. The spatial indeterminacy of the extermination of the kulaks, as with the incapacity to locate the specific space in which the Einsatzgruppen operated, makes it difficult to sacralize such atrocities. There is no place of pilgrimage, no terminus for the physical journey that can mark the negative goal of the soul's spiritual journey as it travels to the hellhole of the past. While sacralized memory can change and the narrative attached to it can be amended or even fall into desuetude, sacralization requires a set procedure. Consequently, there is also a memory of places that once were sacred, but are so no longer. In the modern imagination, Santiago de Compostela does not occupy the place it did in medieval times. But the place must be fixed before it can be transferred. Sacralized memories can change places, but only after they have occupied a place. Thus Santiago de Compostela was a substitute for Jerusalem, just as the Holocaust Museum in Washington DC is a substitute for Auschwitz. Both, however, participate in the aura radiating from the original location for memory.

The sacralization of Auschwitz has a deeper historical meaning. It marks a return of pilgrimage to history. In the nineteenth and early twentieth centuries, pilgrimage continued to be a strong motif in revived religiosity; witness Lourdes and Fatima. Secular pilgrimage, however, was increasingly oriented either to places of constructed national memory, such as the Hermannsdenkmal in Germany, or to the churches of the new religion of culture, the museums. The bankruptcy of these secular ersatz-religions in the wake of World War II left the postwar world with a deficiency of places of sacred memory. The art museum was increasingly displaced by the historical museum as the place for experiencing the memory of meaning. Unlike the art museum, the historical museum, however, was not the place for meditating on the purpose of human existence. This gap in experience was eventually filled by the Holocaust as the focus of the negative myth of origin that characterizes the postwar world. This myth conveys a sense of being orphaned: not only had the Gods flown away, but so had the cultural forefathers. Karl-Heinz Bohrer seeks a way around the Holocaust because he senses this feeling of being abandoned by the past.[5] The past-orientation marked by the Holocaust exists precisely because the Holocaust has become the vanishing point for retrospection, the point beyond which origins can no longer be discerned. Hence the place of the Holocaust is the place for confronting the absence of the past. No other event fills this metaphysical role in postwar culture. Because nothing previous to the Holocaust is thought to continue to subsist, the Holocaust becomes the place for the preservation of absence, since only the memory of that absence makes it possible to seek the trace of the pre-Holocaust past. This sensibility escapes Bohrer, but it can be seen clearly in Derrida.[6]

The conference that stimulated the writing of this chapter witnessed another comparison: that between Nazism and European imperialism and colonialism. Non-German Westerners have a relation to the memory of colonialism much like Germans' relation to the Holocaust. Moreover, colonialism is a memory in many countries of the world. One could have expected that institutional forces would cultivate its memory. Yet this cultivation of memory has not taken place.

There are two reasons for that. First, new states, for obvious reasons, cultivate the memory of their national-liberation movements. They are no longer colonies, their people are no longer victims, and so they have no reason to cultivate victim-memory. There are several analogous cases. In the past few years slavery in the United States has become a focus for organized memory. This memorialization depends on the willingness of the white perpetrators to tolerate and assimilate into their own awareness the commemoration of Afro-American suffering. The political agenda behind this is the inclusion of all ethnic groups in the American consensus. Yet this mixing of perpetrators and victims has prevented the sacralization of slave suffering. In South Africa, a similar process of commemorating apartheid has begun. Here, too, sacralization will be possible only if whites and blacks remain distinct. The problems of mediating between victim-memory and liberation-memory are both different and particularly acute in Israel, which occupies an exceptional position in this regard. So far, these specifically Israeli problems have not been resolved.

The second reason for the memories of slavery and colonial atrocities being less compelling than Auschwitz is those memories' incapacity to be universally applicable. Each colonial atrocity may be well remembered at a particular place, but that place does not become a place of pilgrimage for other peoples, nor does it become a moveable place: there is no museum of a colonial atrocity in a country other than the one in which the atrocity took place. Holocaust museums are everywhere.

This sacral uniqueness of the Holocaust does not mean that Communism was not, in its way, just as unique: the culture of paranoia, the inability of anyone, including the leader, to feel safe from persecution, the need for a constant manipulation of reality in order to feed a virtual meaning-system that claimed to require scientific and empirical confirmation of its achievements, requiring the massive fabrication of data – all this contributed to the construction of as peculiar a cultural system as the world has ever seen. However, as George Orwell noted, this cultural system had one particular trait which the Nazis did not share and which made it impossible to include Communism in the memory dialectics of sacralization and demonization. Namely, Communist culture was a unique culture of institutionalized amnesia.[7] People had to be written out of encyclopedias, air-brushed out of photographs. Not to mention the drive to forget the pre-Communist past, which had to be ruthlessly stripped of any cultic attraction it might still possess. Unlike the Nazis, Communists everywhere sought to destroy the past. For Communists, the past posed the greatest threat, much like racial pollution for the Nazis. In the post-Communist era, the greatest Russian problem has been the lack of an organized capacity to recover and remember the past, in part because these capacities atrophied during 70 years of Communist rule. State-organized amnesia was developed in order to forget both the historical past and the recent Communist past. The question, then, is whether amnesia itself can be remembered; whether a cult that denies memory can become an object of memory.

It is curious that the high moment of Communist totalitarianism in Russia occurred after World War II, whereas the iconic moment of Communist atrocities, both the kulaks and the state-sponsored famines, occurred in the 1920s and 1930s. Hence a problem for the cultural memory of Communism is whether it is the atrocities perpetrated by the regime or its systematic domination and regimentation of the population that should be the object of memory. One could argue that the atrocities were the consequence of a perverted impetus to a misconceived economic rationalization, whereas postwar totalitarianism stemmed in part from the incapacity to provide a viable method for conversion of the war machine into a peacetime economy (and stemmed in part from Stalin's massive paranoia). Nonetheless, the point remains: while totalitarianism and atrocities may be conceptually related, there is no necessary historical link between them. Both atrocities without totalitarianism and totalitarianism without atrocities are possible, although it is probable that Stalin, had he lived, would have initiated new atrocities.

Underlying such discussions is a peculiar conception of memory, one that has grown more culturally prevalent in the postwar period. According to this conception, memories are constructed. Since memories are constructed or reconstructed after the event, the aspect of memory emphasized is recall or retrieval. The idea is that a monument will make present to the viewer something that is also latent in the viewer's mind: the viewer already 'knows' what he or she is about to see. This conception is quite different from Freud's, in which retrieval was intended to unearth from storage the usually traumatic moment of encoding. The problem with this conception is that it can easily be turned into a questioning of the 'reality' of the event being remembered. If memories are constructed, their relations to original events are not fixed, but dynamic. By contrast, a conception that privileges the moment at which memory is encoded also usually presupposes that the relation between event and memory is fixed, as in the theory of an original trauma. Such a conception never questions the 'reality' of the event. However, it makes it more difficult for the act of retrieval to be self-reflective: what we want to remember is the original event, not our memory of it. Nonetheless, the desire to remember the memory of events, and not the events themselves, is often characteristic of organized memory.

This discussion about collective memory is curious, because memory is an intimate experience. Its metaphorical application to public processes is an exportation of intimacy into the public sphere, even while the private ownership of those memories is questioned. The exportation implies that public events are available for sacralization to the extent they can be intimately re-experienced. The point about a visit to a site of sacred memory is that the agreement between those who maintain the site and those who visit it is that the visitors acquire an intimate experience of the event that the site marks. It is not enough to construct a memorial site. If it cannot be intimately experienced it will not be experienced at all. In this sense, memorials of memory are different from historical monuments, which seek to evoke a sense of history. Historical monuments are sacred because of their interrelation with the political order, or with the history of the country. They do not negotiate between the visitor's own memory of the past and the past that they represent.

Furthermore, sacralized memory makes the claim that what is being remembered is somehow ineffable, unlike historical memory, which seeks to make the past transparent. Thus the pilgrimage to a sacred place is capped by the pilgrim's experience of a metaphysical reality that is presented as being greater than this world. Secular sacralized memory applies these categories to places that do not belong to traditional religions.[8] There is something in this world that is ineffable, that cannot be expressed in language. The holiness of the place is marked by its being beyond language.

Thus, sacralized memory requires place, intimacy and ineffability. All three can be transferred from one place to another and from one intimacy to another. What stays the same is the ineffability: the idea is that a visit to a Holocaust museum partakes of Auschwitz. The identity of the memory, the identification of one site of memory with a site of memory that is somewhere else, is then founded on the identity of this ineffability. If the experiences of the two were radically different, then a visit to a Holocaust museum could not be identified as an act of commemoration. It is a question whether all sacralized places promote such an ineffability, or whether ineffability characterizes only some types of sacred memory-places.

If Auschwitz is really a defining public memory-place for contemporary culture, that means that contemporary collective memory assumes that some aspect of the past is ineffable, and that it is that aspect that confers identity.

The idea here is that the difference between Auschwitz and Communist atrocities is not in the degree of atrocity but rather in the meaning ascribed to it. The question is whether the meaning ascribed to atrocity is purely constructive, or whether it has a relation to something about them. I have argued elsewhere that it is not purely constructive (even when we like to think that it is).[9] However, the link is not between memory and event, but rather between the meaning we ascribe to the event and the meaning that was ascribed to the event at the time it happened. Here, however, a curious and terrible shift occurs. We remember the event in the way we do not because we remember the meaning that the victims assigned to the event, but rather because we remember the meaning the perpetrators assigned to it. Even the vivid images we have of the Holocaust are the photographs shot by the perpetrators. In that sense, all memory is perpetrator memory. There is no Jewish memory of the Holocaust that is not affected by the meaning that the Nazis assigned to what they were doing. There can be no memory of the kulaks that does not contain the meaning the Communists assigned to their actions. We cannot remember the kulaks at all; we do not know what they thought or felt. However, that is true even of a comparatively well-documented event like the Holocaust. The Jewish experience of the Holocaust makes no sense if the Nazis are excluded. Thus even Claude Lanzmann, who sought in his film Shoah to transmit the experience of the victims, and to ignore the German perpetrators as much as possible, was constrained to include their point of view at several points in the film.[10] Otherwise the event would not make sense. The question is whether the ineffability that attaches to the experience is a consequence of the impossibility of separating the memory of the event from its perpetrators: we want to remember the victims, not the perpetrators, but this is impossible. That conclusion is obvious for perpetrator memory, which cannot function without the victims; it is less obvious for victim memory.

Much has been made of the Nazi attack on the (Western?) idea of a shared humanity. The argument has been advanced that the Nazis attacked this idea, while the Communists managed to murder their victims in the name of a shared humanity.[11] The counter-argument is made that degrading an ideal is worse than denying it. The memory of the event is then meant to inculcate the idea of a common humanity on the basis of the intimate experience of the past. The Jews become the particular example of a common humanity, just as Christ's passion is designed to provide the focus for an intimate experience of Divinity. Thus, the rejection of the Holocaust is tantamount to an espousal of universalist conceptions and ideals. The memory of the Holocaust, unlike the memory of Christ's passion, is a negative foil for those ideals. Christ is Himself sacred. It is not the victims of the Holocaust who are sacred; they have no salvational power. It is rather the event itself that is sacred. Because the victims cannot be sacralized, the event becomes ineffable: whereas an incarnate God reveals, a sacralized atrocity conceals. On the contrary, there is no narrative that could turn the atrocities perpetrated against the kulaks or the Russian bourgeoisie into sacred events. First, it is misconceived to think that the sacralization of the victims makes the event sacred. In the story of Christ, we are asked to meditate on Christ, not on the Jews. In the twentieth-century atrocity narratives, our attention is constantly diverted to the perpetrators. The reason is, alas, that we have to recognize that the victims were only human; they are permanently unavailable for sacralization.

Since the Holocaust has been interpreted as a unique event, whereas other atrocities and genocides have not, its uniqueness informs others' perceptions of both Germans and Jews. Some will argue that what happened to the Jews was because they have always been unique. Others will say the same thing about the Germans. Still others will claim that the Germans have become unique since the Holocaust, and the same can be said about the Jews.

What is interesting here is the quest for uniqueness, as if a unique event needed unique people, either as perpetrators and victims or as successors and survivors. No such claim has ever been made about the victims of Communism. In the Communist case, uniqueness is at best a category applied to the perpetrators.

What is at stake in the uniqueness debate? Why is it attractive to view either perpetrators or victims as unique? The simple answer is that unique events require unique people, or a unique history, or maybe a unique memory. Hannah Arendt distinguished between the event and the people caught in it: she was unhappy with the behavior of the Jews, both during the Holocaust and thereafter. She was no less unhappy with the Germans, who, she implied, were banal at the time and hypocritical thereafter.[12] In her version, the Holocaust required heroes and villains, but the heroes were not heroic and the villains, while quite evil, were not very villainous. Even she, however, did not deny the uniqueness of the event.

There are at least three issues at stake in the uniqueness debate: first, whether the sacralization of the Holocaust is permissible; second, whether the carry-over from events to people is more than a question of legal responsibility; third, whether the postwar cultural memory-structures that dictate the relations between moral issues and historical issues are valid. To answer all three cases in the affirmative, one must assume that the Holocaust is unique. This, however, does not completely settle the issue of

206

the carry-over between events and people. As recent war-crimes trials show, that issue has not yet been decided. Yet those same war-crimes trials also demonstrate that the Holocaust is being transformed from a unique event in history to an archetypical event for judging future cases and experiences. Thus, on one level it is an intimate and religious event while on another level it establishes the presupposition for legal and moral thinking in the postwar period. That does not apply to Communist atrocities.

The answer to the question of whether the sacralization of the Holocaust is permissible has already been given. First, not only is it permissible, but transforming the Holocaust into just another atrocity would be sensed as a desecration, an obscenity. Any attempt to secularize the memory of the Holocaust is immediately attacked from all sides with vitriol. Second, if the carry-over from events to people were merely a question of legal responsibility, no passion would be attached to the determination of criminality. The Holocaust makes it clear that the legal order of a given state can never trump a general moral consensus. Recent war-crimes trials are based on the same idea. A full-blown legal positivism is simply impossible after the Holocaust. Thus, the uniqueness of the Holocaust, or rather its archetypical role, has legal consequences for the international order and also for the conduct of states and governments towards their own citizens and subjects. Third, the primacy of the ethical framework in the desired construction of the social order must be anchored in memory. Historical positivism is limited by the experience of atrocity. Once again, historical events become subject to moral considerations. In order to secure this primacy of morality over history memory structures have to be constructed, which would moralize memory. The religion of memory is a moral religion: it prescribes conduct by controlling memory. Even a post-secular global memory will be selective.

The reason for the uniqueness of the reception of the Holocaust is clear. The international community in our time is not founded on class universalism, on the idea of an international working class that provides a universal benchmark for interpreting the value of actions. Hence the victims of alleged class warfare suffer from the anonymity of their irrelevance to the universal public morality. The idea of an international community, which at present is positively valued, is based on the possibility of a universal ethics, of applying the same standard to different actions in different places, irrespectively of local cultural conditions and standards. That moral definition of an international community requires a consensus about the rank and order of the severity of crimes and transgressions. The Holocaust is the limit-case of that ethical universalism. It becomes the interpretive matrix for judging current events. The public cultivation of its memory is therefore a necessary component of this specific international order.

The narrative of Holocaust reception has been a narrative of universalization. The victims, much to the displeasure of some Jews, have been detached from their specificity, because it has become necessary to rescue the experience of the Holocaust from its particularity. The memory of the Holocaust has been reconstructed to support a negative cosmopolitanism that assumes that the role of Holocaust victim is transferable: in this narrative anyone is a potential Holocaust victim.

The point was previously made that any Holocaust memory is defined in terms of the perpetrators. The survival of that memory, however, depends on the durability of encoding the victims. Remembering the victims has become a limit-case for defining subjectivity and subjective experience. Any account that was provided for the victims has been couched as an account of the threat to subjectivity when it got exposed to the experience of the Holocaust. While similar accounts have been provided for other events, for other concentration-camp experiences and, in the Communist case, for the threat of brainwashing to subjectivity, the specific meaning of the Holocaust experience of subjectivity has been construed as the question of the worthiness of subjective experience, in contrast to the glorification of subjective experience from the Enlightenment onwards.[13] The much-heralded 'death of the subject' finds its context in the Holocaust-tinted intuition of the provisional nature of subjectivity.

In the Holocaust narrative, the victims have become the heroes, not because of their heroic conduct, but because they have attained the status of martyrdom. But martyrdom for what? For what cause did Holocaust victims die? It is certainly not Judaism. The Holocaust victims have been retrospectively accorded the status of martyrs for the cause of humanity, as is evidenced by the definition of the perpetrators' crime as a crime against humanity. Even Hannah Arendt, in Eichmann in Jerusalem, subscribed to this definition. Accounts of the memory of World War I are often couched in the rhetoric of trauma, because the memory that was intended to be transmitted through memorials was the subjective experience of those who experienced the war.[14] That is not at all the case with the Holocaust: the memory to be transmitted is not that of the victims, but rather the memory of those who heard about the crime somewhere else, some time later. In that memory, the victims are not subjects but icons; icons of human subjectivity. The closest parallel is not the kulaks, but rather the victims of Stalin's show trials. However, those victims, often because of their personal histories as Communist activists, were not amenable to a generalization defining them as icons marking the limits of human experience.

The victims, however, are also a threat. One function of memory, as Freud understood, is protective. Memory is constructed to insulate survivors and successors from the threatening aspects of experience. The memory of the

Holocaust victims raises the possibility that we can all be killed in this fashion and at the same time it is constructed to prevent that possibility from ever occurring again. The procedure of Holocaust memory seeks to recover the victims' subjectivity while insulating those who are in the process of acquiring those memories from that same subjectivity. The victims are, as it were, put in a glass cage of memory. In that cage, they cease to be possible objects of compassion. Yet that incapacity for compassion awakens guilt, not the well-known guilt of having survived while others died, but rather the guilt of a partial intimacy. The experience is intimate, but it has become literary, in the sense of becoming an experience focused on itself: the Holocaust is remembered as a subjective experience of those who remember it, not of those who suffered it. The icons are fixed forever in their ineffability. A suffering God can rouse our emotions, but we can only empathize with Him as human beings, not as one god to another. Setting the victims as victims of a crime against humanity makes them iconic. They become foils for our experience, while their own experiences remain forever transcendent to us. That inability to adopt the point of view of the sacred object, just like the traditional inability to adopt the position of the scapegoat, is a necessary element of sacralization. Memory compensates for the impossibility of true compassion.

In the case of Communism, owing to the fact that Stalin murdered his own people, the line that memory draws between perpetrators and victims is never clear. In the case of Holocaust memory, that line is well marked. The only people for whom that boundary is ambiguous are the Germans. They are victims in two senses. The Nazis themselves were victims: they lost the war. The Germans are also memory-victims, since theirs is the memory-role of condemned perpetrators. It is forbidden to see this because of the terrible dilemma created by viewing the Germans as victims. Hence their victims, those against whom the Germans won their war, become the memory-beneficiaries, the transferees of the loss, of the compassion for the defeated that we are forbidden to feel in this case. The Jew becomes the negative of the Nazi. If the Jewish experience of the Holocaust is taken as the defining experience of subjectivity, the humanity of the Nazis cannot be admitted. Thus, the rite of memory is designed to insulate its practitioners from possible identification with the Nazis.

I have deliberately couched my sentiments in a universalizing vocabulary, implying that any experience could be set as iconic and defining. But I do not really think that experiences are arbitrary in relation to memory. The uniqueness of the reception of the Holocaust is related to the actual Nazi threat to the idea of a common humanity. However, the disjunction between experience and how that experience is remembered by others cannot be overcome. Experience, on the one hand, and remembering the experiences of someone else, on the other, have quite different structures. My point is that moral categories are really applicable to memory and not to experience. It is in terms of those moral categories of memory that there is no comparison between the impact of Communist atrocities and the impact of the Holocaust.

NOTES

[1] Avishai Margalit and Gabriel Motzkin, 'The Uniqueness of the Holocaust', Philosophy and Public Affairs, Vol. 25 (1996), p. 80.
[2] Karl-Heinz Bohrer, 'Erinnerungslosigkeit. Ein Defizit der gesellschaftlichen Erinnerung', Frankfurter Rundschau (16 June 2001), p. 20.
[3] Reinhart Koselleck, 'Die Diskontinuität der Erinnerung', Deutsche Zeitschrift für Philosophie, 47, 2 (1999), pp. 213–22.
[4] Hiroshima mon amour (1959), directed by Alain Resnais, screenplay by Marguerite Duras. See also Robert Jay Lifton and Eric Markusen, The Genocidal Mentality: Nazi Holocaust and Nuclear Threat (New York, Basic Books, 1990).
[5] Bohrer, 'Erinnerungslosigkeit'.
[6] Jacques Derrida, De L'ésprit. Heidegger et la Question (Paris, Galilée, 1987); see also his Mémoires. Pour Paul de Man (Paris, Galilée, 1988) and David Levin, 'Cinders, Traces of Darkness, Shadows on the Page: The Holocaust in Derrida's Writing', in Alan Milchman and Alan Rosenberg, eds, Postmodernism and the Holocaust (Amsterdam, Rodopi, 1998), pp. 265–86. See also James Berger, After the End: Representations of Post-Apocalypse (Minneapolis, MN, University of Minnesota Press, 1999), pp. 106–33.
[7] George Orwell, Nineteen Eighty-Four, a Novel (London, Secker & Warburg, 1949).
[8] For the sacralization of Auschwitz as a site of pilgrimage see Jack Kugelmass, 'Why We Go to Poland: Holocaust Tourism as Secular Ritual', in James Young, ed., The Art of Memory: Holocaust Memorials in History (Munich and New York, Prestel-Verlag, 1994), pp. 175-83.
[9] Margalit and Motzkin, 'The Uniqueness of the Holocaust', passim.
[10] Shoah (1985), directed by Claude Lanzmann.
[11] Margalit and Motzkin, 'Uniqueness of the Holocaust'.
[12] Hannah Arendt, Eichmann in Jerusalem: A Report on the Banality of Evil (New York, Viking Press, 1963).
[13] Arthur Koestler, Darkness at Noon, trans. Daphne Hardy (New York, Macmillan, 1941); Robert Jay Lifton, Thought Reform and the Psychology of Totalitarianism: A Study of 'Brainwashing' in China (New York, Norton, 1961).
[14] Jay Winter and Emmanuel Sivan, 'Setting the Framework', in Jay Winter and Emmanuel Sivan, eds, War and Remembrance in the Twentieth Century (Cambridge, Cambridge University Press, 1999), pp. 6–39.

14

Mirror-Writing of a Good Life?

Helmut Dubiel

The moral sensibility towards genocide, mass murder, rape and torture has increased considerably in recent decades. The attention to mass infringements of human rights even when they affect foreigners living on the other side of the globe is certainly a consequence of the easy access to information that new means of communication have made possible. Another reason is the growing number of people whose political liberties and comfortable living conditions allow them to pay attention and commiserate with the sufferings of others. In the third place, one can argue that higher sensibility to human pain is a historically informed moral reaction, generated under the impact of the unique atrocities of the twentieth century, now condensed under the generic term 'Holocaust'. In what follows, I would like to elaborate on the third point.

The term as we use it today identifies not only the historical event of the 'Holocaust'. It has come to denote, and indeed to connote, the worst that humans can do to one another – simply put, political evil itself.[1]

Pluralism, cynicism and relativism are features of a modern culture gone wild. Religious, traditional and metaphysical sources of certainty dry up. When human beings realize that everything and anything is different and contingent, even their own gods, the common ground of societies is put at risk. My thesis will be that the remembrance of the Holocaust made new certainties accessible, though their nature is only negative.

The division between 'good' and 'evil' is to be found in religious precepts, popular tales and old-time stories, and in political rituals, constitutions, judicial oaths and myths of origin. The emergence of this division of 'good' versus 'evil' is often symbolically linked to a traumatic catastrophe, a despicable crime or, on the contrary, an exemplary heroic deed – or both. I am under the impression that in the Holocaust, that is, in its symbolically abstracted generic form, we can see an emerging transnational political morality.

Yehuda Bauer's opening address to the international forum on the Holocaust, in 2000 in Stockholm, sums up the thesis I am proposing. 'In recent decades, actually in most recent years, we have witnessed an amazing development. A catastrophe that had befallen a specific people at a specific time, in a specific place, has been accepted, all over the world, as the symbol of ultimate evil.'[2] It remains to be explained how the Holocaust was extracted from its time- and place-specific environment and currently operates in the political cultures of perpetrators and victims alike as the symbolic boundary between good and absolute evil. For the Holocaust now provides the meta-narrative for sufferings inflicted for political reasons. It has turned into the supra-denominational passion story of late modernity. Concepts, symbols and images are taken out of their immediate context and are employed to encode, in a single term, the collective pain that people inflict upon others. This symbolic repertoire has been adopted by political groups all over the world who are subjected to extreme pain and distress. The meta-narrative of the Holocaust has transcended the limits of political remembrance socially and existentially. It is present in the political defense of human rights, in the re-moralization of diplomacy, and in the turning away from morally neutral Realpolitik. It is also transparent in newer phenomena, such as the practicing of a 'culture of apology' by leading Western politicians, a new military policy, and the emergence of transnational institutions dispensing justice in cases of crimes against human rights.[3]

To attribute this supra-historical sublimation of the Holocaust to the position of the true symbolic foundation of the moral universalism of late modernity to a Jewish master plan would be no more than anti-Semitic propaganda. The process through which the Holocaust assumed its current meaning of a moral universalism enfolded naturally.[4] The idea was picked up and applied consistently by heterogeneous groups in different countries, who were often in conflict with each other or did not even know of each other's existence, and adopted it in contingent situations and through widely different media – novels, movies, documentaries, historical studies, museums, etc. The question is not whether it is, normatively speaking, right that the concept expanded and acquired such a universal historical meaning. The transformation of the Holocaust into a globally obtaining symbol of political morality is already a historical fact beyond any doubt. What we can ask is the empirical question of how this came to pass.

My attempt to address this problem is sketchy at the best, and is based on an enquiry into the political cultures of Israel, Germany and the USA.[5] The selection of the first two states is self-explanatory. The USA, for its part, given its global military presence, its status as the only superpower, its significant Jewish population, and a universalist, that is, ethnically neutral, civil religion, is an intriguing case in point.

If one steps back and tries to grasp the big picture, there appear to be striking similarities in the dynamic of the political evolution of the Holocaust in all three countries. For totally different reasons, in the immediate post-World War II period in Germany, as the country of the perpetrators, in Israel, the country of the victims, and in the USA not much attention was paid to the Holocaust. In Germany and the USA, the death camps were taken out of the context of the war and considered as an independent phenomenon. For the Germans, the genocide of an entire people was a sealed issue.[6] In a society that had been extensively shaped by Nazi theory and practice, there was still no narrative, no symbolic framework within which the Germans could understand, as a political collective, themselves and their immediate past. The only symbolic interpretive device bequeathed by the Nazis to the Bonn Republic was the concept of the 'nation'. For all political groups – with the exception of the Communists – the nation remained the dominant medium for collective self-reflection, for the institutional frame of the state was fragmented with the division of the country. The forced abjuration of the stigmatized, by the Nazis, but not altogether demolished 'German honor', the assertion of the cultural integrity of the German nation, and the obsessive quest for an ersatz identity betrayed the impression that the overriding symbolic forms of collective self-identification engendered by the nation had been irreversibly destroyed. That national disposition blocked, for a long time, not only the assumption of collective responsibility for the Holocaust but even the possibility to conceive of its real dimensions. The intensification of references to the 'German nation' and the ignorance or depreciation of the genocide were still traceable in the 1980s. It was in this decade that the situation changed perceptibly, in the process of the massive critique of Kohl's policy toward the past. At this juncture, there was a new impetus for the empirical reconstruction of the public remembrance of the historical Holocaust.

Although at the time the state of Israel was formed (1948) many of its citizens were survivors from the death camps, until the trial of Eichmann in 1961 the Holocaust played a surprisingly small role in the public life of the country. The victims kept silent for reasons that can be seen as complementary to the ones for which the perpetrators were silent. In its background was the long-standing conflict between the Zionist founders of Israel and the Jews of the diaspora.[7] The European Jewry victimized by the Nazis did not fit into the heroic historical scheme of the Zionists. It was much more important to the founding generation of Israelis, for political reasons, to represent the Israeli state as the work of those individuals and groups who had actively opposed the Nazis. That is why in the first years after the foundation of the state more attention was lavished on the insurrection in the Warsaw ghetto than on the mass murder in the death camps.

In the public opinion of the USA the inclination was to treat the Holocaust – still not under that name – as a side issue of the war.[8] The genocide of the European Jews was only marginally dealt with during the process at Nuremberg. Here, too, the lack of a narrative structured by the Holocaust, and a traditional perception of war crimes prevented the emergence of a consciousness of the global significance of the phenomenon. Symptomatic of this lack of meaningful paradigms for evaluation of the Holocaust was the regular use of the term 'atrocities' to denote the genocide of European Jews. The concept was a vestige of the terminological apparatus worked out at the end of World War I to denote war crimes. The term allowed at least the implication that the assertion of such atrocities was a propaganda device. The US soldiers had entered the death camps as 'liberators'. In their optimistic, future-oriented mentality, the liberation of the camp inmates was just another step forward bringing closer the victory of democratic civilization. The piles of corpses and the emaciated inmates were only later, when the 'tragic' meaning of the Holocaust set in, turned into icons of human suffering. In the beginning, it was the relatively better-fed political prisoners, who related to the victorious soldiers and whose appearance testified to the triumphal narrative of liberation. The misery of the emaciated, rags-wrapped, half-dead Jews did not conform to this image.[9]

In order to understand the evolution of the remembered Holocaust into a fundamental symbol of a transnational morality one has to take into account what roles were assigned to the actors in this unprecedented political drama by the political cultures of Germany, Israel and the USA. At first sight, everything is quite clear: the Germans were perpetrators, the Jews victims, and the Americans deliverers. Yet against this identification, in the first decades after the war, the overwhelming majority of Germans cast themselves in the role of primary victims – of Hitler and of the war. This perception served many politicians right into the 1980s. It allowed the construction of a universal notion of victimhood that encompassed not only those murdered in the camps but the German soldiers who fought and died in Nazi Germany's enforced war. 'We are all victims' applied even to the graveyards of fallen SS soldiers.[10] The massive critique of this false universalization and the agenda behind it began in the late 1960s and changed the Bonn Republic. The climax, and in a sense the capstone, of the process of moral transformation was the great speech of Richard Weizsäcker in 1985, in which for the first time a representative of a German government officially acknowledged and took responsibility for the Holocaust. Notably, the speech began with a list of all victims of the Nazi terror and of the war. Weizsäcker's symbolic breakthrough was a demonstration of the process of coming to terms with the reality of the Holocaust, a process in the course of which many Germans learnt to distinguish between perpetrators and victims.[11]

214

Similarly, and as a complementary development to the German hesitation to acknowledge themselves as perpetrators, it took the Israelis more than a decade to assume an official role as victims. The turn to a demonstrative identification with the victims of the Holocaust occurred in the wake of the Eichmann trial. Since 1961, the public remembrance of the Jewish victims has been the core of the Israeli civic religion. Until that time, the already mentioned heroic attitude prevailed, fueled in part by the determination never again to be a victim. It was after 1961 that the public all over the world began to accept the representation of the Jews of Israel as victims but the heroic image promoted by the founding generation still persisted. Indeed, it was instrumental in the building of a new political paradigm that the Israeli politicians promoted and put into practice, extracting the concept of victim from its historical context. The double paradigm of victims–perpetrators appeared appropriate to the political confrontation faced by Israel. The casting of the Arabs in the role of new Nazis was the decisive step in the divorcing of the concept of the Holocaust from the historical reality within which it was born.[12]

The victim–perpetrator paradigm did not work in the USA; and not only because the Jewish population was too small to justify the casting of the Israeli state in the role of a victim. The multi-ethnic structure of the USA, a society of immigrants, made the integration of the survivors of the mass murder possible only within the framework of a universalistic narrative. It was an entirely different story in Israel, where the remembrance to this day is ethnically coded. In the USA, where anti-racism was normatively promoted, the persecution of Jews was conceived of as an extreme case of a familiar phenomenon. Within such an interpretive scheme it was, so to speak, 'normalized'. The positive message of this development was that Fascism and racism are best confronted with civic courage and then with military measures.

Jeffrey Alexander distinguishes between what he calls 'progressive' and 'tragic' narratives. During the first years after World War II in Israel and the USA the 'progressive' narrative dominated. From the 1960s, however, it gave way to the 'tragic' paradigm. This division, of course, is based on ideal-types. In reality, the paradigms overlapped but did not blend into one another. A case in point for the tragic paradigm are the postwar writings of Theodor Adorno.[13] He confronts the optimistic, future-oriented progressive narrative with an apocalyptic philosophy of world history, in which the Holocaust solves the mystery of a doomed civilization. Auschwitz was not the gateway to a better world; it was the end of history, the blind alley of civilization. In this picture of the world at 'five minutes past the twelfth hour', the Holocaust marks the end of a negative teleology. For Adorno, it was the sign that the world had already crossed over. The Holocaust happened on the other side of a decisive break. It was the symbol of the entire process of the decline and fall of Western history. Since the Holocaust the clock continues to run, but it does not measure time any longer. What the progress of the clock hands promises is the eternal and inevitable return of a catastrophic evolution. The mass murder at Auschwitz may indeed be over; but the evil for which Fascism stood is still around. Auschwitz could happen again – at any time.

Adorno was not alone in his expectations. There were other authors who, although not in such a forceful manner, testified to the expansion of the tragic narrative of the Holocaust beyond its historical context and its transformation into a wandering motif that was no longer the exclusive property of the victims and perpetrators. In the process, the Holocaust turned into a component of a larger paradigm. A new anthropology emerged, one that locates the communality of humankind precisely in its fragility and vulnerability. Part of this new anthropology is a secularized concept of absolute evil. In this view, evil is not outside the world; it is part and parcel of every society, it is deposited in every individual. The integration of the historical event of the Holocaust into this ahistoric, anthropological paradigm leaves the dichotomy of victim–perpetrator open. Against such a background, anyone could assume either the role of a victim or that of a perpetrator. Moreover, looking back to the historical Holocaust, it becomes possible to identify oneself with victims and perpetrators at the same time. Sublimating the Holocaust to an abstract concept releases the moral potential of its remembrance.

One of the many vehicles for turning the historical Holocaust into a transnationally valid marker of the line between good and evil in a political context was the dispute over its historical uniqueness. The assertion seemed too trivial, however, since all events happening in time are unique. What was really meant was, above all, its incomparability. But even this formulation is inaccurate. Not just historians, all ordinary people can and do compare whatever they see fit. The point is that assertions about the uniqueness and incomparability of the Holocaust are normatively motivated. They are justified with the claim that any comparison of the historical Holocaust with other cases of macro-crime would relativize its meaning. The political message of the insistence on uniqueness is that one can only grasp the magnitude of the new genocide after it has been proven that its dimensions are comparable with those of the Holocaust. The argument seems somewhat circular. Behind it was a psychological demand. On the one hand, there was the survival victims' legitimate need for recognition of their pain. On the other, the nation of the perpetrators had an illegitimate need to relativize their deed and free themselves from guilt. In this ongoing debate, oscillating between the poles of the sacral (for the victims) and the banal (for the perpetrators), the historical Holocaust spiraled upwards to the point where it became the primary measure of political injustice. It assumed this role precisely because of its controversial double nature, being at the same time an historical, empirical event and an ahistorical occurrence transcending history. And with any new crime against humanity the debate is now resolved on a new level.

In the 1990s, the discourse I am presenting in sketchy outline became a factor directly influencing global politics. It is clearly visible in the adjustment of attitudes among the second post-World War II generation of European politicians with reference to the wars in the Balkans. In the beginning of the decade in Germany the slogan 'Never again Auschwitz, never again war!' was the dominant political position. The deployment of German troops in military actions aiming to protect human rights was unthinkable at this juncture. After the mass murders at Srbrenica became public, this position came under pressure. As the Serbian army and the paramilitary detachments began their large-scale ethnic cleansing in Kosovo, NATO intervened. All official representatives of the Western countries in NATO, including German officials, supported the intervention because the mass murders and deportations based on ethnic differences strongly recalled the extermination policies of the Nazis. Back in those hectic days it was not historians who made the analogy; it emerged spontaneously in the imagery of the Western media. Images of people filing in front of trains, clutching all that remained of their possessions, forcefully evoked recollections one could not easily evade. The effect was felt not only by German politicians, who were now for participation in the transnational armed forces defending human rights. The impression was equally strong among other European officials and in the US government. The transformation of the Holocaust into an abstract concept standing for absolute evil reached the point at which it had a direct – and unplanned – impact on political action and decision-making.

At this point, the first attempts to harness the controversial and fluid moral capital of the concept for grounding the political and historical unity of Europe took place. The most spectacular effort to construct a European foundation myth founded on the Holocaust was the turn-of-the-century Forum at Stockholm.

Modern political myths of foundation are constructed narratives which extract an important event of the common past from the historical continuum in which it is embedded, endow it with mythical qualities, and turn it into a starting point of communal history. Their essence is therefore not the recollection of the actual past but the construction of a narrative that shores up collective feelings and identities in difficult times. Myths of foundation can be discovered as well as invented. They are not constructed from scratch, but contain an element of historical occurrences preserved in the collective memory – otherwise the myth would not work. They are, in other words, true inventions, at one and the same time ideological creations and expressions of an authentic desire to make sense of one's existence. Unlike archaic myths, which seek to fit in the flow of time, modern myths stress discontinuity, the caesura of history, be it a triumphal beginning or the admonishing remembrance of a catastrophe. The goal is to revolutionize the normative foundations of communal history and re-orient it toward a new starting point.

Thus, at the invitation of the Swedish prime minister Goran Persson in 2000, an international conference was convened to mark the fifty-fifth anniversary of the liberation of Auschwitz. Historians, politicians and heads of state from 45 countries gathered in Stockholm. The conference took place in an atmosphere informed by right-wing violence and the spectacular success of rightist parties at the voting polls. Nonetheless, the end of the millennium and the anniversary of Auschwitz constituted a reference point for the foundation of a transnational union for struggle against genocide. In the concluding address of the conference the legacy of the Holocaust was clearly sounded out. Through the symbolic representation of the absolute evil embodied in the Holocaust a new, globally obtaining, albeit somewhat defensive concept of the good was worked out. 'The Holocaust put under question the fundamentals of our civilization', stated the address,

> Unique as it is, the Holocaust will always have a general meaning
> ... The self-sacrifices of those who opposed the Nazis are inscribed
> on our hearts. The depths of their pain and the heights of their
> heroism are the foundation stones of our concept of humankind as
> being able to distinguish between good and evil ... In the name of
> the humankind still bearing the scars of genocide, ethnic cleansing,
> racism, anti-Semitism, and hostility to foreigners, the international
> community is united in taking the heavy responsibility to fight these
> evils. Together we must assert the horrific truth about the Holocaust
> against those who claim it is a deception.[14]

In the following paragraph of the address, is it stated once again that the normative foundation of the transnational political community consists in the 'discovery and remembrance of inhuman barbarism, unimaginable cruelty and humiliation that are unthinkable against the background of our common existence'.[15] For the first time in the history of humankind the experiences of the twentieth century, captured in such iconic, self-explicatory symbols as 'Auschwitz', 'Gulag', 'Nanking', 'Hiroshima' and 'killing fields', forge out of the denizens of our globe a world community defined in terms of citizenry of the global 'risk society'. It is not paradoxical that the traumatic contemplation of absolute horror and absolute disregard of the fundamental norms of civilization can engender an ethics transcending the boundaries of a single nation. The category of 'human being', from which concepts such as 'human rights', 'humanity' and 'crimes against humanity' derive, is not – as Carl Schmitt asserted – a hypocritical attempt to mask particular interests. On the contrary, after the catastrophes of the twentieth century the category of 'human' acquired the qualities of a more private concept. It is juxtaposed with the public and political notion of 'citizen'. A 'human' in this sense is a being that has been deprived of the most elementary right, that is, the right to have any rights. By virtue of their destruction of the capillary system of human bonds, genocide, totalitarian terror, wars, civil wars and deportations contribute to the emergence of a new, politically active humanity. The stateless immigrant, the victim of torture and the camp inmate are the exemplary embodiments of the vulnerability that, in the final analysis, is shared by all humans. The tribe, family and nation offer no recognition and protection for such atomized humans. What they are left with is the most abstract and improbable foundation of solidarity: the solidarity of being among strangers.[16]

The idea of the obligation to solidarity with all those who have a human face was formulated in the eighteenth century. It was only after the genocide of the twentieth century, however, that the idea was validated through living experience. Unlike in the eighteenth century, the validity of this idea is no longer staked on the belief of the progressive perfection of humankind. Its foundation is the fear of the barbarian potential unleashed during the past century. The genocide and the total wars of the twentieth century exploded the boundaries of state citizenship and ethnic and class belonging: in short, all particular entities that used to determine who could have claims on one's sense of solidarity. Unlike in previous centuries, too, the thought that we are responsible for diminishing the pain of total strangers does not seem so absurd today.

By way of conclusion, and because the central thesis of this enquiry is open to misunderstanding, I would like to ward off confusion by summing up its main sociological premises and implications.

First, it is not the remembrance of the Holocaust by itself that forges the transnational political entities. The need for the narrative it conditions appears only after the material and institutional prerequisites for a political community have been built, but there is a lack of self-assurance and legitimacy. To put it in other words: the group of people within which there is a mutual obligation for solidarity depends only secondarily on shared cultural identity and common values. The feelings of obligation are to a greater extent socially conditioned. The politico-administrative and economic systems of modern societies create the material framework for the building of the feelings of obligation. As long as the politically autonomous nation-state corresponds to a national economy, a primordial sense of belonging is preserved even in an increasingly internationalizing economy.

It is not so much the extension of global trade and production that condition the growth of moral awareness. Much more important for opening the attitude to the stranger is the depth of the transnational effects on local life caused by globalization.

Second, on a sociological level, these enlarged forms of feelings of obligation and responsibility do not represent new collective identities analogous to national identity. National attitudes are not so easily supplanted by universal, cosmopolitan attitudes. Even in the post-national world order people will not simply stop using the dichotomy 'we–them' in classifying individuals and groups they encounter. But in the future the national encoding of the differences will grow into another level of collective identification. The impact of the Holocaust narrative could help this transformation by causing, through a series of pushes, the further opening of 'we' and the acceptance of new groups. The impact of horror stories and images occurring elsewhere in the world would reinforce, as I postulated, the new, 'negative' paradigm of human bonding that is being built on the legacy of historical catastrophes. The crimes of the Holocaust acquired the status of meta-narrative only because of the extent of their monstrousness.

Third, the norms that emerge in the transformation of an historical occurrence into a political and moral criterion for distinguishing between good and evil have a doubly 'negative' nature. On the one hand, they are negative in the banal sense of not constituting a positive precept. They are avoidance imperatives; they tell us what must be prevented, at any cost. On the other hand, these imperatives are negatively defined in view of their social genealogy. The social and cultural integration not only of transnational societies but of highly differentiated, pluralistic national communities as well is no longer mediated by positive values. It is staked on the social capital derived from conflicts with striking consequences. The potential for a transnational consensus on the minimal standards of civilization generated by the remembrance of the Holocaust exemplifies this postulate best. The catastrophic experiences embodied in the Holocaust triggered a learning process that will not necessarily bring the parties from conflict to consensus. It will, however, most certainly cause them to go ahead with a changed perspective on their own position. And that is enough of an accomplishment.

NOTES

[1] Two recent publications have helped me considerably to clarify my own approach: Daniel Levy and Nathan Sznaider, Erinnerung im globalen Zeitalter: Der Holocaust (Frankfurt: Suhrkamp Verlag, 2001) and Jeffrey C. Alexander,

'The Social Construction of Moral Universals – from War Crime to Trauma-Drama', European Journal of Social Theory, 5, 1 (2002).

[2] Opening of the Holocaust Forum in Stockholm, January 2000. See <www.holocaustforum.gov.se>.

[3] Elazar Barkan, The Guilt of Nations: Restitution and Negotiating Historical Injustices (New York: Norton, 2001).

[4] See Lothar Probst, 'Europaeisierung des Holocaust', Kommune, 7 (2002).

[5] For Germany, see Helmut Dubiel, Niemand ist frei von der Geschichte (Munich: Hanser, 1999), for Israel see Tom Segev, The Seventh Million (New York: Owl Books, 1998), and for the USA see Peter Novick, The Holocaust in American Life (New York: Houghton Mifflin, 2000).

[6] See Dubiel, Niemand ist frei, pp. 72–6.

[7] See Levy and Sznaider, Erinnerung im globalen Zeitalter.

[8] See Novick, Holocaust in American Life.

[9] Alexander, 'The Social Construction of Moral Universals'.

[10] Dubiel, Erinnerung im globalen Zeitalter.

[11] Alexander, 'Social Construction of Moral Universals'.

[12] Ibid.

[13] Theodor W. Adorno and Max Horkheimer, The Dialectic of Enlightenment (New York: Continuum, [1944] 1972), and Theodor W. Adorno, Minima Moralia: Reflections on a Damaged Life (New York: Random House, [1978] 1990).

[14] 'Declaration of the Stockholm International Conference on the Holocaust', February 2000 <www.holocaustforum gov.se>.

[15] Ibid.

[16] See Michael Ignatieff, The Warriors' Honor (New York: Owl Books, 1998).

Notes on Contributors

Ulrike Ackermann is a founder of the European Forum at the Berlin-Brandenburg Academy of Sciences, a frequent commentator in the German print, radio and television media. She focuses on European issues, with particular emphasis on French-German relations, and authored A Case of Intellectual Sin (2000, in German).

Steven E. Aschheim holds the Vigevani Chair of European Studies at the Hebrew University, Jerusalem, where he teaches Cultural and Intellectual History. In 2002/3 he was the first Mosse Exchange Professor at the University of Wisconsin, Madison. Recently he has published three works – Hannah Arendt in Jerusalem (2001, editor.), In Times of Crisis: Essays on European Culture, Germans and Jews (2001) and Scholem, Arendt and Klemperer: Intimate Chronicles in Turbulent Times (2001).

Ruth Ben-Ghiat is Associate Professor of Italian Studies and History at New York University. She is author of Italian Colonialism (2002), Fascist Modernities: Italy, 1922–1945 (2001), and The Fascist Culture (Italian, 2000).

Dan Diner is Director of Simon Dubnow Institute in Leipzig and Professor at The Hebrew University, Jerusalem. His recent book publications include Feindbild Amerika. Über die Beständigkeit eines Ressentiments (2002) and Beyond the Conceivable: Studies on Germany, Nazism, and the Holocaust (2000).

Helmut Dubiel is Professor of Sociology at the Justus-Liebig-Universität in Giessen, Germany. His areas of research are critical theory, political sociology, and contemporary European history. From 1989 to 1997 he was the Director of the Institut für Sozialforschung in Frankfurt. From

2000 to 2003 he held the Max Weber Chair for German and European Studies at the Center for European Studies and the Vernon Center for International Affairs at New York University. Among his many publications are: Theory and Politics (1986), Ungewißheit und Politik (1994), Demokratie und Schuld (1999) and Niemand ist frei von der Geschichte (1999).

Jeffrey Herf is professor of Modern European, especially German, History at the University of Maryland in College Park. His books include Divided Memory: The Nazi Past in the Two Germanys (1997). His current work-in-progress is Narrating the Nazi Era: Goebbels, World War II and the Jews. He is a regular book reviewer for The New Republic and is a contributing editor of Partisan Review.

Berel Lang is Professor of Humanities at Trinity College in Hartford, Connecticut. He has written Holocaust Representation: Art Within the Limits of History (2000), The Future of the Holocaust: Between History and Memory (1999) and Heidegger's Silence (1996).

Steven Lukes is Professor of Sociology at New York University, having previously taught at University of Siena, European University Institute in Florence and serving as Fellow and Tutor in Politics and Sociology at Balliol College, Oxford. He is also co-editor of the European Journal of Sociology. His recent books include Multicultural Questions (editor, 1999) and Moral Conflict and Politics (1991).

Martin Malia is Professor Emeritus of History at the University of California, Berkeley. He is the author, most recently, of Russia Under Western Eyes, from the Bronze Horseman to the Lenin Mausoleum. (2001).

Jean-Louis Margolin is a lecturer at the University of Provence (Aix-Marseilles I) and the Institute of Research on the South-East Asia (IRSEA/CNRS). He was one of the contributors to The Black Book of Communism: Crimes, Terror, Repression (1999).

Sigrid Meuschel is Professor of Political Science at the University of Leipzig. She started her career as the managerial assistant of Jürgen Habermas in the Max Planck-Institute. Her first book was a study in political economy; examining the construction of the railway system in the US. The transformation of eastern Europe has become the subject of her major research, and she is the foremost expert on the history of the former GDR. This reputation was built on her magisterial study Legitimation und

223

Parteienherrschaft in der DDR (1979). She is presently working on the problems of the politics of memory and totalitarianism.

Gabriel Motzkin is Dean of the Faculty of Humanities at the Hebrew University in Jerusalem. He has published on relations between conceptions of history and of memory, the philosophy of history and theories of secularization. Among his publications are: Time and Transcendence: Secular History, the Catholic Reaction and the Rediscovery of the Future (1992), 'The Uniqueness of the Holocaust', Philosophy and Public Affairs, 25 (with Avishai Margalit, 1996), and, most recently, 'Science, Secularization and Desecularization at the Turn of the Last Century', Science in Context, 15 (2002) and 'Déjà Vu in Fin-de-Siècle Philosophy and Psychology' (in Déjà Vu, ed. Gunter Oesterle, 2003).

Tzvetan Todorov is director of research at the Centre National de Recherches (CNRS) in Paris and has been a visiting professor at several universities, including Harvard, Yale, Columbia and the University of California at Berkeley. Recent publications include (1999) and Facing the Extreme: Moral Life in the Concentration Camps (1991).

Irving Wohlfarth is Professor of German literature at the University of Reims. He is co-editor of Nietzsche and An Architecture of Our Minds (1999).

INDEX

225

INDEX

INDEX